# Highway Impact Assessment

# HIGHWAY IMPACT ASSESSMENT

## Techniques and Procedures for Transportation Planners and Managers

### Denver Tolliver

**Quorum Books**
Westport, Connecticut • London

**Library of Congress Cataloging-in-Publication Data**

Tolliver, Denver D.
   Highway impact assessment : techniques and procedures for
transportation planners and managers / Denver Tolliver.
     p.  cm.
   Includes bibliographical references and index.
   ISBN 0-89930-662-4 (alk. paper)
   1. Roads—United States—Maintenance and repair—Costs. 2. Roads—
United States—Maintenance and repair—Environmental aspects.
3. Traffic estimates—United States.    I. Title.
TE220.T65  1994
388.1'0973—dc20      92-1124

British Library Cataloguing in Publication Data is available.

Library of Congress Catalog Card Number: 92-1124
ISBN: 0-89930-662-4

First published in 1994

Quorum Books, 88 Post Road West, Westport, CT 06881
An imprint of Greenwood Publishing Group, Inc.

Printed in the United States of America

The paper used in this book complies with the
Permanent Paper Standard issued by the National
Information Standards Organization (Z39.48-1984).

10 9 8 7 6 5 4 3 2 1

# Contents

Tables and Figures     vii

Preface and Acknowledgments     xi

1. Introduction     1

2. Overview     11

3. The Grain Subterminal Elevator: A Rural Land-Use Change     19

4. Freight Transportation Demand Analysis     27

5. Life-Cycle Pavement Concepts     45

6. Subterminal Land-Use Study     79

7. Shipment Generation Procedure     97

8. Traffic Models     103

9. Network and Impact Models     121

10. Subterminal Case Study & Conclusions     139

11. Branch-Line Abandonment Case Study     161

12. Conclusions and Sensitivity Analysis     197

Appendix     203

Bibliography     205

Index     213

# Tables and Figures

## TABLES

| | | |
|---|---|---|
| 1.1 | U.S. Highway Mileage at or Below Terminal Serviceability, 1988 | 2 |
| 2.1 | Submodels Needed for Subterminal Traffic Analysis | 16 |
| 3.1 | Typical Vehicle Weights and Loaded ESALs for Grain Truck Types | 23 |
| 3.2 | Representative Subterminal-Satellite Elevator Traffic Flows as a Percent of Inbound and Outbound Volumes | 25 |
| 5.1 | Change in ESALs with Decline in PSR for a 16,000-Pound Single Axle | 49 |
| 5.2 | Present Serviceability Rating (PSR) | 59 |
| 5.3 | Truck Tire Pressures in North Dakota | 68 |
| 5.4 | Dry-Freeze Zone Coefficients and Constants for Revised FHWA Model | 70 |
| 5.5 | Estimated ESAL Life of Pavements: By Functional Class | 75 |
| 6.1 | Impact-Year Subterminal Volume Projections | 88 |
| 8.1 | Cost of Double-Handling Grain and Oilseeds at North Dakota Elevators | 111 |
| 8.2 | Hypothetical Shipper Demand Schedule for Railroad and Truck Transport | 113 |
| 8.3 | Distribution of Farm-to-Subterminal Shipments Among Truck Types in the Devils Lake Region by Market Zone | 115 |
| 8.4 | Grain Trucking Costs per Bushel by Truck Type at Various Distance Intervals (in cents) | 117 |
| 8.5 | Average Commodity Payload in Pounds, by Truck Type | 119 |
| 9.1 | Loaded and Empty Axle Weights for Wheat by Truck Type, in Thousands of Pounds | 125 |
| 9.2 | Vehicle Classification Records | 127 |
| 9.3 | Seasonal Adjustment Factors for CO-5AX, SU-2AX and SU-3AX Grain Trucks | 132 |
| 9.4 | Computation of AADT for North Dakota Minor Collectors and Minor Roads | 135 |

9.5     Computation of AADE for Rural Minor Collectors and
        Local Roads                                                      136
10.1    CO-5AX Truck Use as a Percentage of Total Shipments Under
        the Base Case and Scenario 2                                     142
10.2    Projected Distribution of Grain Between Co-op and Non-Co-op
        Elevators                                                        144
10.3    Distribution of Shipments Among Flow Types                       145
10.4    Percentage Distribution of Shipments Among Flow Types            146
10.5    Annual Trips by Truck Class                                      147
10.6    Percent of Annual Trips by Truck Class                           147
10.7    Truck Trips by Functional Class                                  148
10.8    Percent of Truck Trips by Functional Class                       148
10.9    Grain Truck VMT by Truck Type and Functional Class               149
10.10   Percent of Annual Truck VMT by Truck Type and
        Functional Class                                                 150
10.11   Incremental Grain AADE                                           152
10.12   Base-Case Replacement Cost by Functional Class                   153
10.13   Short-Run Incremental Cost                                       154
10.14   Long-Run Incremental Cost                                        155
10.15   Short-Run Incremental Cost                                       157
10.16   Long-Run Incremental Cost                                        157
11.1    Traffic Originating and Terminating on CNW Line Between but
        Excluding Norfolk and Chadron                                    167
11.2    Major Northern Line Elevators                                    168
11.3    Summary of Harvest—Nebraska/South Dakota Counties Along
        CNW Northern Line, 1989: Soybeans                                170
11.4    Summary of Harvest—Nebraska/South Dakota Counties Along
        CNW Northern Line, 1989: Corn                                    171
11.5    Summary of Harvest—Nebraska/South Dakota Counties Along
        CNW Northern Line, 1989: Wheat                                   172
11.6    Summary of Harvest—Nebraska/South Dakota Counties Along
        CNW Northern Line, 1989: Total Crops                             173
11.7    Fertilizer Sold in the Impact Area During 1989                   174
11.8    Gross Weights and Axle Loads for Major Commodities               179
11.9    Maximum Feasible Pavement Lives                                  184
11.10   Build-Sooner Costs for Twenty-Five Years (4,174 Carloads)        190
11.11   Build-Sooner Costs for Twenty-Five Years (6,274 Carloads)        191
11.12   Annual Net Pavement Costs for 4,174 Carloads                     191
11.13   Annual Net Pavement Costs for 6,274 Carloads                     192
11.14   Highway User Costs for 4,174 Carloads                            192
11.15   Highway User Costs for 6,274 Carloads                            193
12.1    Typical Highway Attributes for Rural Functional Classes          198

| 12.2 | Cost Per Ton-Mile (cents) for Rural Functional Class by Design Level | 198 |
| 12.3 | Sensitivity of Impacts to Changes in Structural Design | 198 |

## FIGURES

| 1.1 | Comparison of Growth in Volumes and Loadings on the Rural Interstate System | 6 |
| 1.2 | Percentage Distribution of Average Daily Traffic Volumes and Loadings on the Rural Interstate System | 7 |
| 1.3 | Other Arterials (Rural and Urban) | 8 |
| 3.1 | Typical Grain Flow Within a Subterminal-Satellite Elevator System | 21 |
| 5.1 | Theoretical Pavement Deterioration Function | 46 |
| 5.2 | Pavement Replacement Cycles | 48 |
| 5.3 | Pavement Deterioration and Build-Sooner Costs | 51 |
| 5.4 | Illustration of Incremental Cost Calculations for Different Levels of Highway Design | 57 |
| 5.5 | Estimated ESAL Life-Times Using Revised FHWA Model | 72 |
| 5.6 | Effects of Truck Tire Pressure on Flexible Pavement Life | 73 |
| 6.1 | Subterminal Market Area: Devils Lake & Surrounding Area | 80 |
| 6.2 | Subterminal Market Area: Zones of Equal Relative Attraction | 84 |
| 6.3 | Devils Lake Land Use Zones and Highway Network | 85 |
| 6.4 | Devils Lake Subterminal Volume: 1985-1990 | 89 |
| 6.5 | Flow of Subterminal Impact Assessment Process | 92 |
| 8.1 | Plot of Farm-to-Elevator Impedance Functions | 107 |
| 8.2 | Historic Modal Distribution of Grain and Oilseed Shipments in North Dakota | 116 |
| 8.3 | Transport Cost by Truck-Type and Distance | 118 |
| 9.1 | North Dakota Monthly Grain and Shipment: 1986-87 | 130 |
| 11.1 | CNW Northern Line | 165 |
| 11.2 | (Hypothetical) Natural Pavement Decay Process | 182 |
| 12.1 | Cost per Ton-Mile for a Range of Structural Numbers | 199 |

# Preface and Acknowledgments

During the last decade, highway management and transportation planning have become two major areas of emphasis in federal and state agencies. These activities are much broader in scope than the traditional endeavors of highway design, construction, maintenance, and traffic engineering. There are many excellent books in print that address the traditional areas of highway engineering. However, the set of tools and analytic techniques needed for highway management is different than the set of tools needed for highway design and construction. Highway managers are charged with maintaining the existing system in a cost-effective manner within ever-tightening budget and resource constraints. Topics such as rural land use, freight transportation demand, freight traffic allocation, and heavy truck forecasting techniques represent new and emerging tools that can be of considerable importance to transportation managers and planners.

The goal of this book is to describe an integrated set of impact assessment techniques that can be used to forecast the effects of changes in rural land use and railroad transportation on highway costs. I have spent much of the last ten years developing and integrating the techniques presented in this book. The original idea for the book grew out of my dissertation, which focused on the impacts of grain subterminal elevators on rural highways. Much of the remainder of the book is based on the results of work that I performed for the states of North Dakota, Nebraska, and Washington.

There are many people and organizations that I wish to thank for their contributions to the book. I owe a considerable debt of gratitude to professor John Dickey of Virginia Polytechnic Institute and State University for his suggestion that I write a book in this area, and for his careful review of my dissertation. Similar thanks go to Antoine Hobeika, Donald Drew, Richard Weyer, and Richard Zody of Virginia Tech for their helpful comments and suggestions. Jerry Lenzi of the Washington Department of Transportation, Michael Goings and Robert Wedner of the Nebraska Department of Roads, and Dennis Jacobson, Tim Horner, and Clay Sorensen of the North Dakota Department of Transportation all provided data, comments or helpful suggestions. Special thanks go to John Bitzan of North Dakota State University for his thorough review of the entire manuscript and his helpful comments and suggestions.    While these people and organizations deserve thanks and acknowledgements, they are in no way responsible for the contents of this book.

I wish to thank Martha Struthers, Beverly Trittin, Angela Carroll, and Kathy McCarthy for their diligent work on the manuscript, and the Upper Great Plains Transportation Institute and North Dakota State University for the support they gave me during development of the book.  Thanks also go to Dan Sabin and B. F. Collins of Transportation Operations, Inc. for their comments and insights regarding the railroad abandonment case study.  And last (but certainly not least) I would like to thank my publisher Eric Valentine and my production editor Sally Scott for their comments, suggestions, and patience.

# 1

# Introduction

America has an extensive highway network, consisting of 3.87 million miles of public roads and streets (Federal Highway Administration (USDOT FHWA), 1989). The nation relies on this network for the transportation of goods and materials, commuting, and personal mobility. In 1989, 712 billion ton-miles of freight were moved between American cities by truck. This volume amounted to 2.467 billion tons, or 40.5 percent of all intercity domestic freight tonnage. Furthermore, of the 3 trillion or so passenger-miles logged in America during 1989, over 2.5 trillion were accumulated in intercity highway transport, the majority by private automobile (U.S. Dept. of Transportation, 1990).

The significance of America's sprawling highway system to the nation's economy and quality of life is frequently taken for granted. As part of an integrated transportation system, America's highways allow the movement of raw materials into manufacturing and processing centers and the movement of finished products to consumers. The physical separation of production and consumption afforded by America's extensive transportation network has fostered regional specialization, mass production, divisions of labor, and sophisticated marketing/distribution channels that collectively drive the nation's economy. Just as important, America's extensive highway network has facilitated home-to-work commuting in metropolitan regions, and created an unparalleled world of personal mobility and access for its citizens.

Expenditures for highway construction, rehabilitation, and maintenance constitute a sizable public outlay in the United States. In 1988, state transportation agencies alone expended $47.6 billion on highways (USDOT FHWA, 1988). As large as this expenditure was, it still lagged behind highway needs.

As Table 1.1 shows, over 123,000 miles of U.S. highways in 1988 were rated at or below the critical or terminal serviceability level (USDOT FHWA, 1988). Ideally, these highway sections (which represent over 11 percent of all U.S. mileage) should have been rehabilitated or reconstructed when the terminal serviceability level was reached.[1]  Failure to do has resulted in a more uncomfortable (rougher) ride, increased user costs, and a general diminution of highway safety on these segments.

**Table 1.1**      U.S. Highway Mileage at or Below Terminal Serviceability, 1988

| Functional Class | Mileage | Percent of Class Mileage |
|---|---|---|
| Rural Interstate | 3,844 | 11.7% |
| Rural Other Principle Arterial | 3,958 | 5.0% |
| Rural Minor Arterial | 9,998 | 6.9% |
| Rural Major Collector | 4,456 | 10.4% |
| Rural Minor Collector | 39,470 | 13.4% |
| Subtotal: Rural | 61,726 | 11.5% |
| Urban Interstate | 1,285 | 11.5% |
| Other Urban Freeways | 255 | 3.5% |
| Other Urban Principle Arterial | 3,452 | 6.9% |
| Urban Minor Arterial | 7,085 | 9.6% |
| Urban Collector | 9,933 | 12.9% |
| Subtotal: Urban | 22,010 | 10.7% |
| Total: All Classes | 83,736 | 11.3% |

In some states, the projected highway needs for the next twenty years greatly exceed the projected revenues. For example, in a recent study, the North Dakota Department of Transportation projected that highway needs could exceed anticipated revenues by nearly 100 percent. On a nationwide scale, the potential discrepancy is mammoth. In a recent (1987) study, the National Council on Public Works Improvement estimated that America's highway and bridge system was being underfunded by roughly $20 billion per year.[2]

Management and funding of the highway system in America pose a major challenge for state and local governments. Highway rehabilitation and maintenance expenditures are usually programmed over a multi-year period. Typically, state and local governments formulate a five-year capital plan, frequently referred to as a *Transportation Improvement Program* or TIP. The TIP allocates a limited set of funds among highway routes and sections. Forecasts of highway needs are based on present pavement condition, traffic levels, and user costs. The TIP functions as intended under *stable* traffic conditions, or when past traffic growth trends continue. However, when historical traffic patterns change on certain highway routes or sections, the rational improvement process envisioned by the TIP starts to unravel. Impacted highway sections may require rehabilitation or reconstruction sooner than anticipated. Moreover, the cost of improvements may be greater than expected.

Traditional traffic forecasting and data collection techniques focus on a highway section or route. Estimates of truck and automobile traffic (e.g. average daily trips) are generated from automatic vehicle classifications and traffic counts. Typically, the vehicles that travel a highway section are counted and classified for a multi-year period. From these data, the average growth rates in automobile and truck traffic are computed. Two major shortcomings are evident in this approach. First, historical traffic data may not be reflective of future traffic conditions. Second, statistics such as the average daily trips over a highway section do not reflect the origins and destinations of the traffic. Moreover, traffic counts do not reflect land-use patterns, economic activity, or the travel desires they create.

This book poses an alternative method of traffic and highway needs forecasting. The book presents a system of techniques (collectively referred to as highway impact assessment) that can be used to supplement existing methods of transportation forecasting. Highway impact assessment is *the process of forecasting changes in programmed highway costs resulting from exogenous changes or forces.* Exogenous forces are those that cannot be controlled by highway engineers or planners. They generally result from shifts in land-use patterns, transportation conditions, or regional economic activity.

The construction of a large processing facility such as a grain subterminal is an example of an exogenous change in land-use patterns. Subterminal elevators are typically built in nonmetropolitan regions where only limited zoning authority exists. The new facilities may dramatically alter truck traffic patterns, generating additional traffic on low-volume highways. Consequently, the expected service lives of highways in the impact region may be significantly shortened.

Railroad branch-line abandonment is a primary example of an exogenous transportation change that can affect highway costs. Over 60,000 miles of railroad lines have been abandoned in the United States since 1960.[3] Many more miles have been downgraded, resulting in a loss of railroad traffic. When branch lines are downgraded or abandoned, heavy bulk commodities such as farm products, lumber, and chemicals are diverted to highways. Since most railroad branch lines are located in rural areas, the adjacent highway network usually consists of light-duty, low-volume roads not designed for heavy truck traffic. In general, changes in investment and capacity of railroad and waterway systems can divert traffic to or from highways.

Broader shifts in regional activity can also change highway traffic patterns. Rapid or cyclical natural resource extraction poses a particular problem for highway planners. Coal, petroleum, ore, or timber extraction can generate high levels of heavy truck traffic in concentrated areas. The "boom" nature of these activities tends to place heavy demands on low-volume roads over a short period of time.

Readers familiar with intermodal transportation issues can probably think of additional examples. To some extent, each case is unique. However, most of these problems exhibit common features and require a similar problem-solving process. In each instance, the highway planner must: (1) predict the level and composition of the incremental or diverted traffic, (2) determine the routes the traffic is likely to follow, and (3) translate this information into revised estimates of future highway needs in the impact region. Although this process sounds simple, it requires an understanding of a broad range of topics including freight demand, modal traffic allocation, highway networks, pavement deterioration models, and present value analysis.

## OBJECTIVES AND FOCUS

This book includes some technical material in pavement impact analysis. However, it is not intended as a reference in highway engineering or pavement design. A library of references already exist in this subject area including Yoder and Witzack (1990), The American Association of State Highway and Transportation Officials (1986), and a number of Transportation Research Board publications. The purpose of this book is to present a system of techniques that can be used to project changes in highway rehabilitation and reconstruction costs, resulting from changes in land use, regional economic activity, or traffic distribution among modes. Therefore, the focus is on the rehabilitation of existing highways, not on new construction. Moreover, the book focuses on freight transportation demand analysis, modal traffic allocation, and truck trip generation—topics that are generally not covered in depth in highway engineering texts.

The goal of the book is to assist transportation managers and analysts in planning and financing the rural and nonmetropolitan highway network. The major objectives are to: (1) provide managers and analysts with a better understanding of the forces and decisions that affect highway costs, (2) introduce an integrated set of procedures that can be applied to specific problems, and (3) supplement existing engineering and transportation planning textbooks. The book is primarily intended as a tool or guide for the practitioner. However, it may also prove useful as a supplemental text for courses in highway maintenance, traffic forecasting, or statewide transportation planning.

## BACKGROUND ISSUES

The remainder of this chapter presents some background information in transportation planning and finance. The purpose of the discussion is to highlight some important issues in transportation that drive the need for highway impact assessment. Specifically, three major topics are discussed: (1) growth in heavy truck traffic and axle loads, (2) the aging and deterioration of the rural highway system, and (3) the current transition to intermodal and multimodal statewide planning.

### Growth in Heavy Truck Traffic

As will be detailed later, the principal traffic-related component of highway deterioration is heavy truck traffic. Automobile traffic places few structural demands on a highway, and figures only marginally in the structural design of new roads. Structural design focuses on the strength of a pavement, which is a measure of its ability to withstand repeated heavy loads within a given environmental setting. Automobile traffic helps determine the capacity needs of a highway (e.g., number of lanes) and the geometric design considerations (such as horizontal and vertical alignment, sight distance, and cross section). However, automobile traffic has little effect on the life of a pavement or the thickness of the pavement layers required.[4]

Heavy trucks (and heavy axle loads in particular) are the primary determinants of future highway needs in rural areas. When many of the nation's roads were first constructed, the "design truck" was a single-unit vehicle with relatively light axle weights. In 1918, the Bureau of Public Roads described a heavy truck as one carrying eight to twelve tons and being of the single-unit variety.[5] However, by 1949, the median state gross vehicle weight (GVW) limit for combination five-axle (CO-5AX) trucks had risen to 61,000 pounds and was still climbing. In 1974, Congress mandated a uniform 80,000 GVW limit on interstate highways. The states shortly followed suit. By 1982, the median state GVW limit for major highways had risen to 80,000 pounds, where it stands today.

Although important, the increase in combination truck traffic and GVWs are only surface manifestations of the heavy truck problem. The real problem for pavements lies with the axle configurations of trucks and the increased axle load limitations that have occurred in recent years. The weight of a truck is transmitted to the pavement and subgrade through its set of axle and tire configurations. Recognizing this effect, Pennsylvania adopted the first axle load limitations in 1913 (18,000 pounds).[6] In the Federal Aid Highway Act of 1956, Congress adopted the recommendations of the American Association of State

Highway Officials (AASHO) and mandated a maximum load of 18,000 pounds on a single axle and 32,000 pounds on a tandem axle for interstate highways. In the Surface Transportation Act of 1982, Congress required that all states standardize interstate load limitations at 20,000 for a single-axle and 34,000 for a tandem axle.[7]

With increasing GVWs, many combination trucks are operating at or near the axle weight limits today. This trend is illustrated in Figure 1.1, which graphs changes in equivalent axle loads (EAL) and truck interstate traffic over time. As Figure 1.1 shows, part of the problem is attributable to increased truck travel. However, growth in standardized axle loadings has far outstripped traffic growth since 1972.

**Figure 1.1**        Comparison of Growth in Volumes and Loadings on the Rural
                       Interstate System

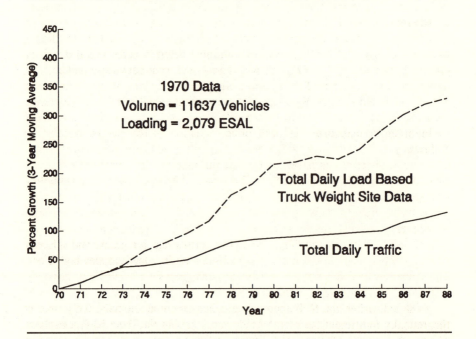

Figure 1.2 shows more specific trends for CO-5AX trucks. In 1970, CO-5AX trucks comprised 8 percent of daily interstate traffic volume. By 1988, CO-5AX volume rose to 15 percent of average daily traffic. During this same period, the CO-5AX's percentage of daily axle loadings increased from 74 to 92 percent. In short, *trends toward more frequent combination truck trips, heavier combination truck weights, and heavier axle loads are placing more and more stress on America's highways.*

**Figure 1.2**     Percentage Distribution of Average Daily Traffic Volumes and Loadings on the Rural Interstate System

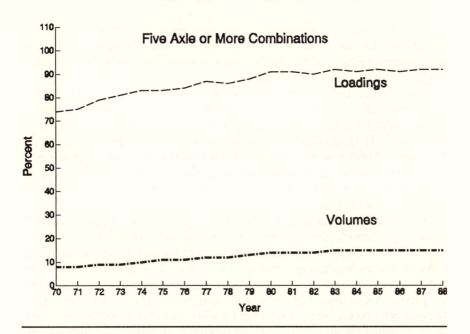

### The Aging and Deterioration of America's Highways

Many of America's highways were built during the post–World War II construction era. With underinvestment and deferred rehabilitation, much of the highway network is deteriorating. As Figure 1.3 shows, 42 percent of America's arterial highways in 1987 was classified as either deteriorated or deteriorating by the U.S. Department of Transportation (USDOT FHWA, 1988). This percentage remained relatively constant from 1982 to 1987, suggesting that federal and state governments were unable to rehabilitate an aging, deteriorating system despite recent motor fuel tax increases.

**Figure 1.3**        Other Arterials (Rural and Urban)

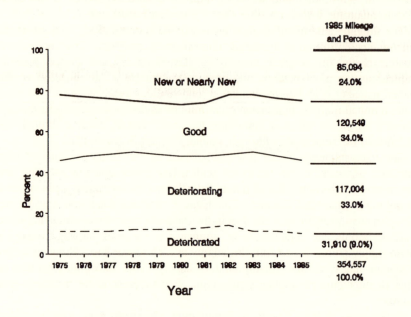

Deteriorated highways exacerbate the heavy truck problem. As the serviceability of a highway declines, the pavement's capacity to absorb (and recover) from a heavy axle pass decreases. Thus, the impact of an axle passage of a given magnitude (e.g., 20,000 pounds) is greater on an older, deteriorated highway than on a recently rehabilitated road.[8]

The combined effects of increased truck traffic, heavier axle loads, and deteriorating rural highways provide a strong impetus for improvements in highway impact assessment. The need for statewide multimodal planning analysis provides another strong justification for state transportation departments to develop highway impact assessment techniques.

**Transition to Intermodal Statewide Transportation Planning**

The Intermodal Surface Transportation Efficiency Act of 1991 (ISTEA) requires each state to establish a statewide transportation planning process and implement an intermodal management system (IMS) by 1995. In effect, the ISTEA ushered in an era of intermodal planning and investment. It is no longer sufficient to focus on highway investment and planning in a purely modal sense. Instead, states must "encourage and promote the development of transportation systems embracing various modes of transportation in a manner that will serve all areas of the state efficiently and effectively." Moreover, Section 1034 of ISTEA stipulates that the IMS shall: "provide for integration and improvement of all of a State's transportation systems and shall include methods for achieving the optimum yield from such systems, methods for increasing productivity in the State, methods for increasing use of advanced technologies, and methods to encourage the innovative use of marketing techniques such as just-in-time deliveries."

The highway impact assessment procedures described in this book can be a valuable tool in state intermodal planning and management. First, the techniques can be used to forecast the impacts of shifts in traffic distribution among modes. Thus, the procedures can be used to evaluate tradeoffs among highway, railroad, and waterway investments. The railroad abandonment problem mentioned earlier illustrates the concept. In many cases, the lack of investment in railroad branch lines can divert traffic to trucks, which in turn accelerates the deterioration of highways resulting in increased highway investment. Although railroad investment is primarily a matter of private financing, these investment decisions can have a significant impact on public highway investment. The tools described in this book give state transportation managers a method for assessing the effects of investment in railroads and waterways on highway funding needs.

## NOTES

1. This present serviceability level is typically 2.5 for interstate highways and 2.0 for other classes of roads.

2. Part of the highway finance dilemma relates to the fact that the Highway Trust Fund, the primary funding mechanism for interstate and primary highways, is part of the unified federal budget. Consequently, annual expenditure or obligation ceilings are typically placed on highway funds.

3. United States Department of Agriculture.

4. For reasons of safety, a minimum pavement thickness is usually required, even in the absence of truck traffic.

5. USDA. 1918b. "The Highways of the Country and Burden They Must Carry." *Public Roads* 1,2.

6. TRB, Truck Weight Limits, 1990, page 35.

7.  A detailed history of axle weight limitations is contained in Transportation
Research Board (TRB) Special Reports 211 (1986) and 225 (1990).

8.  This relationship is illustrated in Figure 5.1.

# 2

# Overview

This chapter presents an overview of the highway impact assessment process beginning with a survey of the types of highway impacts typically encountered. The survey is followed by a discussion of the analytical approach and philosophy of the impact assessment process. The objective in this section is to orient the reader away from traffic classification and toward systems analysis as a solution technique. The chapter concludes with an overview of the procedures and models involved in highway impact assessment, each of which will be detailed later in the book.

## SCOPE OF THE HIGHWAY IMPACT ASSESSMENT PROCESS

Changes in heavy truck traffic patterns may generate a wide range of impacts. These include

1. highway capacity impacts,
2. user cost impacts,
3. safety impacts,
4. environmental consequences,
5. community impacts, and
6. pavement rehabilitation and reconstruction costs.

Increased heavy truck traffic consumes a portion of the available capacity of a highway (as measured in vehicles per lane per hour). In general, on a rural, two-lane highway over level terrain, a single-unit two-axle truck occupies 1.2 times the capacity of a standard passenger car in a stream of traffic (USDOT FHWA, 1984). The passenger car equivalents (PCEs) are even higher for single-unit three-axle trucks and combination trucks: 1.5 and 3.0, respectively. Furthermore, the PCEs increase considerably in areas of rolling terrain.

Operating speed on rural highways is a function of the design speed and the volume-to-capacity (V/C) ratio. As the V/C ratio of a highway section increases due to additional truck traffic, the costs of other users (as measured in travel time) rise. If user costs rise substantially due to congestion, lanes may have to be widened or added.

Low-volume roads are typically constructed to lower geometric standards than interstate highways or freeways. Thus, additional heavy truck traffic may impact the safety of operations on rural highways. Narrow lanes and shoulders may pose both vehicle and pedestrian hazards. Curves and winding roads may limit a driver's line of vision and impair operating safety. Furthermore, a basic increase in accident exposure at railroad grade crossings and other areas of potential hazard may occur due to increased truck vehicle miles of travel.

The environmental consequences of heavy truck traffic consist principally of noise, air pollution, and dust in the impact region. These externalities are particularly noticeable in instances where CO-5AX trucks are routed over gravel-surface, low-volume roads.

Community impacts are those experienced by non-highway users residing in an impact area. Community impacts can be environmental, such as increased noise, pollution, and dust on unpaved roads. However, community impacts can also be perceptual in nature. The obtrusiveness of transportation into the everyday lives of residents can be exacerbated by additional truck traffic on low-volume highways.

Some exogenous changes (such as branch-line abandonment) may result in non-highway costs to communities. These economic impacts are generally caused by three off-shoots of abandonment or traffic diversion. First, truck shipping rates are usually higher than railroad or waterway rates for bulk commodities. Second, shippers' distribution costs may increase due to the purchase of trucks, construction of transloading and storage facilities, or other capital expenditures. Third, jobs and income may be lost in the transportation, agricultural, processing, and manufacturing sectors of the economy. These primary effects can result in an overall decline in gross business volumes and tax revenue in affected communities and counties.

Community economic impacts are sometimes considered in abandonment impact studies and railroad benefit-cost analyses. However, they are not addressed in this book. The primary focus of the book is on pavement costs. The exclusion of other types of costs does not imply that they are unimportant. However, branch-line abandonment, resource extraction, and grain subterminal development occur primarily in rural areas where the scale of capacity, environmental, and noise impacts tends to be relatively small. Rural areas usually exhibit low V/C ratios, good ambient air conditions, and low population densities. Thus, environmental, community, and highway capacity impacts are somewhat mitigated. On the other hand, infrastructure costs per vehicle mile of travel (VMT) tend to be relatively high on low-volume roads. Thus, pavement costs are a major concern of highway managers.

## APPROACH AND PHILOSOPHY

The underlying philosophy of highway impact assessment is that *traffic data alone cannot provide timely and adequate analysis of changes in heavy truck traffic*. Analysis of *before* and *after* traffic data may provide hindsight into truck traffic patterns, but, this approach places the highway manager in a reactive rather than in a proactive planning situation.

### The Traffic Approach Versus Systems Analysis

There are severe problems and limitations associated with traditional traffic analysis. First, the traffic approach focuses on vehicle volumes rather than transportation demand. Traffic data collected at particular sites can show what is occurring (the results), but cannot explain why. The truck volume at any given monitoring site at any particular time is determined by the demand for the transportation of the commodities to and from specific locations. The traffic approach treats the determinants of demand as exogenous forces that are reflected in trend lines and patterns. Because the traffic approach does not explicitly account for underlying causal relationships, forecasts are subject to considerable uncertainty. Furthermore, simulation and sensitivity analysis cannot be properly performed because the underlying demand relationships are unknown.

Second, the traffic approach typically deals with classes of vehicles or traffic, rather than with classes of commodities. For example, short-term changes in the Federal Highway Administration's vehicle class six (single–unit three-axle trucks) can be captured by classification data. However, the farm truck movements that comprise a portion of these counts may be obscured by the group data. Yet, these farm truck movements could be the focus of the impact study.

Third, the traffic approach does not identify origins and destinations for the traffic. The classification data tell how many vehicles of a particular type pass a monitoring site during a particular time interval, but do not say where the trips originated and where they will terminate. Again, this limits the simulative and analytical capabilities of the approach.

This book presents an alternative to reliance on traffic counts and classifications. This does not mean that traffic data are not important inputs. Traffic counts and weigh-in-motion (WIM) data, properly adjusted for seasonal variance, help paint a picture of the historical traffic stream and its composition. However, the process of highway impact assessment is much broader. In this book, a systems approach is adopted that explicitly models the location and level of economic activities and commodity flows in the impact region. The process is centered on the desires for travel, not the vehicle count on a particular highway section.

The advantages of highway impact assessment over traditional traffic analysis are:

1.   In addition to vehicle class data, specific commodity flow data within each vehicle class are accounted for;
2.   The origin and destination zones are explicitly defined;
3.   Long-run facility operating strategies and economic shifts are considered;
4.   Uncertainty and the dynamics of the land-use and transportation system are better accounted for;
5.   The results are available in a timely, usable fashion.

Most traffic forecasts are deterministic in nature. However, a great deal of uncertainty exists in forecasting future traffic flows. A variety of forces acting in isolation or in concert can affect and dramatically alter the patterns of commodity flows that exist in a region. Such uncertainty lends itself to the use of scenario analysis.

## Scenario Analysis Versus Forecasting

The use of future or scenario analysis has received greater attention lately in transportation and economic forecasting, as the capability to predict exogenous forces has become circumspect.[1] In scenario analysis, the analyst does not have to forecast the future. Instead, he or she forecasts a set of likely, alternative futures. This approach admits the incapability of analytic techniques to adequately account for all major economic, political, and environmental forces.

In lieu of a single deterministic forecast, scenario analysis yields a range of forecasts that might hold true under different assumptions. By looking at a range of impacts, the analyst can identify both the worst and the best possible cases. Furthermore, an *expected value* of future flows can be  calculated simply by assigning probabilities to each scenario.[2]

In the subterminal case study presented later in the book, the technique of scenario analysis is used in conjunction with a Delphi survey to generate estimates of future commodity flows.[3] Then, using the expected values of the scenarios, a range of possible highway impacts is identified.

## SYSTEM OF MODELS

The highway impact assessment process actually consists of a  chain of analytic procedures. These submodels collectively translate the demand for transportation and the abstract traffic flows that it creates into estimates of future highway costs. Four basic types of models are discussed in this book:

1. transportation demand models,
2. traffic models,
3. network models, and
4. pavement impact models.

Transportation demand models relate the type, intensity, and location of economic activities to the demand for the movement of goods between various locations in space.[4] Intuitively, the demand for transportation is the *potential* for traffic flow between spatially separated points or zones.

Traffic models translate abstract commodity flows into traffic volumes over space and time. Collectively, traffic models predict the distribution of shipments among zones, the mode taken, the classes of highway equipment utilized, the gross vehicle weights and axle loads.

Network models assign the predicted highway traffic flows between origins and destinations to specific highways and routes. Then, based on the attributes of the highway sections in each route, the equivalent single axle loads (ESALs) per VMT are estimated.

The impact models utilize the ESALs and axle passes generated by the network models to simulate use-related pavement deterioration on highway sections. The highway cost model, the final link in the chain, estimates the absolute level and distribution of future highway needs among functional classes.

Sequentially, the output of one submodel in the chain generally becomes the input to the next. The order of analysis shown in Table 2.1 is typically followed. However, the truck weight and axle load procedures may be combined. Weigh-in-motion (WIM) equipment exists today that can simultaneously classify and electronically compute a vehicle's equivalent axle loads. The use of WIM data in highway impact assessment is illustrated in chapter 10.

This chapter has highlighted the highway impact assessment process and discussed its philosophical underpinnings. Both the breadth and focus of highway impact assessment have been defined, and distinctions have been drawn between highway impact assessment and traffic analysis. Scenario analysis has been introduced as a means of dealing with uncertainty. In conclusion, a system of analytical procedures has been presented that can be used to analyze changes in land-use, transportation, or regional economic activity. These procedures will be the focus of much of the remainder of the text.

**Table 2.1**        Submodels Needed for Subterminal Traffic Analysis

| Category | Submodels |
|----------|-----------|
| Demand | Land-Use<br>Shipment Generation |
| Traffic | Shipment Distribution<br>Modal Split<br>Truck Distribution<br>Truck Weight |
| Network | Route Assignment<br>Highway Attribute<br>Equivalent Axle Load |
| Impact | Pavement Damage<br>Highway Needs |

**NOTES**

1. For a recent example of the application of future or scenario analysis to public transportation, see Rutherford and Lattemann (1988). In this study, an expert panel was assembled with a knowledge of "economics, demographics, social sciences, development, law, trade, and business," which provided technical input on national and regional trends. The panel was asked to assign probabilities to future regional scenarios and estimate the impacts of each scenario on the various jurisdictions involved.

2. The concept of scenario analysis lends itself to the formulation of contingency plans. Instead of developing a single financial strategy that is valid only if the underlying assumptions and forecasts hold true, transportation planners may formulate a set of alternative plans that might be implemented under various circumstances.

3. The Delphi technique was originally developed by the Rand Corporation in the early 1960s as an alternative to committee forecasting. The Delphi procedure employs the concepts of anonymity and feedback to arrive at an approximate consensus within a panel of experts. Briefly, the Delphi technique works as follows. First, a panel of experts is identified. Second, a survey instrument is

designed and administered to the panel. Third, the results are tabulated and used in a second round of questionnaires. In the second round, participants are allowed to compare their answers against those of other (anonymous) committee members, and adjust their initial response if appropriate. The iterations continue until there is no longer a great deal of convergence in the answers.

4. Two points should be noted here concerning transportation demand analysis. First, as mentioned earlier, the demand for freight transportation is a derived demand, derived from the underlying demand for the use of a commodity at a particular point in space during a particular interval in time. Although the expressed demand may be for truck trips or ton-miles, the true underlying demand is for the commodity itself. Second, and following from the first point, transportation demand analysis is distinct from traffic forecasting. The two are obviously related, but traffic forecasting may involve the use of trending, extrapolation, or other techniques in an effort to forecast future volumes. Consequently, this process may be removed from underlying commodity demand relationships. Demand analysis, on the other hand, focuses on the relationships, linkages, and decision rules that give rise to the flow of commodities or people between zones. Demand analysis thus begins at the level of abstract commodity flow, and converts these flows into traffic volumes.

# 3

# The Grain Subterminal Elevator:
# A Rural Land-Use Change

Many of the concepts introduced in chapters 4 through 9 are generic in nature. Consequently, they can be applied to a variety of problems. However, many of these concepts are also very abstract and theoretical in nature. Thus, it may prove useful for the reader to have a concrete example of an exogenous change in mind before delving into the theory and mechanics of highway impact assessment.

This chapter describes a sample problem—the subterminal-satellite elevator system—that will be used to illustrate many of the concepts presented in chapters 4-9. An actual case study of a grain subterminal system will be presented in chapter 10.

There are several reasons why the grain subterminal problem is a good example of an exogenous change. First, it is one of the most complex problems the highway analyst is likely to encounter. The subterminal system generates five types of truck flows. In comparison, branch-line abandonment generates only three types. Thus, the subterminal problem more fully illustrates the major aspects of highway impact assessment. In addition, the cooperative subterminal elevator system described in this chapter is an example of a multiplant business. Multiplant businesses typically trans-ship commodities among facilities or warehouses within the system. The multiplant model tends to characterize many types of extractive and industrial activities. Third, the subterminal system exemplifies resource-based economies in which multiple supply points feed central processing or transloading facilities. Timber and coal enterprises tend to exhibit these same characteristics.

## OVERVIEW OF THE PROBLEM

Prior to 1980, the predominant grain flows in many rural areas of America consisted of farm-to-country–elevator and country–elevator-to-market shipments. The majority of farm-to-elevator trips occurred in two-axle, single-unit farm trucks over relatively short distances.[1] Outbound elevator shipments originated primarily by rail. The remainder moved via long-haul commercial trucking services, which primarily utilized interstate and principal arterial highways.

Today, under a cooperative organizational structure, many of these small, previously independent grain elevators function as "satellites." As such, they are primarily used for the assembly and storage of grain that is reshipped to a subterminal at a later date. In many rural states, trans-shipments or elevator-to-subterminal shipments have largely supplanted the traditional country–elevator-to-market flow. Consequently, railroad or long-haul trucking services at the country elevator have been replaced by short-haul trucking to the grain subterminal.

The subterminal traffic problem entails three dimensions or facets: grain flows, highway equipment, and highway attributes. Each dimension is highlighted in the following paragraphs.

## GRAIN FLOWS

Subterminal-satellite systems generate five classes or types of grain flows (Figure 3.1):

1. farm to satellite elevator,
2. farm to subterminal elevator,
3. satellite elevator to market,
4. satellite elevator to subterminal,
5. subterminal elevator to market.

Only two of these flow types (1 and 3) occurred prior to the advent of subterminal-satellite systems. Of the three new flows, most of the concern has been expressed over flow-type 4 (trans-shipments). When a trans-shipment occurs, it represents the second truck movement within the subterminal-satellite market area. The first movement is the farm truck trip to the satellite elevator (flow-type 1). In addition to trans-shipments, direct farm-to-subterminal movements (flow-type 2) are prevalent in some subterminal systems today. The primary concerns of this flow-type are the increased distance of haul and the type of truck used. Subterminal-to-market shipments (flow-type 5) are important in all systems. However, these flows primarily occur via rail, engendering little if any highway concern.

**Figure 3.1**         Typical Grain Flow Within a Subterminal-Satellite Elevator System

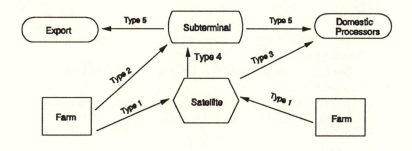

## TRUCK TYPES

Three types of vehicles are used extensively in the highway transportation of grain:

1.   the single-unit, two-axle farm truck (SU-2AX),
2.   the single-unit, three-axle farm truck (SU-3AX),
3.   the combination, five-axle truck (CO-5AX).

The three classes of vehicles have different tare (empty) weights, capacities, and axle configurations. Consequently, the axle loads applied to the pavement by each type of vehicle usually differ. Furthermore since the capacities differ among vehicle types, the annual number of trips required to haul a fixed annual tonnage tends to vary.

The density of the commodity affects the net weight. Certain grains and oilseeds are denser than others. As a result, more net tons can be loaded into a given truck before the cubic capacity of the vehicle is reached. The reverse is true of less-dense, light-loading commodities.[2] Thus, denser commodities require fewer annual trips. However, dense commodities result in heavier axle weights. The axle weights may constrain the net weight of the vehicle, thus offsetting some of the economies of commodity density.

## HIGHWAY ATTRIBUTES

The impacts of a fully loaded truck of a given type carrying a given commodity are determined in part by the axle weights. But they are also governed by the type and characteristics of the highways used.

The principal highway attributes that will determine the effects of truck shipments for a given climatic zone are:

1. the thickness of the surface course, the base course, and the subbase course of flexible pavements,
2. the thickness of the concrete slab for rigid or Portland Concrete Cement (PCC) pavements,
3. the composition, characteristics, and strength of the materials used,
4. the composition and character of the supporting soil,
5. the age of the highway section, and
6. the present condition or serviceability.

The chain of cause-and-effect in highway deterioration is as follows: (1) The truck type and the commodity determine the axle weights or loads. (2) The axle weights, in combination with the attributes of a highway section, determine the amount of damage that each truck pass will inflict. (3) The number of annual trips required to haul a given level of commodity will decide the number of axle passes that will occur during a year. (4) The accumulation of axle passes over time will eventually result in the rehabilitation or reconstruction of the highway section.

Grain flows constitute mixed traffic flows; that is, they consist of different types of vehicles with different axle weights. In pavement damage analysis, a mixed traffic stream is analyzed through the use of a "reference axle." Using the reference axle, all other axle weights are translated into equivalent axle loads. If the reference axle is a single axle, then the term "equivalent single–axle load" or ESAL is used. In almost all instances, the reference axle is the 18,000–pound single axle.

The damage that a particular axle configuration and load will cause is evaluated by first converting the axle to ESALs. For example, on a typical low-volume road a 22,000 pound single axle load is expressed as 2.35 ESALs.[3] Once the ESALs are determined, the truck trips can be related to pavement deterioration through means of a damage model.

Table 3.1 gives typical tare weight, net weight, and gross vehicle weight for grain trucks operating over low-volume roads. Note that while the CO–5AX operates at higher gross weights, it carries substantially more payload than the SU–3AX or SU–2AX truck.

**Table 3.1**        Typical Vehicle Weights and Loaded ESALs for Grain Truck Types

| Truck Types | Tare Weight (lbs) | Net Weight (lbs) | ESALs Per Loaded Mile | ESALs Per Ton Mile |
|---|---|---|---|---|
| SU-2AX | 12,407 | 15,412 | 1.68 | .22 |
| SU-3AX | 16,671 | 27,435 | 1.24 | .09 |
| CO-5AX | 26,650 | 53,350 | 2.42 | .09 |

Source: North Dakota Truck Weight Survey (1988)

Table 3.1 also illustrates the difference in ESALs and resulting pavement damage that may result from different patterns of vehicle use. The CO–5AX has by far the highest number of ESALs per loaded vehicle mile of travel (VMT), followed by the SU–2AX farm truck.[4] However, because of differences in payload capacity, the CO-5AX and the SU-3AX generate approximately the same ESALs per net ton-mile (.09). In contrast, the SU-2AX farm truck generates approximately .22 ESALs per ton-mile. Thus, shifts in grain flows that increase the length of haul of SU-2AX trucks or divert traffic from railroads to CO-5AX trucks can increase the level of highway costs in rural areas.

## HIGHWAY IMPACTS

The manner in which a given subterminal-satellite system impacts a highway section depends on the extent to which the dimensions of the problem are altered or affected by the development of the subterminal. In general, subterminal-satellite systems impact grain flows in two ways: (1) they create new types of flows (flow-types 2, 4, and 5), and (2) they alter the level of existing flows.

In a 1988 study, Zink surveyed nine major grain cooperatives in the Upper Great Plains region. Some of the unpublished survey data obtained in the study shed light on the shipping patterns of subterminal-satellite systems. On the average, 61 percent of the inbound grains and oilseeds were trans-shipped from satellite elevators to the subterminal (Table 3.2). The remaining 39 percent were drawn directly from farms to the subterminal. On the average, only 11 percent of total elevator-to-terminal market volume was shipped from satellite elevators. The remaining 89 percent of outbound shipments originated at the subterminal.

The formation of subterminal-satellite systems has increased the average trip distance from farms to delivery points. Prior to 1980, the majority of farm-to-elevator shipments were relatively short in distance. A typical farm truck trip in 1980 covered twelve miles (Griffin, Wilson and Casavant, 1984). Now, direct farm-to-subterminal shipments are occurring over considerable distances. Zink (1988) found that the average distance from farms to the subterminal elevator within the seven North Dakota systems surveyed ranged from 10.5 to 37.2 miles, with a grand mean of 23 miles. Furthermore, it is not unusual for farmers on the periphery of a trade area (which constitute the extreme cases in a distribution) to truck up to 50 miles in order to reach the subterminal.

Trans-shipment is a major trend in truck usage attributable to subterminal-satellite systems. An increase in trans-shipments typically implies a shift in traffic from railroads to CO–5AX trucks. This has important implications for pavement damage, as illustrated by Table 3.1.

As grain flows change, so do the highways utilized. Prior to 1980, the majority of CO–5AX truck miles in rural areas were accumulated on interstate and principal arterial highways. These highways were specifically designed to accommodate heavy truck traffic. Today, the pattern has changed. The frequency of CO–5AX truck use has risen within subterminal market areas. Consequently, a large number of CO–5AX truck miles are now being accumulated on low-volume roads.

In many rural areas, the highways that connect the subterminal to its satellites are minor rural arterials or local roads. Unlike the interstate and principal arterial network, these highways were not designed to accommodate heavy truck traffic. Furthermore, the rural minor arterial system is aging and in deteriorated condition. Much of it needs to be replaced. Unfortunately, the effect of a CO–5AX truck-mile on an old, deteriorated road designed for low volumes is much greater than an interstate truck-mile over high-design pavements.

The purpose of this chapter has been to define a concrete example of an exogenous change. The grain subterminal is a major change in rural land use. The location of these facilities has changed truck traffic patterns in many rural and western states during the last two decades. The facilities generate heavy truck traffic that creates a mismatch between structural demands and the existing low-volume road network. The subterminal example is prototypical of many types of natural resource or extractive activities that are primary traffic generators

**Table 3.2**          Representative Subterminal-Satellite Elevator Traffic Flows as
                       a Percent of Inbound and Outbound Volumes

| Flow-Type | Mean | Median | Low Value | High Value | Range |
|-----------|------|--------|-----------|------------|-------|
| Trans-shipment (#4) | 61% | 65% | 25% | 99% | 74% |
| Direct Market (#3) | 11% | 7% | 0% | 40% | 40% |

Source:  Unpublished UGPTI survey data.

in nonmetropolitan regions.  For these reasons, the subterminal problem is used
to illustrate some of the major concepts and procedures in freight transport
demand analysis presented in Chapter 4.

**NOTES**

1. A 1980 survey by the Upper Great Plains Transportation Institute found that
84% of the farm truck fleet in North Dakota consisted of two-axle, single unit
trucks.  The average length of haul in 1980 was 12 miles.  Source: Griffin,
Wilson and Casavant (1984).

2. The commodity plays its most important role with respect to the single-unit,
two-axle truck.  Because of the axle configuration, the SU-2AX may reach
payload capacity before legal axle load limitations (e.g. 20,000 pounds).  This is
particularly true with light-loading commodities such as barley and sunflowers.

3. This example assumes the following conditions: (1) a flexible pavement, (2)
a structural number or strength rating of 3.0, and (3) a terminal present
serviceability rating of 2.0.  The structural number (SN) is an abstract index
which reflects the composite strength of the layers of a flexible pavement section.
In computing the SN, .44 of a point is typically added to the index for each inch
of surface course, .14 for each inch of granular base and .11 for each inch of
granular sub-base.  The present serviceability rating (PSR) is a composite measure
of a highway's condition at a given interval in time.  The terminal PSR is the
condition rating which prevails at the time the highway section reaches functional
failure.  Usually, at this point in a pavement's life cycle, the section is either
replaced or upgraded.

4. Note that the SU-3AX farm truck has lower ESALs per loaded VMT than does the SU-2AX truck. The reason for this lies with the axle configuration of the vehicles. The SU-3AX has a tandem rear axle, typically with eight tires. Thus the load per wheel which is transmitted to the pavement is less than that for the SU-2AX.

# 4

# Freight Transportation
# Demand Analysis

The demand for freight transportation is a derived demand. It is derived from the demand for the commodity. Freight demand has both temporal and spatial dimensions. The demand for freight transport is a function of the demand for a commodity at a certain location during a certain interval of time. In the terminology of transportation economics, freight transport creates place and time utilities for shippers and producers.

The purpose of this chapter is to set forth some fundamental concepts in freight transportation demand analysis. In section one, a simple yet intuitive model of freight demand relationships is set forth. Section two introduces spatial interaction modeling, illustrating the process through the use of the grain subterminal problem outlined in chapter 3. Section three introduces optimization techniques as an alternative to spatial interaction modeling. The general transportation and trans-shipment algorithms are defined and illustrated within the context of agricultural traffic flows.

## COMMODITY TRANSPORTATION DEMAND

Kananafi (1983) identified three basic approaches to commodity transportation demand analysis: microeconomic approach, spatial interaction approach, and macroeconomic approach. Both microeconomic theory and spatial interaction modeling play key roles in the commodity transportation demand models formulated in this chapter.

Commodity demand analysis is based on the theory of the firm, particularly its production processes and level of technology. In the theory of the firm, commodities constitute factors of production; that is, they are inputs to the production, sales, or marketing processes of a firm. The firm requires (demands) the commodities, thus establishing economic linkages with producers or suppliers.

The discussion of demand theory begins with the formulation of some simple yet intuitive relationships. Assume (for purposes of illustration) that a supplier in zone $A$ sells an input to a firm located in zone $B$. The demand for the commodity at $B$ is a function of the delivered (or FOB) price. Algebraically, this relationship is expressed by:[1]

$$Q_B = f(P_B)$$                 (4.1)

where:

$Q_B$    =    Quantity demanded at $B$
$P_B$    =    Price at $B$

The price of a good at $B$ is comprised of two components; the price at $A$ $(P_A)$ plus the transportation cost between $A$ and $B$ $(TC_{AB})$. Thus the quantity demanded at $B$ may be restated as:

$$Q_B = f(P_A + TC_{AB})$$                 (4.2)

The demand for the transportation of a commodity between $A$ and $B$ results in a commodity flow or volume $(V_{AB})$. Theoretically, the volume of flow between $A$ and $B$ is a function of the demand for the commodity and the level of transportation service $(S)$:[2]

$$V_{AB} = f(Q_B, S)$$                 (4.3)

Since the level of service affects operator costs, it implicitly has an effect on the cost of transportation between $A$ and $B$ $(TC_{AB})$. Therefore, with little loss of explanatory power, equation (4.3) may be condensed to:

$$V_{AB} = f(Q_B) = f(P_B)$$                 (4.4)

Alternatively (by substitution) the demand for transportation between $A$ and $B$ becomes:

$$V_{AB} = f(P_A + TC_{AB})$$                 (4.5)

Equations (4.1)–(4.5) make two important points concerning commodity transportation demand: (1) if the firm's demand for a good is known, then the demand for transportation of the commodity can be derived, and (2) the firm's demand for a given commodity is a function of its supply-point price and the transportation cost between $A$ and $B$.

## Spatial Interaction Modeling

The major problem with the simple demand model presented above is that it does not explicitly account for the competitive relationships and spatial linkages that exist within a particular market region. Only one commodity and firm are contemplated. In reality, there are usually multiple commodities, purchasers, and suppliers within a given geographic region. There is competition among firms (demand-point competition) and competition among suppliers (supply-point competition). When these competitive relationships are strong, they tend to distort the restrictive model presented in equation (4.5).

An alternative formulation of equation (4.5) can be derived by moving to a spatial interaction approach. Spatial interaction models are typically aggregate in nature, dealing with zones of excess supply and demand rather than with individual firms and suppliers. Fairly large regions or zones have been used in previous studies. For example, Black (1972) modeled subnational, inter-regional commodity flows with a spatial interaction model. However, the level of aggregation does not necessarily have to be great. For example, Rimmer and Black (1981) modeled the flow of goods within a metropolitan region. In fact, the smaller the level of aggregation and the more concise the demand relationships, the more accurate the spatial interaction model will be.

## Theory

Blunden and Black (1984) have extensively developed the theory behind spatial interaction modeling. In their 1984 study, they conceived traffic flow as a *potential/flow problem* with analogies in physics. On page 21, they write:

> Interaction between land-use activities and transport facilities may be conceptualized as a potential/flow problem. The analogy in physics is a mass, electric charge, or a magnetic pole, setting up a gravitational, electric, or magnetic field which exerts a force or influence on a remote counterpart. Similarly, a zone of land-use activity creates a socioeconomic *field* which causes attraction forces among other complementary land-uses. This force of attraction acts on people giving rise to the flow of person trips. Intuitively, the strength of attraction is directly proportional to the intensity of the land-use activity but diminishes as the effort of making the trip increases.

Although referring to person-trips in the quote, the basic concepts advanced by Blunden and Black (and others) are equally applicable to all modes and types of transportation, freight or passenger.[3] The central idea is that a land-use zone containing processing plants or industry will exert an economic attraction over complementary production or supply zones within a given geographic region.[4] The force of attraction will be directly proportional to the intensity of the land-use activity in the zone (as measured by the size, number, and output level of firms), and inversely proportional to the distance or cost of transport.

**Laws**

Spatial interaction is governed by three fundamental laws: (1) a law of attraction, (2) a law of flow, and (3) a law of interaction. Although originally stated in terms of person-trips, the laws are general enough so that they can be restated in terms of commodity flows.

The attractive force exerted over an origin supply zone $O$ by a destination demand zone $D$ is directly proportional to the level of the economic attractors at $D$ and inversely proportional to the *impedance* to flow that exists between $O$ and $D$. This relationship is given by:

$$A_{OD} = \frac{X_D}{Z_{OD}} \qquad (4.6)$$

where:

$A_{OD}$ = the attractive force exerted over zone $O$ by destination zone $D$

$X_D$ = a measure of economic attraction

$Z_{OD}$ = a variable representing the impedance to flow between zone $O$ and zone $D$

$X_D$ is typically some function of the bid price for the commodity at $D$, the number and size of firms, the amount of available storage, the adequacy of unloading and transloading facilities, and a range of related factors. The impedance factor ($Z_{OD}$) is typically some function of the distance between $O$ and $D$, the level of transportation services, the travel time, and operator costs.

If the level of transportation services is low, the impedance to flow will be high. Conversely, if the distance is small and the travel time short, the impedance will be low.

Since the level of transportation services, the distance, and the travel time all affect operator costs, the cost of trucking between zones $O$ and $D$ may be used to represent the impedance function. Similarly, since the size and number of firms and their processing and handling capabilities are somewhat reflected in the bid price for the commodity, price may be utilized as a measure of the economic attraction between supply and demand zones.

The law of attraction defines the intensity of the economic linkages that exist between complementary land-use zones within a region. The law of flow translates this attractive force into a potential volume or flow.

The law of flow is given by:

$$F_{OD} = \frac{S_O X_D}{Z_{OD}}$$

(4.7)

where:

$F_{OD}$ = the potential volume of flow between $O$ and $D$

$S_O$ = the amount of commodity available (the supply) at $O$

The law of flow describes the *potential* volume between $O$ and $D$ given the level of supply at $O$, the intensity of the economic attraction at $D$, and the impedance to flow. But the law of flow does not actually say what the interzonal volume will be. This depends upon the attractiveness of $D$ relative to all other destination zones in the region. In other words, the interzonal volume of flow will be determined in part by demand-point competition.

Demand-point competition is addressed in spatial interaction modeling through the law of interaction. Algebraically, this law states that:

$$V_{OD} = S_O \frac{\dfrac{X_D}{Z_{OD}}}{\displaystyle\sum_D \dfrac{X_D}{Z_{OD}}}$$

(4.8)

where:

$V_{OD}$ = the volume of flow between supply zone $O$ and demand zone $D$

Recall from equation (4.6) that the term $X_D/Z_{OD}$ is the attractive force exerted over zone $O$ by destination zone $D$ ($A_{OD}$). Thus, by substitution, equation (4.8) becomes:

$$V_{OD} = \frac{S_O A_{OD}}{\displaystyle\sum_D A_{OD}}$$

(4.9)

Intuitively, equation (4.9) states that the volume of flow between two land-use zones is a function of the attractiveness of the destination zone relative to the attractiveness of all other zones. Thus, the law of attraction might be more accurately termed the law of "relative attraction."

The discussion thus far has focused on commodity transportation demand in a broad, general sense. In the following section, the principles of spatial interaction are illustrated using the grain subterminal problem. A specific law of interaction is formulated that characterizes flows within a subterminal-satellite system.

### A Subterminal-Satellite Elevator Spatial Interaction Model

A subterminal market area constitutes a special case of a "land-use/transportation system." Within the system, three types of land-use are of particular importance—farms or production zones, satellite elevators, and the subterminal elevator.

Farms function solely as supply or origin zones within the system. They generate truck shipments headed for satellite or subterminal elevators. Satellite elevators function as both originating and terminating zones. On one hand, they receive inbound farm truck shipments. On the other hand, they generate outbound traffic to the subterminal or terminal market. In similar fashion, the subterminal constitutes both a receiving and a generating zone.

Rephrasing the law of attraction, it may be said that the attractive force exerted over a particular production zone by a given grain elevator is directly proportional to the bid price at the elevator, and inversely proportional to the cost of trucking from farm to elevator. Within a subterminal-satellite system, each elevator including the subterminal will establish a bid price. Producers within the region will react to the prices and to the perceived farm truck costs involved, and make decisions regarding where to sell their grains.

Given this arrangement, the law of flow may be restated for subterminal-satellite systems as follows:

$$F_{OD} = \frac{S_O \, P_D}{FT_{OD}} \tag{4.10}$$

where:

$\qquad S_O \qquad =$ The amount of grain and oilseeds available for shipment at zone $O$ (computed as production minus consumption minus storage minus loss).

$\qquad P_D \qquad =$ Elevator price at $D$

$\qquad FT_{OD} \quad =$ Farm truck cost from $O$ to $D$

Within a subterminal-satellite elevator system, each elevator theoretically will exert some attractive force over each production zone (albeit weak over long distances). The effects of these attractive forces on grain flows can be modeled by restating the law of interaction so that it applies specifically to subterminal-satellite elevator systems. This is the purpose of equation (4.11).

$$V_{OD} = S_O \frac{\dfrac{P_D}{FT_{OD}}}{\displaystyle\sum_D \dfrac{P_D}{FT_{OD}}} \tag{4.11}$$

As equation (4.11) implies, the price relationships among elevators within a cooperative system will determine in part the relative attractiveness of each destination zone. Zink (1988) found that with few exceptions the price at a satellite elevator consists of the price at the subterminal elevator minus the trucking cost between the satellite and the subterminal. Given this pricing scheme, the attractiveness of a satellite elevator relative to the subterminal elevator for a given production zone is a function of two items: (1) the farm truck cost to the satellite, and (2) the farm truck cost to the subterminal.

Assuming the price relationship described above holds true, $P_D$ may be defined as follows:[5]

$$P_D = P_T - GT_D \tag{4.12}$$

where:

| | | |
|---|---|---|
| $P_T$ | = | Bid price at the subterminal |
| $GT_D$ | = | Grain trucking cost between subterminal and satellite elevator (located at $D$) |

## OPTIMIZATION TECHNIQUES

Optimization techniques are mathematical algorithms that generate a best or optimal solution within a given set of constraints. Linear programming (LP) is a well-known example of an optimization technique. For the most part, optimization algorithms either minimize or maximize an objective function. For example, LP has been widely used to maximize profits or minimize costs. Goal and multi-objective programming algorithms are exceptions to this rule.[6] In goal programming, several objectives are considered simultaneously. The resulting optimal solution is neither a maximum nor a minimum. Instead, it is a satisfactory solution.

Optimization procedures can be used to model the behaviors and choices of travelers. In fact, a set of optimization procedures exists for solving freight transportation problems. Two such techniques are discussed in this section: (1) the transportation algorithm, and (2) the trans-shipment procedure. Again, the use of these procedures is illustrated through the use of the grain subterminal problem.

Two classes of optimization models are of particular importance in analyzing agriculture shipments. The first is a farmer (or producer) optimization model. The second is an elevator or cooperative (system) optimization model. The former relates to inbound elevator shipments, the latter to outbound elevator traffic.

## Behavioral Motivations and Determinants of Grain Shipment Flows

Agricultural optimization techniques are based on the behavioral motivations of producers, transporters, and processors. The farmer's decision framework can be summarized in three words: price, proximity, and patronage. Price and proximity are both economic variables that can be measured quantitatively but patronage is a human factor that cannot. Nevertheless, patronage can be an important factor in the selection of an elevator.

Farmers may patronize a local elevator for two basic reasons. First of all, they may be members of a local cooperative and thus have interests and equity in the elevator. Second, they may want to ensure the survival of the local elevator and support economic development within the community. Such patronage, in and of itself, is not likely to be a decisive factor in the farmer's decision-making equation. However, when combined with proximity, patronage tends to enhance the relative attractiveness of a local facility.

Proximity is a composite measure of two underlying factors—distance, and time. The interrelationship between the two is quite important in the formulation of an impedance function. Certain farm truck costs such as fuel, use-related maintenance, and use-related depreciation tend to increase in proportion to distance. However, others do not. In particular, it is unlikely that the cost of a farmer's time will increase in a linear fashion. As the length of a journey increases, the inconvenience, discomfort, boredom, and fatigue of a traveler increases more-than-proportionately to distance. Thus the real value that a farmer places on time spent behind the wheel of a truck may not be consistent with a comparable hourly wage for labor.[7]

The intuitive logic set forth above is supported by the results of previous farm truck studies. Griffin, Wilson, and Casavant (1984) found that North Dakota farmers transported their grain to the closest elevator approximately 67 percent of the time. Eighty-one percent of those surveyed indicated that they traveled 15 miles or less in order to reach their most frequent destination. Furthermore, 86 percent said that they spent 30 minutes or less driving to the elevator of their choice. These findings have two important implications. First, they support the contention that the combined influence of proximity and patronage tends to favor the selection of nearby elevators. Second, they indicate that because of the value that farmers place on time, the impedance function (with respect to farm-to-elevator shipments) is probably nonlinear in nature.

Although patronage and proximity are strong influences in the distribution of farm-to-elevator shipments, they are not necessarily the decisive factors. Griffin et al. (1984) found that one–third of the farmers surveyed did not deliver their grain to the closest facility. When asked why they bypassed the local elevator, the majority of those responding (74 percent) gave low prices as the reason. This is not a surprising conclusion, but it does provide empirical support for the theoretical model of grain flows presented in equation (4.10), in which price was defined as the measure of attraction and farm truck costs as the impedance factor.

The role of price in the farmer's decision-making equation can best be represented through the concept of "net farm price." The net farm price is the price the farmer receives at an elevator minus the farm truck cost associated with positioning the grain at the facility. If the effects of patronage and time are ignored, then net farm price (NFP) becomes the primary decision variable. In this case, the farmer will logically deliver the grain to the facility which offers the highest NFP.

In many respects, the behavior of an elevator manager is easier to model than that of a farmer. A primary motivation of an elevator manager is to maximize the net price received for a given commodity (the market price minus the distribution cost). In pursuing this objective, the manager usually has a choice among modes of transport and sometimes routes. If the non-transportation components of the distribution cost are roughly equal, then the manager will generally choose the mode that offers the lowest freight rate.[8]

The motivations of subterminal managers are somewhat different than those of the traditional elevator managers. They must be concerned with revenues and costs for the cooperative system of elevators as a whole, rather than for any individual facility. Their primary motivation is to minimize the aggregate distribution cost for shipping grain from all elevators in the system to all potential markets.

The purpose of the preceding discussion has been to describe the motivations of agricultural producers and shippers so that their transportation behavior can be effectively modeled. The chapter now turns to a discussion of farm-to-elevator optimization models that are largely premised on assumptions concerning the farmer's motivations and transportation behavior.

## Farm-to-Elevator Optimization Models

The producer optimization model mentioned earlier may have one of two objectives as its optimizing function. The algorithm can maximize net farm prices. This is somewhat analogous to a profit maximization objective function in operations research. Maximizing net farm price may be a logical extension of economic theory. However, proximity and patronage are not accounted for in the

NFP maximization model. In the net farm price model, a farmer will theoretically be indifferent between an elevator that is seventy-five miles away and one that is two miles in distance, provided that the two have the same net farm price. When the effects of time, convenience, and patronage are considered, this is an illogical conclusion.

Instead of maximizing net farm prices, the algorithm can minimize producer transportation costs. Since farm truck costs represent only one component of the net farm price equation, a cost minimization approach paints only a partial picture of the producer's decision-making formula. However, the cost minimization model does give an explicit advantage to nearby elevators. Thus, it reflects (in a limited and indirect sort of way) the influence of proximity and patronage on the farmer's decision process.

The farm-to-elevator optimization problem can be handled with the transportation algorithm.[9] The general formulation of the transportation problem is:

$$Minimize\ Z = \sum_i \sum_j C_{ij} X_{ij} \qquad (4.13)$$

subject to:

$$\sum_j X_{ij} = S_i\ (supply\ at\ zone\ i)$$
$$\sum_i X_{ij} = D_j\ (demand\ at\ zone\ j) \qquad (4.14)$$
$$X_{ij} \geq 0$$

where:

$$X_{ij} \quad = \quad \text{Volume shipped between zones } i \text{ and } j$$

$$C_{ij} \quad = \quad \text{Unit cost of transportation between zones } i \text{ and } j$$

In this general formulation, supply and demand are balanced. The balance condition is given by:

$$\sum_i S_i = \sum_j D_j \qquad (4.15)$$

However, an exact balance between supply and demand rarely exists in a subterminal market area during a given interval of time. Instead, the supply typically exceeds the collective demand expressed by the system of cooperative elevators. The remainder flows to other elevators (in or outside of the region), or is stored temporarily on-farm. A special variant of the transportation algorithm can be employed to handle an imbalance between supply and demand. An unbalanced transportation algorithm that can be used to model a grain subterminal system is given by:

$$Minimize\ Z = \sum_o \sum_d FT_{od} V_{od} \qquad (4.16)$$

subject to:

$$\sum_d V_{od} \leq S_o$$
$$\sum_o V_{od} \geq V_d \qquad (4.17)$$
$$V_{od} \geq 0$$

where:

| | | |
|---|---|---|
| $V_{od}$ | = | Volume between zones $o$ and $d$ |
| $FT_{od}$ | = | Farm truck cost between $o$ and $d$ |
| $S_o$ | = | Supply at $o$ |
| $V_d$ | = | Demand at elevator $d$ |

In order to maximize net farm price, equation (4.16) can be restated as follows:

$$Maximize\ Z = \sum_o \sum_d NFP_{od} V_{od} \qquad (4.18)$$

where:

| | | |
|---|---|---|
| $NFP_{od}$ | = | Net farm price for grains and oilseeds originating in zone $o$ at elevator $d$, or $P_d - FT_{od}$ |

As stated earlier, the NFP approach entails a potential anomaly; the farmer is theoretically indifferent between two elevators having the same NFP regardless of proximity or other factors. Specifying a nonlinear farm truck cost function can mitigate this problem to some extent. Alternatively, an impedance function for proximity can be used in lieu of farm truck costs in the NFP equation. Unfortunately, no such function has been calibrated to date for agricultural movements.

**Elevator-to-Market Flow Optimization Models**

The general objective in modeling outbound elevator flows is to minimize the total cost of distribution including transportation. The primary components of the distribution cost equation for a cooperative system of elevators are:

1.         the grain trucking rate from the satellite elevator to the subterminal,
2.         the cost of double-handling the grain at the subterminal,[10]
3.         the transportation rates from the subterminal and satellite elevators to terminal markets.

The cost of distribution between a given satellite elevator and market can be minimized through the application of a simple decision rule. In general, the grain that is stored at a satellite elevator will be trans-shipped through the subterminal as opposed to being shipped directly to terminal market if the following condition holds true:

$$GT_{ce} + DH + SR_{ct} \leq ER_{ct} \qquad\qquad (4.19)$$

where:

$$GT_{ce} \quad = \quad \text{Grain trucking rate for commodity } c \text{ from satellite elevator } e$$

$$DH \quad = \quad \text{Cost of double-handling grain at the subterminal}$$

$$SR_{ct} \quad = \quad \text{Rate for commodity } c \text{ from the subterminal to terminal market } t$$

$$ER_{ct} \quad = \quad \text{Rate for commodity } c \text{ from the satellite elevator to terminal market } t$$

In other words, if the sum of the grain trucking rate to the subterminal, the additional cost of handling the grain at the facility, and the outbound elevator rate is less than the transportation rate from the satellite elevator to terminal market, then the commodity will be trans-shipped.[11] Otherwise, it will be shipped directly to terminal market.

While equation (4.19) may produce an optimal flow pattern between a given satellite elevator and market, it will not necessarily produce an optimal flow for the network of elevators as a whole. All possible commodity flows from all elevators in the system to all potential markets must be considered simultaneously in order for this to happen. A special form of the transportation model (the trans-shipment model) is especially designed to handle the combination of flows and routings that are possible within a cooperative system of elevators.

In the trans-shipment problem, a company is trying to minimize the total transportation cost of shipping products from several origins to several destinations. Instead of shipping everything directly from origin to destination, the company has the option of routing shipments through intermediate locations or "trans-shipment points." Thus, a shipment that is consigned at a given location may be shipped through another supply point or destination enroute to market in order to attain the lowest possible shipping or distribution cost.

The shipping patterns of a subterminal-satellite system closely conform to the structure and definition of the classic trans-shipment problem. There are several possible origins for a given commodity (the elevators) and several possible destinations (terminal markets and processing centers). The objective of the general manager is to ship the volume of commodities available at each elevator to the terminal markets in a manner that minimizes the total cost of distribution. In doing so, he or she may trans-ship the grain; that is, route it through the subterminal (or conceivably through another elevator in the system).

The trans-shipment model is a special case of the balanced transportation problem. As such, it can be solved with a few minor adjustments using the transportation algorithm. Recall that in the balanced transportation problem, total supply must equal total demand. This balance condition must hold true for the trans-shipment problem as well. But in the trans-shipment formulation, all of the available supply can conceivably be originated at (or trans-shipped through) a single supply point. As a result, the supply at each source must be increased by an amount that is at least equal to the total supply. This allows the algorithm to route all shipments via another supply point, if this represents the minimum-cost solution.

In the trans-shipment problem formulation, shipments may also be routed through an intermediate destination. This means that the total number of units that either pass-through or are terminated at a given destination can conceivably equal the total supply which in turn equals the total demand. Consequently, the amount demanded at any given destination must be increased by an amount that is at least equal to the total demand.

A thorough discussion of the theory and solution procedures that underlie the trans-shipment problem is beyond the scope of this book. For a more detailed description of the problem formulation and some sample tableaus the reader is referred to Hillier and Lieberman (1980) or Lee, Moore, and Taylor (1985).[12]

## EVALUATION OF ALTERNATIVE MODELING TECHNIQUES

As the preceding discussion has pointed-out, the transportation analyst has several options available with respect to the modeling of farm-to-elevator grain flows. Producer optimization models offer the advantage of a relatively simple, standardized solution process. There are several software packages available that can be used to derive the optimal solution. However, the analyst should be aware of several potential problems associated with the use of the producer optimization models.

1.    The typical assumption of linearity may be inappropriate within the context of producer cost minimization (or NFP maximization);

2.    The optimization procedures are not designed to account for the effects of time, convenience, and patronage on producer transportation decisions; and

3.    The models are deterministic in nature, although the flow problem itself has a great deal of uncertainty involved.

The farm truck cost procedure involves some uncertainty because price is not included in the modes. However, farm truck costs are a function of distance. Thus, nonprice factors such as patronage and proximity are indirectly reflected in the truck cost minimization procedure.

Both the NFP and the farm truck cost models are based on assumptions and motivations relevant at the level of the individual producer or traveler. However, it may not be possible to model the travel of each farmer within a 1,000 square mile area.[13] Thus, the aggregation of data to the level of supply zones may be necessary. Within a large supply zone, the highway analyst may be dealing with ten or more producers, all represented by a single centroid. At this level of aggregation, the optimization models become somewhat divorced from their underlying assumptions.

The optimization models permit the analyst to draw upon a set of "canned" software packages to derive an optimal solution. However, there is no existing computer program that will generate a solution to the farm-to-elevator shipment problem via the spatial interaction model.[14] Instead, analysts must write the computer code themselves. Nevertheless, the spatial interaction model has some attractive features that may make the effort worthwhile. First, the spatial interaction model explicitly incorporates the transportation demand and impedance functions into the predictive equation via a logical relationship. The attractiveness of a given elevator is assumed to be directly proportional to the bid price for the commodity and inversely proportional to the impedance to flow. Second, the spatial interaction model is expressly designed to function at the zonal level of aggregation. The model directly addresses the effects of demand-point competition on individual producers in the zone through the law of "relative attraction." Even though a single centroid is used to represent many producers, the flow patterns that emerge reflect the fact that producers situated in different subregions of a zone (potentially thirty miles apart) will prefer different elevators.[15] Third, the impedance function in the spatial interaction model can easily be modified to assume any functional form, linear or nonlinear.

In general, the greatest degree of precision is likely to be achieved with a spatial interaction model. However, this approach also entails the highest resource cost for both data collection and computing. At the other end of the spectrum, the basic farm truck cost model can generate modest levels of precision at relatively low resource costs. The basic farm truck cost model could be enhanced through the use of a non-linear function that more realistically reflects the value of operator time and the inconvenience of lengthy trips. Moreover, an impedance function could be developed that reflects highway service level, speed, or other factors in addition to cost. The NFP model falls somewhere in between the farm truck and spatial interactive procedures. A higher level of precision can be achieved in the NFP approach by using an impedance function in lieu of linear farm truck costs. However, the resource costs will also increase.

In terms of outbound elevator flows, the trans-shipment model presented earlier is sound in both logic and procedure. However, the analyst should be aware of some potential drawbacks. The major problem relates to the assumption of determinism. The analyst assumes that distribution costs (including the freight rate) are known with certainty for the duration of the analysis period. In reality, distribution costs are subject to many forces and can quickly change during any given year. Thus, uncertainty in the parameters of the function clearly exist. Uncertainty in parameters can be handled somewhat through sensitivity analysis, or by re-solving the transportation algorithm using different values for the distribution costs. Alternatively, uncertainty can be handled through scenario analysis, as discussed in Chapter 2.

The purpose of this chapter has been to define and illustrate some fundamental freight demand concepts and procedures. Many of these techniques are applied to specific problems in subsequent chapters of the book, including a grain subterminal case study. The grain subterminal example can be easily extended to other types of economic activities, particularly multiplant businesses. The timber industries that are characterized by several supply zones and sawmills exhibit similar demand linkages. Similarly, the trans-shipment algorithm is applicable to a wide range of distribution flows. In fact, the branch-line abandonment problem involves the same trans-shipment decision presented in equation (4.19). Only in abandonment cases, the decision facing shippers is whether to truck directly to terminal market or trans-ship to a nearby railhead.

## NOTES

1. This simple relationship assumes that all other factors or forces are held constant. The prices of complements and substitutes for the commodity are assumed fixed and competitive relationships or reactions (e.g., supply-point and demand-point competition) are assumed to be constant. The model is thus quite restrictive, and is useful mainly for providing an intuitive understanding of

fundamental demand relationships.

2. The level of service is an abstract rating that defines the availability, capacity, congestion, and general condition and performance of the transportation network.

3. For a description of the land-use/transportation modeling process (particularly as it relates to urban transportation planning) see Dickey (1983) and Mannhiem (1979).

4. Land-use is a generic term referring to the type, intensity, and level of economic activity occurring at a particular location in space during a particular interval of time. In this study, agricultural production and processing are the two types of land-use that are of primary importance in highway impact assessment.

5. The bid price at the subterminal elevator may be a weighted-average of the bid prices for individual commodities handled at the facility. In this case, $P_T$ is given by:

$$P_T = \frac{\sum_i Q_i P_i}{\sum_i Q_i}$$

where:

$Q_i$     =          Quantity handled of commodity $i$
$P_i$     =          Price of commodity $i$

6. For more detailed information, see Lee, Moore, and Taylor, 1985.

7. This is particularly true during harvest or other periods of peak work demand. During these intervals, the opportunity cost of a farmer's time (particularly the time spent behind the wheel of a truck) may be quite high due to the competing demands for his or her time.

8. Nontransportation or more correctly nonrate distribution costs consist of expenses other than the freight rate that are associated with the positioning of grain in a particular market. These costs can include: (1) warehousing or storage costs, (2) inventory costs, (3) packaging, and (4) loss and damage. The nonrate components of distribution costs may vary among modes. For example, one mode may require special packaging or dunnage of freight while another does not. Similarly, loss and damage or accessorial charges (fees in addition to the freight rate) may vary between truck and rail. Typically, these nonrate distribution costs are not a major concern in the transportation of grain. This does not mean that one mode may not have service advantages over another. What it does mean is that in the case of grain, the transportation rate is the primary element of the

distribution cost that affects mode choice.

9. The transportation algorithm is explained in a variety of operations research and management science texts, including: Hillier and Lieberman (1980) and Lee, Moore, and Taylor (1984).

10. The cost of double-handling grain at a subterminal consists of: (1) the variable cost of elevation, (2) interest on the grain while it is stored at the facility, and (3) other variable interest costs. Fixed interest payments on capital (construction) outlays, fixed depreciation, insurance costs and other constant expenses related to the existence of the facility are not considered in the cost of doubling-handling grain.

11. Because of volume loading capabilities and rail mainline location, the subterminal manager, unlike the substation manager, typically has access to low trainload or contract rail rates. Consequently, the outbound rail rate from the subterminal is typically low relative to the rates at the satellites.

12. In the case study presented in chapter 10, the TRANS procedure contained in the SAS operations research computer package is used to formulate and solve the subterminal transshipment problem. See SAS (1985) for details.

13. For example, the trade area of the Devils Lake subterminal-satellite system in North Dakota is over 1,000 square miles.

14. There is a software package used in urban transportation planning that calibrates the "gravity model," a particular type of spatial interaction model. This program (developed by the FHWA) is called the Gravity Model Calibration Program, or GMCP. Although the shipment distribution procedure is analogous to the trip generation model in urban transportation planning, the processes, the variables, and the relationships involved are different. So the GMCP is not really a viable option for agricultural analysis. For a description of the GMCP see FHWA (1977).

15. Recall that in the spatial interaction model (according to the law of relative attraction), the amount available for shipment in a given zone is distributed among competing elevators based on the relative attractiveness of each. So the model predicts that some grain will flow to most or all of the feasible elevators in the given area. Thus, the predicted flow pattern reflects the fact that some farmers within a twenty-five or thirty square mile area will ship to different elevators.

# 5

# Life-Cycle Pavement Concepts

In the previous chapter, the forces of demand that generate heavy truck traffic were described. However, heavy truck trips are only part of the problem. The focus of this chapter is on highway attributes, particularly pavements, and the role they play in highway deterioration. The objectives of the chapter are:

1.  to introduce some fundamental theoretical concepts in pavement life-cycle analysis,
2.  to define marginal and incremental costs specifically within the context of pavement damage analysis,
3.  to formulate a theoretical model that describes the impacts of heavy truck traffic on pavement costs, and
4.  to specify equations for estimating the incremental cost of heavy truck traffic.

## A THEORETICAL MODEL OF PAVEMENT LIFE

A pavement, like any other asset or resource, has a useful life. Pavements deteriorate with time and axle loads, as illustrated by Figure 5.1. The exact rate of deterioration and shape of the function will depend on factors such as climate, the composition of the supporting soil, the strength of the pavement, and other design considerations. For the moment, however, only the general nature of the relationship is important.

The effects of time and non–use–related pavement decay are difficult to isolate and model. Theoretically, a pavement that has never been exposed to traffic may last up to one hundred years (Balta and Markow, 1985). However, this has never been verified empirically. So, while it is known that time is partially responsible for pavement decay, highway deterioration models are typically condensed to "damage models," wherein the decline in pavement serviceability is attributed solely to axle passes.

**Figure 5.1**        Theoretical Pavement Deterioration Function

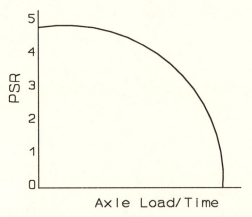

PSR - Present Serviceability Rating (an index ranging from 0.0 to 5.0)

Assuming away the effects of time, pavement life is typically viewed as a function of the cumulative number of axle passes in a given climatic zone, the soil support factor, and the strength of the highway section. This fundamental relationship is depicted in equation (5.1).

$$PL = f(N, C, SSN, STR)$$                         (5.1)

where:

|         |                                                              |
|---------|--------------------------------------------------------------|
| $PL =$  | Pavement life                                                |
| $N =$   | Cumulative passes of a given axle type and load              |
| $C =$   | Climatic zone or regional factor                             |
| $SSN =$ | Soil support number or index                                 |
| $STR =$ | Strength of the highway section (some function of D or SN, TH1, and/or TH2) |

where:

|         |                                                              |
|---------|--------------------------------------------------------------|
| $D =$   | Slab thickness (Portland Concrete Cement pavements)          |
| $SN =$  | Structural number (flexible or asphaltic concrete pavements) |
| $TH1 =$ | Thickness of asphaltic concrete layers                       |
| $TH2 =$ | Thickness of the aggregate base                              |

If values are defined for the soil support index and the regional factor, equation (5.1) can be simplified as follows:

$$PL = f(N, STR) \qquad (5.2)$$

For a mixed traffic stream, the effects of different axle passes can be translated into ESALs. Thus, if the strength of a pavement section is held constant, pavement life becomes a function of ESALs. Consequently, equation (5.2) may be simplified as follows.

$$PL = f(ESAL) \qquad (5.3)$$

The life of a highway section is composed of a sequence of cycles. Typically, pavements are rehabilitated or reconstructed prior to the full expiration of pavement life. When a pavement is replaced, the highway section enters a new phase or stage. As illustrated in Figure 5.2, the section is typically restored to some acceptable level of condition, from which the deterioration process starts all over again.

To summarize the major concepts presented thus far:

1.      Each pavement section has a useful life, which expires with traffic over time;
2.      The useful life of a highway section may be expressed in ESALs;
3.      A typical section moves through a series of pavement life cycles over its entire existence; and
4.      Heavy axle loadings shorten the interval between rehabilitation or capital outlays.


## COST CONCEPTS

The expiration or consumption of pavement life constitutes an economic cost that is different from a financial outlay or expenditure. Expenditures occur only at discrete time intervals, as illustrated by Figure 5.2 (e.g., at times $T_1$, $T_2$, and $T_3$). Costs occur whenever a portion of the remaining useful life of a pavement is consumed.[1]

Two types of economic cost are of primary importance to this study: marginal cost (MC), and incremental cost (IC). Each type of cost may be either short run or long run in nature.

In the context of pavement life cycles, the short run is the period of time for which the capacity of a highway section to absorb ESALs is fixed. In other words, the short run may be viewed as the cycle between replacement activities. At the end of each cycle, the pavement is replaced as before, or rebuilt to a

**Figure 5.2**       Pavement Replacement Cycles

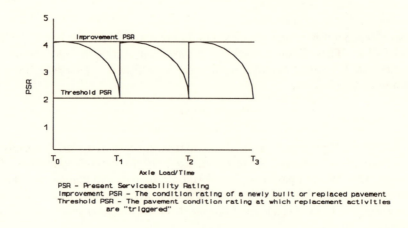

PSR - Present Serviceability Rating
Improvement PSR - The condition rating of a newly built or replaced pavement
Threshold PSR - The pavement condition rating at which replacement activities
          are "triggered"

higher standard. In either case, the capacity to handle traffic once again becomes fixed, and another short run period ensues. The long run, on the other hand, reflects the entire existence of a highway section from the time of initial construction until the time the roadway is abandoned. In the long run, the capacity to handle traffic may be freely adjusted.

**Marginal and Incremental Pavement Cost**

Within the context of highway impact analysis, short run marginal cost (SRMC) reflects the additional consumption of highway capacity resulting from the addition of one more ESAL to a highway section. SRMC depends on three factors: (1) the ESAL life of a section, (2) the replacement cost incurred at the beginning of the cycle, and (3) the current condition of the highway section.

Recall from Figure 5.1 that the decline in pavement serviceability is a nonlinear function of traffic over time. Logically then, the short run marginal cost of an axle pass will vary over time, increasing with age and accumulated passes. Mathematically, SRMC is the derivative of PSR with respect to axle passes.

$$SMRC = \frac{\partial PSR}{\partial N} \tag{5.4}$$

Standardized axle loadings can be computed from the AASHTO axle equivalency equations given in Appendix A. An example presented in this section illustrates the effects of axle passes at different serviceability levels (or ages). Assume that the 16,000–pound single axle is the axle of interest and that the terminal serviceability of the impacted highway is 2.0. Table 5.1 illustrates the change in ESALs resulting from a single axle–pass at different PSRs as the PSR declines from 4.0 to 2.1.

**Table 5.1**     Change in ESALs with Decline in PSR for a 16,000–Pound Single Axle

| Pavement Serviceability Rating | ESALs |
|:---:|:---:|
| 4.0 | 0.47 |
| 2.5 | 0.55 |
| 2.1 | 0.79 |

Unlike SRMC, long-run marginal costs (LRMC) have nothing to do with the present serviceability of a highway section. LRMC are the result of an increase in pavement strength necessitated by the addition of one more ESAL to the existing traffic base. If pavement thickness is defined on a ratio scale from zero to some practical maximum thickness, then the LRMC of an ESAL is the additional layer required to maintain the service life of a highway as before. However, in practical terms the addition of a single ESAL to a traffic stream does not require an overlay of existing pavement. It is only the accumulation of ESALs over time that leads to the upgrading of pavements.

Although long-run marginal cost is not a practical concept in pavement impact analysis, it does provide a theoretical understanding of the relationship between traffic and pavement design. An important distinction to remember is that LRMC is related to pavement thickness, not to current serviceability. Mathematically then, LRMC is the derivative of pavement thickness with respect to ESALs.

$$LRMC = \frac{\partial THI}{\partial ESAL} \tag{5.5}$$

The addition of an ESAL to a traffic stream results in a real cost, however infinitesimal. But it is only when many ESALs are combined over time that capital expenditures actually flow. For this reason, incremental cost is frequently a more relevant concept to highway planners than marginal cost.

Incremental pavement costs arise from considering the effects of classes of traffic or relatively large traffic increases as opposed to a single ESAL analysis.[2] For example, the total volume diverted from an abandoned branch line would constitute an incremental class of traffic. In such instances, highway planners are dealing with a potentially sizable class of trucks rather than with a single vehicle or operator. Thus, incremental cost rather than marginal cost is the most relevant concept or measurement.[3]

## Replacement Versus Upgrading Costs

The previous discussion loosely introduced the concepts of replacement and upgrading costs. Replacement cost, as the name implies, is the cost associated with the periodic "replacement" of pavements so that the highway section may continue to provide service at roughly the same functional level as before. Upgrading costs, on the other hand, are the capital expenses associated with increasing the capacity of a highway section to handle heavy traffic.

Pavement replacement encompasses a range of potential improvements usually referred to as resurfacing, rehabilitation, restoration, or reconstruction. Resurfacing and rehabilitation typically entail an overlay of existing pavement with a new asphaltic concrete surface layer. If a pavement has been allowed to deteriorate to a very low level of serviceability, an overlay is unlikely to restore the section to its intended functional use. In such cases, full-scale pavement reconstruction may be required wherein the existing pavement is completely removed and replaced. Regardless of the implemented improvement type, the idea is that the pavement is replaced essentially as before.

If the traffic and axle loads change appreciably during a given pavement cycle, replacing the pavement may not provide satisfactory service other than for a short period of time. As the intervals between replacement become increasingly short, the most economical solution is to strengthen the existing pavement.

There are several ways to strengthen an existing pavement. Yoder and Witczak (1975, page 73) state that, "in order to reduce the subgrade stress of flexible pavements to some tolerable design value, one can either increase the base-course thickness and the surface thickness of the same layered material or replace the quality of the layered material with a more rigid material." Typically for low-volume rural roads, strength is added by increasing the thickness of the surface or asphaltic concrete layers.

In this book, the upgrading of impact highways is assumed to entail an asphaltic concrete overlay.

## Build-Sooner Costs

Employing the concepts of incremental and replacement costs, the concept of *build-sooner* cost can be introduced.[4] Build-sooner costs constitute the incremental highway impacts of increased heavy truck traffic, arising from the timing of future replacement activities. More specifically, build-sooner costs are concerned with the shortening of replacement cycles as illustrated in Figure 5.3.

**Figure 5.3**     Pavement Deterioration and Build-Sooner Costs

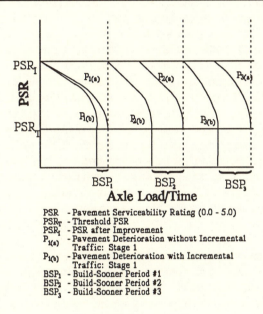

PSR     - Pavement Serviceability Rating (0.0 - 5.0)
$PSR_T$ - Threshold PSR
$PSR_I$ - PSR after Improvement
$P_{1(a)}$ - Pavement Deterioration without Incremental
          Traffic: Stage 1
$P_{1(b)}$ - Pavement Deterioration with Incremental
          Traffic: Stage 1
$BSP_1$ - Build-Sooner Period #1
$BSP_2$ - Build-Sooner Period #2
$BSP_3$ - Build-Sooner Period #3

The logic of Figure 5.3 is as follows. Over the life of a highway section, the pavement is replaced periodically when the PSR or serviceability reaches some threshold or trigger level (e.g., 2.0). Upon restoration, the section is replaced essentially as before, and the condition rating is returned to its previous level (e.g., 4.2). This threshold is called the improvement PSR, or $PSR_I$. Assume that in Stage 1 of the section's life, a significant increment of heavy truck traffic is added to the traffic stream. The baseline pavement deterioration curve $P_{1a}$ is shifted to the left in response. This shift (represented by curve $P_{1b}$) reflects the accelerated rate of decay attributable to the new traffic stream. Build-Sooner Period 1 ($BSP_1$) may be thought of as the reduction in pavement life in Stage 1 due to incremental traffic.

A fundamental concept in the economic analysis of highways is the time value of money. Money has a different value to highway officials, users, and taxpayers over time. If given a free choice, everyone would prefer to receive a dollar today rather than five years from now; all else being equal. The same is true for capital outlays. Highway officials, given a free choice, would prefer to spend a dollar on highway improvements five years from now rather than today; all else being equal.[5] Differences in the value of money over time are accounted for by expressing all future outflows (or inflows) in present dollars. The present value of a dollar ten years in the future is calculated by "discounting" the dollar to reflect the fact that highway officials and users value it less than a dollar available today. Discount rates for transportation analysis are typically based on the opportunity cost of public sector capital.

Returning to the concept of build-sooner cost, if the capital outlays incurred at the end of the baseline replacement cycle $(P_{1a})$ and the altered replacement cycle $(P_{1b})$ are both discounted to present value, then the build-sooner costs in Stage 1 assume a real monetary value. They are equal to the difference between the present value (PV) of the capital outlay that would have occurred at the end of the baseline replacement cycle, and the PV of the outlay that now occurs at the end of the altered replacement cycle. If acted out over stages 2, 3, and so forth, the accumulated difference in present value represents the build-sooner cost associated with a particular increment of heavy traffic over the life of a highway section.

To summarize the major concepts presented in this section, it may be said that build-sooner costs:

1.      constitute incremental, replacement costs,
2.      represent the reductions in pavement life cycles attributable to incremental truck traffic,
3.      are concerned with the timing of future monetary outlays,
4.      are premised on the time value of money, and
5.      are expressed as the difference in the present value of the discounted capital outlays between the baseline and the altered traffic streams.


## Upgrading Costs

Purnell (1976) developed a procedure for estimating increased costs on Indiana highways due to rail branch–line abandonment. The procedure entailed the estimation of the incremental pavement thickness required for an altered traffic stream that would (hypothetically) result from the abandonment of rail branch lines in an area.

According to Purnell, the incremental thickness of the asphaltic concrete (AC) layer for a flexible highway section can be calculated as follows:

$$IT_i = \frac{SNA_i - SN_i}{a_1} \qquad (5.6)$$

where:

$IT_i =$    incremental thickness for section $i$

$SN_i =$    structural number of section $i$ under conditions of *normal* traffic

$SNA_i =$    structural number of section $i$ under conditions of *altered* traffic

$a_1 =$    coefficient of the surface AC layer (generally taken to be .44)

Purnell's procedure involves three basic steps. First, the SN required to handle the ESAL load under "normal" traffic conditions is determined using the AASHTO design equation. Second, a revised structural number is determined (again using the AASHTO design equation) based on the estimated ESAL load after the addition of the incremental traffic to the normal traffic stream. Third, the incremental dollar cost associated with the required thickness is estimated from unit costs for material and labor.

As noted previously, the introduction of incremental heavy truck traffic onto a highway section will reduce the interval of time between replacement cycles. Upgrading the section according to Purnell's formula essentially returns the replacement cycle to its previous duration (that which existed prior to the alteration of the traffic stream). For example, if the SN of a highway section provides for a twenty-year life at current traffic levels, then the revised structural number (SNA) will similarly provide for a twenty-year life at higher traffic levels.

In contrasting upgrading and replacement costs, it may be said that build-sooner costs represent the short run incremental costs (SRIC) of additional truck traffic. That is, build-sooner costs are the costs incurred during a given replacement cycle, during which time the capacity of a highway section to absorb ESALs is fixed. In contrast, upgrading costs, as estimated via Purnell's method, represent the long run incremental costs (LRIC) associated with the new traffic stream.[6]

The problem with Purnell's approach is that it does not consider the impacts of incremental truck traffic during the current replacement cycle. On page 2 he writes: "Since the adopted procedure is concerned strictly with the incremental impact arising from increased truck traffic due to service elimination along a nearby rail line, the present condition of a pavement structure is not directly considered."

Although Purnell did not directly address the costs incurred during the current replacement cycle, he did acknowledge their existence and the need for evaluation. Later on page 2 he writes:

> Nevertheless, service discontinuance on railroad branch lines can alter the setting of priorities associated with upgrading and routine maintenance of a rural road. A rural highway which is forced to assume additional trucks transporting commodities previously moved by way of the railroad may have to be repaved earlier than had been specified in a state or county's maintenance program. Thus, the current condition of a facility's pavement structure must be considered via an analysis of the manner in which a study section's need for upgrading is escalated by the effects of railroad abandonment.

The procedure used in the subterminal case study (shown in Chapter 6) measures both effects that Purnell spoke of. The incremental cost of subterminal-generated traffic is defined as the sum of the SRIC incurred during the current replacement cycle (the build-sooner cost) and the LRIC incurred if the section must be upgraded at the end of the current cycle.[7]

### Time Value of Money

The present value of a future sum accruing at time $n$ is given by:

$$PV = \frac{FS_n}{(1 + r)^n} \qquad (5.7)$$

where:

$$
\begin{array}{ll}
PV = & \text{Present value of a future sum} \\
FS_n = & \text{Future sum accruing at year } n \\
r = & \text{Rate of interest or discount rate}
\end{array}
$$

As an illustration, consider the following hypothetical case. The replacement cycle for a principal rural arterial extends for twenty years under normal traffic conditions. After the location of a subterminal, the cycle is reduced to fifteen years. As a result, expenditures are encountered five years earlier than originally anticipated. Assume that the replacement cost per mile is $288,000 and that the discount rate $r$ is 10 percent. Using equation (5.7), the present value of replacement expenditures for a one-mile section of highway fifteen years in the future is approximately $69,000. In contrast, the present value of the same expenditure twenty years in the future is $43,000. The build-sooner cost (the difference between the two) amounts to $26,000. In a similar fashion, an upgrading expense encountered twenty years in the future must be expressed in present dollars.

## Incremental Method and Cost Allocation Problems

The highway impact techniques outlined thus far comprise an incremental cost method. Their purpose is to quantify the change in highway cost resulting from shifts in land-use, regional economic activities, or the distribution of traffic among modes. The incremental approach is applicable to a wide range of problems, such as the grain subterminal problem analyzed in Chapter 6. However, many transportation problems involve multiple classes of commodities and traffic generators, or exhibit special characteristics that are inconsistent with the incremental method. Some of these special cases are highlighted in this section. Moreover, an alternative approach to the incremental method is illustrated in Chapter 11.

Many transportation problems (such as branch-line abandonment) involve several shippers, commodities, and types of trucks. In branch-line studies, the analyst may wish to simulate the diversion of traffic from highways to railroads as a result of rail-line investment. An incremental method could be devised for forecasting reductions in highway costs resulting from investments in railroads or waterways (such reductions are call *decremental* costs). However, a decremental cost approach involves several potential pitfalls. First, the upgrading and build-sooner cost models may not work as well in reverse order. Most highway departments specify a minimum pavement thickness for purposes of safety and reliability. Thus, the effects on pavement thickness of traffic diversions to railroads are not be clear-cut. Second, identifying changes in common highway costs resulting from the removal of traffic from a facility is difficult. Third, if highway traffic levels decline, the transportation agency might not react by reducing pavement thickness as Purnell's model simulates. Instead, the agency may move to another design (e.g. gravel surface road). In such cases, the techniques outlined in this chapter would not be applicable. Railroad and waterway investment analyses usually involve other nuances that may be inconsistent with the incremental approach. The costs attributable to certain classes of vehicles or commodities are usually a major concern in a multimodal investment study. However, costs cannot be assigned to commodity or vehicle classes using the incremental method. Figure 5.4 illustrates the dilemma. Suppose that traffic increments 1-4 represent different commodities hauled in different vehicle types. Traffic increments 2 and 3 are roughly comparable. Yet, the analyst will obtain much different estimates of cost responsibility if increment 2 is added to (or removed from) the traffic stream before (or after) increment 3. In effect, the arbitrary ordering of vehicle or commodity classes by the analyst affects the costs assigned to each group.

This very problem has been the bane of highway cost allocation for many years. Federal and state highway cost allocation studies in the 1960s and 1970s employed an incremental method in which vehicle classes were removed from the traffic stream in inverse order of weight. However, as Figure 5.4 illustrates, highway design and construction involve economies of scale. In essence, the ESAL capacity added to a pavement section is much less for thin pavements than for thick ones.

In its 1982 highway cost allocation study, the U.S. Department of Transportation discarded the incremental method, noting that:

> The old incremental approach fails to follow equitable design theory by charging one set of axle weights a different thickness-requirement-per-ESAL than another set of axle weights. The order of hypothetical ESAL removal, i.e. which vehicle class is removed first, has a profound effect on pavement cost assignment.

In summary, the incremental method should not be used in these instances:

- when highway cost responsibilities, user fees, or developer impact fees are analyzed;
- when the removal of existing traffic from highways is simulated; and
- in rail-line abandonment studies where the analyst assigns costs and benefits to commodity or vehicle classes.[8]

However, highway analysts should not stampede away from the incremental approach. In many cases, the relevant objectives and concerns of a study are purely incremental in nature. For example, a highway manager's concerns frequently lie with additions to estimated outlays or budgets; that is, *how much more do I have to spend?* The subterminal problem is such a case. The highway manager has little control over zoning regulations or the firm's location decision. Thus, additional information regarding the allocation of costs among vehicle classes is largely irrelevant.

**Figure 5.4**      Illustration of Incremental Cost Calculations for Different Levels of Highway Design

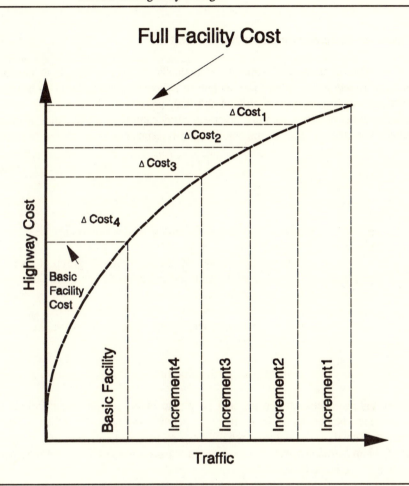

Source: Adapted from U.S. Department of Transportation (1982), modified by author.


## PAVEMENT DETERIORATION MODELS

Pavement deterioration functions constitute an essential element of the highway impact assessment process.  This section discusses the theory behind pavement deterioration models, and introduces and evaluates some of the major pavement damage functions in existence today. The discussion begins with some general background concepts in pavement damage analysis.

## Pavement Damage Functions: Background

The deterioration of pavements is typically analyzed through means of a damage function that relates the decline in pavement serviceability to traffic or axle passes. Figure 5.1, it will be recalled, presented a theoretical pavement deterioration curve in which the pavement serviceability rating declined with axle passes over time. This general relationship is expressed by equation (5.8):

$$g = \left(\frac{N}{\tau}\right)^{\beta} \tag{5.8}$$

where:

$g =$      an index of damage or deterioration

$N =$      the number of passes of an axle group of specified weight and configuration (e.g. the 18,000–pound single axle)

$\tau =$      the number of axle passes at which the section reaches failure

$\beta =$      rate of deterioration

At any time between construction (or replacement) and pavement failure, the value of $g$ (the damage index) will range between 0.0 and 1.0. When $N$ equals zero for a newly-constructed or rehabilitated section, $g$ equals zero. On the other hand, when $N$ (the number of cumulative axle passes) equals the life of a highway section ($\tau$), $g$ equals 1.0.

There are several ways to model the deterioration of pavements and the decision to rehabilitate or reconstruct. A "distress approach" may be taken in which the occurrence of specific distresses (such as rutting or fatigue cracking) is modeled. In this approach, a damage function is developed for each distress, and the decision to replace a pavement is modeled collectively from the occurrence of individual distresses.[9]

Modeling individual distresses requires considerable data and is not practical for use in most studies. Instead, the traditional approach in pavement deterioration analysis is to model the decline in pavement serviceability rating. A pavement serviceability rating (PSR or PSI) is a composite index that reflects the general serviceability of pavements at the time of evaluation. The verbal rating scheme used in determining the PSR (Table 5.2), considers the smoothness of the ride as well as the extent of rutting and other distresses. Thus, by modeling the decline in PSR, one is to a certain extent modeling the occurrence of individual distresses as well.

**Table 5.2**        Present Serviceability Rating (PSR)

|   | Verbal Rating | Description |
|---|---|---|
| 5 | Very Good | Only new (or nearly new) pavements are likely to be smooth enough and sufficiently free of cracks and patches to qualify for this category. All pavements constructed or resurfaced recently should be rated very good. |
| 4 | Good | Pavements in this category, although not quite as smooth as those described above, give first-class ride and exhibit few, if any visible signs of surface deterioration. Flexible pavements may be beginning to show evidence of rutting and fine random cracks. Rigid pavements may be beginning to show evidence of slight surface deterioration, such as minor cracks and spalling. |
| 3 | Fair | The riding qualities of pavements in this category are noticeable inferior to those of new pavements, and may be barely tolerable for high-speed traffic. Surface defects of flexible pavements may include rutting, cracking, and patching. Rigid pavements in this group may have a few joint failures, faulting and cracking, and some pumping. |
| 2 | Poor | Pavements that have deteriorated to such an extent that they are in need of resurfacing. |
| 1 | Very Poor | Pavements that are in an extremely deteriorated condition and may need complete reconstruction. |

Source: USDOT, *Status of the Nation's Highways, July, 1983.*

To return to the general damage function presented earlier, if the ratio of the decline in pavement serviceability relative to the total capacity of a highway section is used to represent the damage index, then equation (5.8) may be rewritten as follows:

$$\frac{P_i - P}{P_i - P_t} = \left(\frac{N}{\tau}\right)^\beta \qquad (5.9)$$

where:

$P_i =$    Initial pavement serviceability rating
$P_t =$    Terminal pavement serviceability rating
$P =$      Current or present serviceability rating

The term $P_i - P$ on the left-hand side of the equation represents the decline in pavement serviceability rating from the time the highway was initially constructed or replaced until the present. The denominator in the expression $(P_i - P_t)$ represents the total decline in pavement serviceability that is possible from the time the pavement is built or replaced until it reaches failure (terminal serviceability). Intuitively, equation (5.9) is saying: *the deterioration of a highway section at any time can be measured by a damage index representing the proportion of total capacity or pavement life consumed to-date.*

Five major pavement damage models are discussed in the remainder of this chapter. They are:

1.      The AASHO damage function,
2.      the HPMS deterioration model,
3.      the revised AASHTO pavement design equation,
4.      the FHWA pavement damage model (the Rauhut model), and
5.      the revised FHWA model.

Because most rural arterials, collectors, and local roads consist of asphalt pavements (as opposed to Portland Concrete Cement), the examples and equations presented in this section deal with flexible rather than with rigid pavements. However, each model described has an analogous rigid pavement deterioration function that can be obtained from the references given.

## The AASHO Damage Function

Perhaps the best-known pavement deterioration function is the one developed by the American Association of State Highway Officials (AASHO). The AASHO damage model is based on the results of a road test conducted in Ottawa, Illinois, between November 1958 and November 1960.[10]

### AASHO Variables and Relationships

In order to track pavement decay on the test sections at Ottawa, a serviceability measure known as the Present Serviceability Index (PSI) was constructed. The PSI is a composite index that reflects the extent to which certain physical distresses affect the serviceability of a pavement section.

Four major types of distresses were considered in the calculation of the PSI for flexible pavements during the road test: cracking, patching, slope variance or longitudinal roughness, and rut depth. The extent to which each of these distresses altered the PSI for a given pavement section during the road test was measured by the following formula:

$$PSI = 5.03 - 1.91 \, LOG_{10}(1 + SV) - 0.01 \sqrt{(c + p)} - 1.3 \, RD^2 \qquad (5.10)$$

where:

| | |
|---|---|
| $SV =$ | slope variance |
| $RD =$ | rut depth |
| $c =$ | extent of cracking |
| $p =$ | extent of patching |

Using the PSI, AASHO officials were able to relate accumulated traffic and axle loads to changes in pavement serviceability. Each highway section was evaluated at two–week intervals throughout the road test. From the occurrence of distress (or lack thereof) the current PSI was calculated. Given the current PSI and the cumulative axle loads, the value of the damage index (g) was calculated (for each test section) based on the original and terminal PSI.[11] The unknown parameters in the equation ($\beta$ and $\tau$) were estimated through regression analysis. The form of the regression equation for each parameter is given by equations (5.11) and (5.12), respectively.

$$LOG_{10}(\tau) = 5.93 + 9.36 \, LOG_{10}(SN + 1) \\ - 4.79 \, LOG_{10}(L1 + L2) + 4.33 \, LOG_{10}(L2) \qquad (5.11)$$

$$\beta = 0.40 + \frac{0.081(L1 + L2)^{3.23}}{(SN + 1)^{5.19} \, L2^{3.23}} \qquad (5.12)$$

where:

| | |
|---|---|
| $SSN =$ | AASHO soil support index |
| $R =$ | Regional factor |
| $L1 =$ | Axle load (in kips or thousand pounds) |
| $L2 =$ | Axle type (where $1=$ single axle and $2=$ tandem |

axle)

Equations (5.11) and (5.12) may look intimidating, but the primary concern of the reader should be with understanding the intuitive logic of the relationships. Equation (5.11) states that the life of a highway section is positively related to its structural strength *(SN+1)* and negatively related to axle loadings *(L1)*. The impact of *L2* in the term *L1 + L2* is relatively insignificant, since it can only assume a value of 1 or 2. In contrast, *L1* can assume legal values as high as 34. However, *L2* is the only variable in the last term of the equation. Here, pavement life is directly related to the type of axle, as illustrated by the expression: *+4.33LOG$_{10}$(L2)*. When *L2* assumes a value of *2* for a tandem axle, pavement life increases. Intuitively, this relationship makes sense. Spreading a given axle weight over two axles instead of one results in less damage.

Similar intuitive relationships can be found in equation (5.12). The rate of pavement deterioration *(β)* is directly related to axle loadings *(L1)*, and inversely related to pavement strength and axle type. Furthermore, a combination of high structural design and tandem axles reduces the rate of pavement decay in a multiplicative fashion. Again, both relationships fit the intuitive models presented earlier.

In pavement damage analysis, the 18,000–pound single axle is typically used as a reference axle for developing traffic equivalence factors. Thus, the values of $\tau$ and $\beta$ for this axle type are of particular importance. Substituting a value of *18* for *L1* and *1* for *L2* in equation (5.11) yields a condensed function for $\tau$ that is specific to the reference axle (referred to as $\tau_{18}$). A similar substitution into equation (5.12) yields $\beta$ for the reference axle $(\beta_{18})$.

$$LOG_{10}(\tau_{18}) = 9.36\,LOG_{10}(SN + 1) - 0.2 \qquad (5.13)$$

$$\beta_{18} = 0.40 + \frac{1094}{(SN + 1)^{5.19}} \qquad (5.14)$$

The intuitive logic of these equations is even more straightforward. Pavement life is directly related to pavement strength in equation (5.13). However, the rate of pavement decay is inversely related to pavement strength in equation (5.14). Both relationships make sense.

Recall from equation (5.8) that $\tau$ represents the number of axle passes of a given configuration and load at which the damage index equals 1.0. Consequently, $\tau$ may be thought of as the theoretical life of a pavement in axle passes. It follows then that $\tau_{18}$ represents the theoretical life of a pavement in 18,000–pound single-axle passes or ESALs.

While equation (5.13) represents the life of a pavement in theory, the effective or actual life of a section may be much shorter. Equation (5.13) assumes that the pavement will be allowed to deteriorate until its reaches a terminal serviceability of 1.5 (at which time safe and economic transport over the section will be impractical).[12] In actuality, most highway sections are replaced or upgraded much earlier. Federal Aid Highways which include the Interstate and much of the principal arterial system are typically replaced when the PSR reaches 2.5. Other arterials, collectors, and local roads are usually rehabilitated when the PSR declines to 2.0. In these instances, equation (5.15) may be used in lieu of equation (5.13) to predict the *effective* ESAL life of a highway section. The terminal serviceability level in the equation ($P_t$) may be set at either 2.5 or 2.0 to reflect the expected replacement cycle for a given class of highway.

$$LOG_{10}(ESAL) = 9.36\,LOG_{10}(SN + 1) - 0.2 + \frac{G}{\beta} \qquad \text{(5.15)}$$

where:

$$LOG_{10}(ESAL) = \text{Log of effective ESAL life}$$
$$G = LOG_{10}\left(\frac{4.2 - P_t}{2.7}\right) \qquad \text{(5.16)}$$

### Problems and Qualifications

The AASHO damage function has been widely criticized by practitioners and academics alike.[13] The major criticisms are:

1.  only one climatic zone was evaluated at the road test;
2.  all test sections had essentially the same type of soil;
3.  only one level of load was applied to a test section for a given axle type (thus the effects of mixed traffic and axle loads were not analyzed);
4.  the range of axle loads applied to the test sections was small; and
5.  because of accelerated testing, the effects of the environment over a relatively long period of time were not accounted for.

For all of its criticisms, the AAHSO model has been widely used (Van Til et al., 1972). To its credit, a recent study by Wang (1982) found that the decay of test sections at the Pennsylvania Transportation Research Facility tended to follow the AASHO power function shown in Figure 5.1. So, while the AASHO damage function must be qualified whenever it is used outside of the climatic and soil regions for which it was intended, it has been shown to provide at least "ballpark" estimates of pavement life. Furthermore, the causal relationships and formulas presented in this section set the stage for the HPMS model introduced next.

## The HPMS Damage Function

The Highway Performance Monitoring System (HPMS) employs a modified AASHO damage function. The original AASHO function has been modified in three major ways. First, HPMS uses the PSR instead of the PSI used at the road test. The difference is that the PSR entails a verbal rating scheme (as shown in Table 5.2) whereas the PSI is derived from the mathematical relationship shown in equation (5.10). Second, the original or design serviceability rating is set at its theoretical maximum (5.0) instead of at 4.2. This has the effect of increasing the range over which the pavement serviceability index is allowed to decline. Third, the rate of decay of flexible pavement has been modified. In order to illustrate this change, the HPMS flexible pavement damage function is first introduced in equation (5.17).[14]

$$LOG_{10}(ESAL) = 9.36\,LOG_{10}\left(SN + \sqrt{\frac{6}{SN}}\right) + \frac{G}{\beta} \qquad (5.17)$$

where:

$$G = LOG_{10}\frac{5 - PSR}{3.5} \qquad (5.18)$$

$$\beta = 0.4 + \frac{1094}{\left(SN + \sqrt{\frac{6}{SN}}\right)^{5.19}} \qquad (5.19)$$

Note that the term $SN+1$ in the AASHO equation has been replaced by the term $(6/SN)^{0.5}$ in the HPMS function. In practice, this modification has the effect of predicting higher ESAL life-times on highways with lower structural numbers (e.g. 2.5 or lower).

One of the applied problems associated with the AASHO pavement damage function is that it exhibits poor predictive capabilities at the lower end of the range of highway structural numbers.[15] For example, on a highway section with a structural number of 2.0, equation (5.15) predicts on ESAL life of 16,458. On the same highway section, equation (5.17) predicts a pavement life of 115,011 ESALs.

## The Rauhut Model

While the AASHO model has been roundly criticized, until recently a strong effort had not been made to come up with a workable alternative. In the Federal-Aid Highway Act of 1978, Congress stipulated that DOT must conduct a new highway cost allocation study and report the findings to Congress by January 1982. As part of a set of studies funded by the FHWA, a new set of pavement damage functions was developed by Rauhut, Lytton, and Darter (1982).

### Background

The form of the equation relating damage to axle loads in the Rauhut model is the same as the one shown earlier in equation (5.8). Damage is defined as an index ranging from 0.0 to 1.0, as a pavement moves from initial or design serviceability to terminal serviceability. Like the AASHO model, $\tau$ denotes a constant that represents the number of cumulative axle passes that accrue at terminal serviceability.[16]

In the Rauhut study, a regression model was formulated that will predict either $\tau$ or $\beta$ based on the thickness of the pavement layers for a given highway section and the resilient modulus of elasticity (an indicator of soil support). The function (shown in equation (5.20)) has the same form for either parameter. However, the values of the constants and the coefficients in the equation are different for each.

$$\tau, \beta = C + A (L1 + L2)^{X_a} \cdot L_2^{X_b} \cdot E_S^{D} \cdot SN^{E} t^{F} \tag{5.20}$$

where:

| | | |
|---|---|---|
| $t =$ | thickness of all asphaltic concrete layers (in inches); |
| $E_s =$ | subgrade modulus of elasticity (psi). |
| $X_a =$ | $(B_1 + B_2 t + B_3 t^2 + E_2 E_s + E_3 E_s^2)$ |
| $X_b =$ | $(C_1 + C_2 t + C_3 t^2 + G_2 E_s + G_3 E_s^2)$ |

Values for the constants and coefficients were estimated for each of four different climatic zones—a wet freeze, a dry freeze, a wet no-freeze, and a dry no-freeze zone.

### Calibration

The flexible pavement damage functions developed in the Rauhut study reflect a combination of mechanistic and statistical techniques. Mechanistic models consist of a set of mathematical relationships that depict the way in which multilayered pavements respond to applied loads over time. The models are based on elastic theory in which a flexible pavement can be modeled as a system of elastic layers resting on an elastic foundation. From the theory, analytical solutions can be derived for the stresses in the system, and the strain or deflection caused by applied loads can be computed at a given point (or points) beneath the surface. The concepts of multilayered elastic systems and the occurrence of stress in flexible pavements are fully developed in Yoder and Witczak (1975, chapter 2).

Mechanistic models do not directly predict pavement deterioration. Instead, they simulate structural responses. The structural responses are related to pavement deterioration through means of a performance model that predicts the level of distress or loss of serviceability that occurs from wheel loadings or environmental conditions. The mechanistic-statistical modeling process is essentially as follows:

1.  A mechanistic model is applied to a range of hypothetical axle loads, pavement types, and subgrade conditions in order to generate a "data base" of structural responses;

2.  The *output* of the mechanistic model is used to calculate the values of the parameters in the damage function ($\tau$ and $\beta$) for various combinations of input variables;

3.  The manner in which $\tau$ and $\beta$ vary with changes in the independent variables in the model (e.g., pavement thickness or subgrade modulus) is determined through regression analysis on the data base of observations; and

4.  The formulated regression model is then used to predict the values of $\tau$ and $\beta$ for any given load level, axle configuration, and soil support measure.

Generally (as a check against the reasonableness of the estimates), the distress or loss of serviceability predicted by the regression model is compared to observed values for sample pavement sections. In fact, the predicted results may be correlated with actual observations (if sufficient data are available) and the equations for $\tau$ and $\beta$ refined to reflect real-world effects and experiences.

The major inputs in the Rauhut study consisted of: (1) the environmental region, (2) the subgrade modulus, (3) the thickness of the surface course, (4) the structural number, and (5) the load level. Within each environmental zone, three subgrade values were simulated. In addition, three different levels of surface thickness, three subgrade thicknesses, three structural numbers, and eight different load levels were analyzed. Altogether, 216 computer runs resulting from the combinations of these variables were made in each of the four environmental zones. In the author's words, the computer runs represented "separate, miniature versions of the AASHO Road Test in each of the four climatic regions with the important distinction that three different subgrades were used instead of one as at the AASHO Road Test."[17]

In addition to equation (5.20), a second regression model for $\tau$ and $\beta$ was formulated that included the thickness of the aggregate base as an independent variable.


## The Revised FHWA Model

The original FHWA pavement damage model (the Rauhut Model) was updated in 1987 by Villarreal, Garcia-Diaz, and Lytton. The updated deterioration model employs an "S-shaped" decay function in lieu of the power function shown in equation (5.20). In addition to the revised functional form, the updated FHWA model utilizes an expanded and improved data base. With these exceptions, the theory and calibration of the model are essentially the same as those described previously with respect to the original version.

Perhaps the major enhancement contained in the revised edition (from a predictive standpoint) is the inclusion of explanatory variables in the model to account for the effects of different types of tires (bias versus radial) and variations in truck tire pressure. This modification has the potential for greatly enhancing the predictive capabilities of the model. However, it requires detailed information regarding the distribution of tire usage in the impact area and actual tire pressures (by type of truck).

### Model Inputs

The revised FHWA model (like the original function) can be used to predict the loss of serviceability on a given highway section caused by accumulated axle passes. However, before the model can be applied the analyst must specify values for three types of parameters: tire characteristics and use, pavement surface thickness, and subgrade support.

In describing tire use in the impact area, the analyst must estimate typical values for three important truck operating factors: the type of tire which is used (radial versus bias), the number of tires (dual or single), and the tire pressure (in psi).

A recent study in Montana sheds some light on typical tire-use patterns on rural interstate highways. In fall 1984, the Montana Department of Highways conducted a truck tire survey at various sites along the interstate and arterial network. Altogether, over 2,300 tires were sampled. The major conclusions of the study were:

1.      over 82% of the truck tires employed in Montana consist of belted radials;

2.      the average (statewide) air pressure for truck radial tires is 105 pounds;

3.      the average tire pressure for bias-ply tires is 84 psi;

4.        on the average, tire pressures in eastern Montana are higher than in the
          West, ranging between 100 and 110 psi.

The North Dakota Highway Department also conducted a truck-tire study in
fall 1984. The type of tire was not determined in the North Dakota study.
However, sample data were compiled regarding truck tire pressures. The results
of the North Dakota survey are summarized in Table 5.2. As Table 5.2 depicts,
the mean tire pressure in North Dakota (for CO-5AX trucks) is somewhat lower
than the average in Montana. However, both estimates tend to support the same
general conclusion: *truck tire pressures are considerably higher today than the
75 psi reflected in the AASHO damage function.*

**Table 5.3**        Truck Tire Pressures in North Dakota

| Truck-Type | N | Mean | Standard Deviation |
|------------|-----|------|--------------------|
| CO-5AX     | 530 | 97   | 13.7               |
| SU-3AX     | 35  | 92   | 12.7               |
| SU-2AX     | 12  | 85   | 9.0                |

Source: Unpublished NDHWD survey data.

Differences in projected pavement life attributable to truck tire pressure and
usage are illustrated later in the chapter. To summarize the major implications
of the North Dakota and Montana studies, it may be said that (1) truck tires
(particularly on heavy trucks) consist primarily of steel–belted radials, and (2) the
average pressure per tire on combination trucks ranges from 95 to 105 psi.

*Model Structure and Form*

Predicting the ESAL life of a flexible pavement section using the revised
FHWA model is a multistep process. First, the values of $\tau$ and $\beta$ must be
predicted based on the characteristics of the highway and patterns of tire use. The
form of the predictive equation for either parameter is given by:

where:

$$LOG_{10}(\tau, \beta) = (L1 + L2 + L3)^{K1} \cdot L2^{K2} \cdot L3^{K3}$$
$$\cdot (L4 + 1)^{K4} \cdot T1^{A17} \cdot ES^{A18} \cdot P^{A19} - C \qquad (5.21)$$

$$K1 = A1 + A2 \times TH1 + A3 \times ES + A4 \times P \qquad (5.22)$$

$$K2 = A5 + A6 \times TH1 + A7 \times ES + A8 \times P \qquad (5.23)$$

$$K3 = A9 + A10 \times TH1 + A11 \times ES + A12 \times P \qquad (5.24)$$

$$K4 = A13 + A14 \times TH1 + A15 \times ES + A16 \times P \qquad (5.25)$$

| | | |
|---|---|---|
| $L3$ | = | Tire code (*1* for one tire, *2* for dual tires) |
| $L4$ | = | Tire type (*1* for radial, *2* for bias) |
| $TH1$ | = | Thickness of AC surface layer |
| $ES$ | = | Subgrade modulus of elasticity |
| $P$ | = | Tire inflation pressure |

As noted previously, the revised damage function is a sigmoidal or S-shaped curve (rather than a concave function).  The form of the damage function is given by:

$$g = c\, e^{\left(\frac{\tau_{18}}{N_{18}}\right)^{\beta_{18}}} \qquad (5.26)$$

**Table 5.4**        Dry-Freeze Zone Coefficients and Constants for Revised FHWA
                     Model

| Coefficient | $\tau$ | $\beta$ |
|:---:|---:|---:|
| A0 | 8.54580997 | -0.86987349 |
| A1 | -1.92636492 | 0.00000000 |
| A2 | 0.00000000 | 0.09442385 |
| A3 | 0.00000900 | -0.00001860 |
| A4 | -0.00087092 | -0.00022683 |
| A5 | 1.79275336 | 0.00000000 |
| A6 | 0.00000000 | 0.10482985 |
| A7 | -0.00001170 | 0.00001300 |
| A8 | 0.00000000 | 0.00000000 |
| A9 | 1.85872192 | 0.00000000 |
| A10 | 0.00000000 | -0.10122395 |
| A11 | -0.00000860 | 0.00002340 |
| A12 | 0.00000000 | 0.00000000 |
| A13 | -4.37832061 | -0.08745997 |
| A14 | 0.67225250 | 0.01632584 |
| A15 | 0.00000930 | -0.00000080 |
| A16 | 0.00000000 | 0.00000000 |
| A17 | 0.00000000 | -0.84335410 |
| A18 | -0.12346038 | 0.63703782 |
| A19 | 0.00000000 | 0.00000000 |
| C | 0.00000000 | 11.00000000 |

where:

$$c = \frac{P_i - P_f}{P_i - P_t}$$

$N_{18}$ = ESAL life
$P_i$ = initial or design PSR                    (5.27)
$P_f$ = final terminal PSR
$P_t$ = effective terminal PSR

The true terminal serviceability rating (that which occurs at structural failure) is
generally assumed to be 1.5, while the effective terminal serviceability rating is

typically much higher (2.0–2.5). In the subterminal case study, the terminal PSR ($P_t$) was assumed to be 2.5 for interstates and principal arterials, and 2.0 for all other highways.

In order to predict ESAL life, equation (5.26) must be solved for $N$. Taking the natural log of the equation and manipulating the terms yields:

$$N_{18} = \frac{\tau_{18}}{\left(-\ln\dfrac{g}{c}\right)^{\frac{1}{\beta_{18}}}} \qquad\qquad (5.28)$$

which can be used to predict the effective life of a flexible pavement for an assumed terminal serviceability rating.

### Sensitivity to Inputs

Because of the number of factors involved and the newness of the model, the effects of changes in important inputs (such as tire pressure and subgrade modulus) were investigated in the subterminal case study (shown in Chapter 6). A range of reasonable values was established for each variable. For example, the subgrade modulus was allowed to vary between 4,500 and 8,000 psi, while the tire pressure was permitted to range from 75 to 100 pounds.[18]

Figure 5.5 shows the difference in projected ESAL life for a range of surface thicknesses due to variations in tire type and pressure. In this example, the tire pressure was set at 75 pounds for bias-ply tires and 100 pounds for radials.[19] As Figure 5.5 depicts, the difference between the two types of tires on thinner pavements is minimal, with bias-ply tires actually yielding lower (projected) pavement lives. However, on thicker pavements, the effects of steel–belted radials are quite noticeable, markedly reducing the predicted pavement life of a section.

Figure 5.6 more clearly isolates the effects of tire pressure on pavement life, showing the projected life of a typical low-volume highway section when tire pressures are set at 75, 90, and 100 psi, respectively.[20] As the graph depicts, increasing the average tire pressure on a five-inch pavement from 75 to 100 psi reduces the projected ESAL life by 6.25 percent.

In summary, it may be said that the revised FHWA model is

1.    relatively insensitive to moderate changes in the subgrade modulus of elasticity,;
2.    moderately sensitive to changes in truck type pressure;
3.    quite sensitive to the type of tire specified on thick pavements; and
4.     relatively insensitive to the type of tire when the thickness of the surface layers is six inches or less.

**Figure 5.5**        Estimated ESAL Life-Times Using Revised FHWA Model

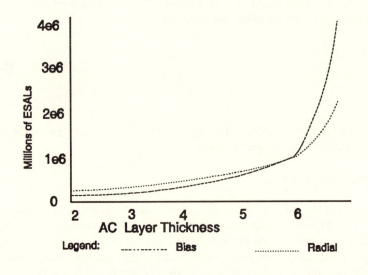

**Evaluation of Flexible Pavement Deterioration Models**

The sensitivity analysis presented above was just one element of an overall evaluation process used to determine the most appropriate pavement deterioration model for the subterminal case study. Each of the deterioration models discussed in this chapter was evaluated with respect to:

1.       theory and estimation techniques;
2.       the reasonableness of the estimates when contrasted with the estimates of other models; and
3.       the reasonableness of the estimates when compared with real-world experience and engineering expectations.

**Figure 5.6**     Effects of Truck Tire Pressure on Flexible Pavement Life

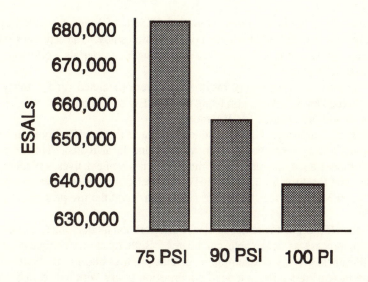

As part of the evaluation process, each model was used to predict the ESAL life of 30 sample sections in the Devils Lake region of North Dakota. For each highway section, data concerning the SN, the thickness of the AC surface layers, the thickness of the aggregate base, the likely elastic modulus of the subgrade, and the current PSR were collected.

### Reasonableness of the Estimates

The reasonableness of the estimates was assessed in three major ways. First, the ESAL lives predicted by the various models were arrayed and compared. Second, the predicted ESAL lifetimes were compared to national averages (by functional class of highway) developed by the FHWA (1982). Third, the results of the models were evaluated in light of the experiences and expectations of North Dakota Highway Department engineers familiar with the nature and rate of pavement decay in the soil and climatic regimes of the Upper Great Plains.

With respect to the first test of reasonableness, two of the models predicted very similar results over the range of structural numbers represented by the thirty test sections. These were: (1) the HPMS deterioration function and (2) the revised FHWA model.[21] Both the original AASHO formula and the revised AASHO model predicted little or no ESAL life at the lower end of the range.

Furthermore, both models were quite sensitive to modest changes in the soil support variable (the SSN or the MR). The Rauhut model was particularly problematic on highway sections with moderate or high SNs, predicting extremely high ESAL lives.

Column (b) of Table 5.5 gives estimates of ESAL lifetimes developed by the FHWA for use in their 1982 highway cost allocation study. The estimates reflect the average pavement condition rating and strength of arterials, collectors, and local roads nationwide.[22]

For purposes of comparison, mean values were predicted for the thirty test sections in the Devils Lake region using the AASHO equation (column d), HPMS (column c) and the updated FHWA model.

As Table 5.5 indicates, HPMS produces estimates that are roughly in line with the national averages (particularly on arterials and local roads). However, the AASHO model does not, predicting much lower pavement lives, especially on collectors and local roads. The new FHWA model generates estimates which are similar to HPMS when the tire type is set to "bias" and the tire pressure is set at 75 psi.

Both the HPMS and the revised FHWA deterioration models emerged from the evaluation process as acceptable candidates. Both functions predicted similar ESAL lifetimes, given the assumptions of bias-ply tires and tire pressures of 75 psi. The increasing tendency toward combination trucks with belted radials and tire pressures of 100 pounds or more may make these assumptions unrealistic in future years. However, the HPMS damage function can be applied in such a manner that the results reflect higher tire pressures. This adjustment process is illustrated in the abandonment case presented in chapter 11. The techniques employed in chapter 11 also account for another shortcoming of pavement damage models; they do not directly account for the effects of time. In order to better simulate time-related deterioration, a natural decay process is introduced in chapter 11. This function is used in conjunction with the HPMS damage procedure to estimate highway impacts.

The purpose of this chapter has been to describe the process of pavement deterioration and present some frequently used damage models. None of the models are perfect. However, several of them yield reasonable results. Highway engineers in various states may have empirically modified the AASHTO design equation, or developed statistical cost functions from historical pavement data. State-specific models can easily be substituted for the HPMS or TTI functions in the highway impact assessment process. However, these functions may not be transferable to other states or regions. Regardless of the damage function used, the highway impact assessment principles and methods are the same.

**Table 5.5**          Estimated ESAL Life of Pavements:  By Functional Class

| Functional Class (a) | FHWA Averages (b) | HPMS Predicted Values (c) | AASHO Predicted Values (c) |
|---|---|---|---|
| Arterial | 1,500,000 | 1,762,734 | 422,858 |
| Collector | 400,000 | 88,051 | 5,053 |
| Local | 80,000 | 76,711 | 208 |

**NOTES**

1.  Expenditures are related indirectly (albeit casually) to ESALs.  Economic costs, on the other hand, are directly related to ESALs and may be expressed in terms of the pavement life expired or consumed.

2.  Unlike the effects of a single vehicle, the impacts of a class of traffic are usually measurable on some meaningful scale, and can be translated into dollars or resource costs.  The statement, "an additional 2 inches of pavement might be required in order to handle heavier vehicles" is a much more relevant bit of information to highway managers that the theoretical concept of .00011 inches per ESAL.

3.  There is a key linkage between marginal and incremental cost.  The cost of an increment of traffic is roughly (although not precisely) the sum of the marginal costs occasioned by the individual units of traffic that comprise the class.  For example, if 1,000 annual CO-5AX truck trips constitute the class of traffic under evaluation, then the incremental cost of the class is approximately equal to the sum of the cost of each individual truck trip.

4.  The term *build-sooner* cost was originally coined by Bisson, Brander, and Innes (1985) during their evaluation of the incremental effects of heavy truck traffic on New Brunswick highways.  On page 10 they write: "Build-sooner cost is related to the hypothesis that loading a large increment of heavy traffic onto a link will cause two conditions to evolve.  First, pavement life cycles are likely to become shorter, and, second, future capacity improvements will be needed sooner."

5. This is only rational behavior. The retention of the dollar(s), all things being equal, provides highway officials with greater management flexibility, and allows funds to be used for some competing, alternative purpose. This preference, it should be noted, is independent of inflation.

6. In the long run, the capacity of a highway section to absorb ESALs can be freely adjusted. For practical purposes, the long run period begins at the *end* of the current replacement cycle, and extends over all remaining cycles in the section's life.

7. This approach explicitly assumes that impacted highways will be upgraded at the end of the current replacement cycle. The alternative to upgrading is to continue to replace the section periodically at ever-shortening intervals throughout its life. Upgrading the section represents the most rational and economic course of action (in most instances), as the savings in life-cycle maintenance costs should more than offset the initial upgrading expenditure. However, upgrading will not always be necessary for each section. The occurrence of upgrading costs on a highway section will depend on two factors. The first is the existing design of the section. A relatively strong rural section may be able to handle some additional truck traffic without the need for increasing the structural strength of the pavement. On the other hand, relatively weak or underdesigned sections cannot accommodate additional ESALs without unduly increasing user costs and dramatically shortening the rehabilitation cycle. The second factor governing the occurrence of upgrading costs is the absolute level and composition of the incremental traffic. A large increase in ESALs even on a relatively well-built highway section may necessitate upgrading. In the case study shown in Chapter 6, highway sections that show little or no reduction in pavement life (as measured in years) are not upgraded.

8. In rail-line abandonment analyses, it is frequently necessary to bifurcate a branch line and analyze the two segments as free-standing lines in addition to analyzing them as a single rail line. Under the incremental method, different highway costs could result for the two segments even if they generate exactly the same number of ESALs. The outcome will depend on the order of the analysis. Moreover, in branch-line studies, it is frequently desirable to assign benefits to commodities for determining the subsidy or rehabilitation burden each shipper should pay. Again, the incremental method cannot handle this special case.

9. In this approach, the relative contribution of each distress in terms of the decision to rehabilitate is determined empirically. For example, rutting may account for 14 percent of the decision to replace a pavement. Consequently, 14 percent of the cost of replacement is assign to rutting. For a detailed discussion of this approach and the development of damage functions for individual

distresses, see Rauhut, J.B., R.L. Lytton, and M.I. Darter. *Pavement Damage Functions for Cost Allocation*, FHWA Report No.: FHWA/RD-841018, Washington, D.C., 1984.

10. Six test loops were constructed in Ottawa over which 110 vehicles operated between six and seven days a week (except in spring thaw). Altogether, the vehicles applied 1.14 million axle loads to the test sections over the duration of the project. Tractor semi-trailer combinations operated over the four largest test loops. To control for axle configuration, both single- and tandem-axle combination trucks were used. The load levels on the four loops were 14, 18, and 22 kips, respectively, for single-axle vehicles, and 18, 26, 34, and 38 kips for tandem-axle trucks.

11. AASHO officials found, somewhat surprisingly, that the PSI of a new section that had never been exposed to traffic was 4.2. In other words, none of the sections were ever rated at their theoretical maximum of 5.0. The terminal PSI for pavements at the road test was determined to be 1.5. This figure represents actual pavement failure; that is, the point at which the serviceability of the section is such that safe and reasonably economic transport is no longer possible. True pavement failure is different from effective terminal serviceability, in which a threshold or trigger PSI is established (e.g. 2.5) that, when reached, results in the decision to rehabilitate.

12. At a terminal serviceability of 1.5, user costs will rise dramatically and the quality of ride will be at an unacceptable level.

13. An implicit assumption of the AASHO Road Test is that the decline in pavement serviceability (PSI) is due entirely to the effects of traffic (axle loads) upon pavements. A recent critique by Coree and White (1988) suggests that the initiation of significant deterioration in the test sections at Ottawa was linked to springthaw, which critically affected the performance of test sections in subsequent evaluation periods. In addition, the flexible pavement layer coefficients used in the calculation of the structural number were criticized by Coree and White as "secondary regression coefficients with no physical significance as indicators of pavement strength."

14. The term $G$ represents the damage index in the HPMS function. When the PSR is set to 1.5 (terminal serviceability), the term $G/\beta$ becomes zero. The log of G then becomes 0 and the entire term $(G/\beta)$ resolves to zero.

15. This observation is based on conversations with NDHWD engineers, and is felt to be a fairly common perception of the AASHO formula.

16. But unlike the AASHO function, the Rauhut model assumes a higher terminal serviceability rating (2.5). This is based on the observation that Federal Aid highways are rarely allowed to deteriorate to a serviceability rating of 2.0 or lower.

17. Rauhut, Lytton, and Darter 1984, p. 152.

18. Estimates of the typical subgrade modulus of elasticity for highway sections in the Devils Lake region were developed as follows. The low-range estimate (4,500) was adapted from AASHTO (1986), and is considered to be a conservative estimate for low-volume roads in the dry-freeze zone (Region VI). The upper-end estimate (8,000 psi) was calculated from guidelines contained in Rauhut et al. (1984) using descriptions of the typical soil composition, density, and moisture content provided by Clay Sorenson, NDHWD district engineer. The FHWA model is apparently not very sensitive to reasonable or moderate variations in the subgrade modulus. For example, increasing the ES from 4,500 to 8,000 psi on a five-inch pavement decreases the projected pavement life from 678,819 ESALs to 657,159, a change of 3.2 percent.

19. As the Montana study illustrated, steel–belted radials are usually inflated to a higher pressure than bias-ply tires.

20. This example assumes: (1) radial tires, (2) a surface thickness of five inches (roughly equivalent to a SN of 2.6 in the Devils Lake region), and (3) a subgrade modulus (ES) of 4,500.

21. When the revised FHWA model was set to a tire-type of "bias" and a PSI of 75, it closely paralleled HPMS predicted values for pavement life.

22. While it cannot be contended that the attributes of North Dakota's rural highways are identical to national "averages," there should be similarities within functional classes.

# 6

# Subterminal Land-Use Study

Chapters 4 and 5 defined much of the theoretical and analytic framework of highway impact assessment. The purpose of the next three chapters is to describe and illustrate the process. The individual submodels and procedures are covered in depth, and many of the required data inputs are highlighted. The analytic and data collection procedures are illustrated through the use of the subterminal problem. An actual subterminal case study is introduced in this chapter.[1] Because the illustrations relate to actual places, problems, and events, they will hopefully allow the reader to better visualize the spatial and geographic dimensions of the land-use study. The Devils Lake North Dakota elevator system and its surrounding transportation network are shown in Figure 6.1.

The subterminal problem requires a much more detailed and complex land-use study than a railroad abandonment case. Before land-use zones can be defined, the subterminal market area must be demarcated. The impact zone in a subterminal analysis typically coincides with the boundaries of the facility's drawing region. Therefore, the market study is very important. Although the subterminal example is complex, it has its rewards. The analysis of trade area boundaries and elevator linkages presented in this chapter have analogies in other types of multiplant operations. Plus, the subterminal problem is ideal for illustrating spatial interaction modeling techniques.

## DESIGN OF THE LAND-USE STUDY

Subterminal impact analysis involves a series of steps, starting with an aggregate picture of the impact zone and culminating with a microscopic examination of individual highway sections and interzonal traffic patterns. The initial task is to bound the impact region and subdivide the area into origin zones. This can be accomplished through a top-down process involving the following tasks (in descending and sequential order):

1.      The impact area is delineated or "cordoned off";
2.      The impact zone is subdivided into broad zones of subterminal market

**Figure 6.1**        Subterminal Market Area: Devils Lake & Surrounding Area

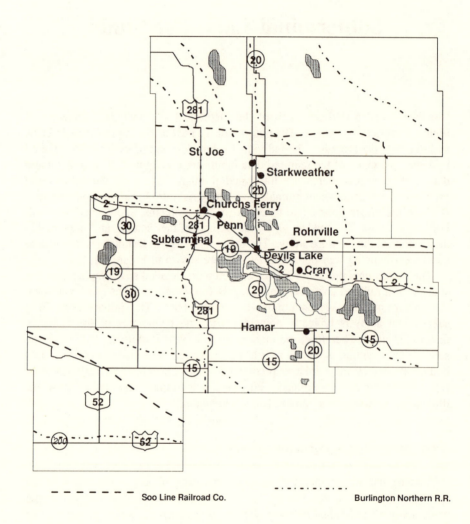

------------        Soo Line Railroad Co.          -.-.-.-.-.-.        Burlington Northern R.R.

power;
3.      The zones of subterminal market power are partitioned into agricultural production or supply zones;
4.      Within each agricultural production zone, one or more "centroids" or traffic-loading points are identified.

## Delineating the Impact Zone

In some cases, the subterminal may already be built. In others, the facility may only be in the planning stages. Even if the subterminal has not yet been constructed, a market feasibility study should have been completed. If accessible, this market feasibility study can help the highway analyst demarcate the impact zone and define the land-use regions.

One method of defining the trade area is to use price relationships among satellite elevators and competing elevators at the periphery of a subterminal's market area. In this method, farm truck costs and elevator bid prices are used to define points of equal drawing power along the subterminal's trade area boundary. A point of equal drawing power is defined by the equality:

$$SNFP_{MAX} = ONFP_i \qquad\qquad (6.1)$$

where:

$SNFP_{MAX}$ = Highest net farm price of any elevator within the subterminal-satellite system

$ONFP_i$ = Net farm price at closest competing elevator in direction $i$

Theoretically, farmers situated on an imaginary line connecting two points of equal drawing power will be indifferent with respect to where they truck their grain. However, farmers situated on one side of the line or the other will tend to favor one of the elevators. This is because the net farm price (the price paid at the elevator minus the farm truck costs) will be greater at one elevator than at the other. If this process of demarcation is repeated in each direction, a set of points will emerge representing approximate locations of equal drawing power. When connected, these points will tend to approximate the outer boundary of an elevator's trade area. For an illustration of this approach see Cobia, Wilson, Gunn, and Coon (1986), particularly pages 14 through 18. The shortcomings of this approach are: (1) it has some detailed data requirements attached, (2) it ignores farmer patronage and other factors unrelated to price and distance, (3) the boundary line may be different for individual commodities, and (4) the line may change with fluctuations in prices and variations in farm truck costs.

Defining trade area boundaries in this manner requires detailed and precise information concerning price relationships among satellite elevators and their competitors at the fringe of a trade area. This information is not readily available and must usually be obtained by survey. An alternative method of defining the trade area is to ask the subterminal manager to delineate the outer boundary based on his or her knowledge of the price relationships and competitive pressures that exist. If the facility is already operational, this approach may be feasible. In the Devils Lake case study, the subterminal manager was given a map of the region with a rough boundary line sketched-in, and asked to modify the line based on his knowledge of:

1.      competition from nonmember elevators or competing subterminal systems,
2.      the distribution of production in the region,
3.      geographic constraints and barriers,
4.      the capacity of his system, and
5.      the perceived optimum volume at the subterminal.

Several iterations of the process were performed before the final boundary line emerged.[2]

Once the outer boundary of the subterminal's market area has been demarcated, the impact region can be partitioned into origin or supply zones. This task was accomplished in the Devils Lake study via a two-step process. First, the market area was subdivided into broad zones of subterminal market power. Second, within each zone of subterminal market power, specific production or supply zones were identified.

**Defining Zones of Subterminal Market Power**

Of all of the elevators in the impact region, the subterminal will exert the strongest attractive force over supply zones. This force will be at its greatest close to the facility (where the absolute attraction is strong) and in zones which are not adjacent to a local or satellite elevator. In the latter instance, the relative attraction of the subterminal will exceed that of the closest local elevator due to price advantage.

The market power of the subterminal elevator will directly affect two important variables in the highway impact assessment process. First, the drawing power of the subterminal elevator will strongly influence the allocation of grain between the subterminal-satellite system and competing (nonsystem) elevators in the region. Second, the attractive force exerted by the subterminal elevator (relative to its satellites) will determine the allocation of grain between flow–types *1* and *2*. The allocation of grain among flow–types is important for two reasons: (1) farm-to-subterminal shipments (flow-type *2*) will generally involve longer trip distances, and (2) the distribution of farm-to-elevator shipments among truck types is partly a function of the type of flow. Thus, the market power of the subterminal elevator will indirectly determine the distribution of grain shipments among truck types in the region.

Figure 6.2 shows the zones of equal market power for the Devils Lake subterminal. The zonal boundaries consist of concentric rings about the subterminal at various distance intervals. The innermost zone includes points within twenty-five miles of the subterminal (approximately). The second zone consists of locations less than thirty-eight miles away, while the third zone includes locations up to fifty-five miles in distance. Within each zone, the subterminal exerts approximately the same level of attraction over grain flows. However, the attractive force exerted by the subterminal will differ from zone-to-zone, typically declining with distance.

### Subterminal Market Share

The percentages shown in Figure 6.2 represent the projected market shares of the Devils Lake subterminal-satellite system in 1990 (the year in which the system should reach its long-run output level).[3] For example, within twenty-five miles of the subterminal, the cooperative should capture roughly 75 percent of the grains and oilseeds produced. However, in zone 2 the projected market share is only 50 percent, and it drops even further in zone 3 (declining to 25 percent of total production). This is a typical pattern of subterminal market influence, wherein the market share of the system declines with distance from the subterminal.

The share of grain captured by a subterminal-satellite system in the region will depend, in part, on the scope and intensity of demand-point competition.[4] In general, the only demand-point competition that arises close to the subterminal is that which stems from nonmember elevators situated in the immediate geographic vicinity. Consequently, the percentage of grain captured by the system in the innermost zone will typically be quite high. However, as the distance from the subterminal increases, the percentage of grain captured by the system will generally decline. This is because at greater distances the attractive power of the subterminal tends to weaken and nonmember elevators begin to compete directly with nearby satellite elevators rather than with the subterminal. Also, as the distance from the subterminal increases, competition from independent elevators located at the fringe of the market area (as well as competition from neighboring satellite-subterminal systems) tends to intensify. The zones of subterminal market power (shown in Figure 6.2) reflect these dynamics, depicting a decline in market share with distance.

**Figure 6.2**       Subterminal Market Area:  Zones of Equal Relative Attraction

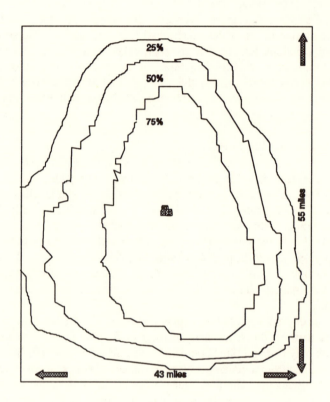

## Defining Agricultural Production Zones

The third step in demarcating the impact area consists of subdividing the region into agricultural production or supply zones. Altogether, fifty-four supply zones were identified in the Devils Lake study (Figure 6.3). Six major criteria were followed in the definition of the zones:

    1.        A given zone should be large enough to generate a significant flow, and yet small enough to provide specific information concerning which farm-to-elevator highways are used;

**Figure 6.3**        Devils Lake Land Use Zones and Highway Network

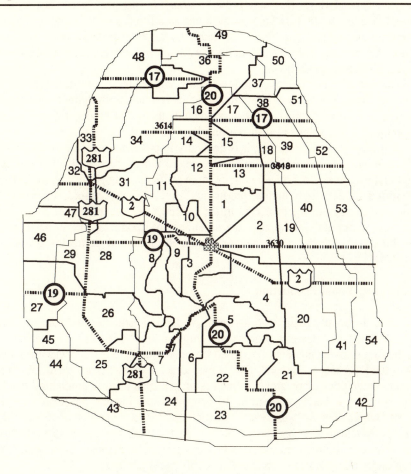

2.      Zones should recognize and follow natural boundaries (such as lakes and rivers) wherever possible;

3.      The boundaries of the zones should consider the coverage and characteristics of the highway network, and if possible include one or more access highways (such as a collector or minor arterial);

4.      The zones should be defined so as to facilitate the identification of logical centroids (traffic loading points);

5.      Each production zone should fall entirely within the boundaries of a single zone of subterminal market power; and

6.      The zones should be as homogenous as possible with respect to the types of nonagricultural land-uses present.

One option for defining production zones is to make them consistent with township boundaries. This may prove desirable in instances where few natural boundaries or variations in land-use or highway attributes exist. However, using township boundaries may fail to consider important natural barriers and may ignore the characteristics of the highway network in the area, both of which can potentially affect grain flows.

The resource costs of the land-use study will increase with the number of zones defined. For a low-budget study, the analyst may wish to limit the number of zones. However, larger zones may preclude the use of producer optimization techniques in the shipment distribution phase of the study.

In highway impact analysis, it is generally impractical to define every source of traffic generation and identify exactly where it originates or "loads-onto" the first highway link. So, typically one or more traffic loading points (*centroids*) are identified in each agricultural production zone. Each centroid represents a weighted average of the projected traffic loadings in a given zone or area. The use of centroids minimizes the number of possible origin-destination combinations, thereby reducing the data collection and computer resources required.

**Estimating Zonal Production**

Once the supply regions are defined, production estimates and forecasts can be developed. A three-step process was employed in the Devils Lake case study. In the first step, the number of acres under cultivation in each zone was estimated from land-use maps. Second, the cultivated acres in each zone were allocated among the various crops grown in the region based on historic production levels. For example, if barley comprised 40 percent of the historic production in the county where the zone was located, then 40 percent of the cultivated acres in the zone were allocated to barley production. In the final step, the crop production levels in each zone were computed by multiplying the number of acres of each crop under cultivation by the average county yield per acre.[5]

**The Planning Horizon**

Changes in highway costs are computed by comparing the ESALs generated from the baseline traffic stream to the ESALs generated from the altered traffic stream. However, a simple before and after analysis may provide only limited data regarding subterminal highway impacts. There are several reasons for this. First, even if the subterminal has been built, full-scale operations may not be achieved for several years. Second, even after full-scale subterminal operations commence, changes in traditional trade-flows and highway routes may not occur immediately. Third, changes in agricultural production or transportation conditions may alter the level and distribution of flows in the impact region.

Essentially, two types of traffic effects will be felt in the impact area during the analysis period. The first effect is due to the redistribution of existing volumes among flow types. For example, some portion of the base-year farm-to-elevator volume may shift to flow-type 2 at some time during the analysis period. This change is strictly a function of the establishment of a subterminal elevator in the area. However, the traffic flows generated in the region may also change during the analysis period due to variations in production levels or crop patterns over time. These effects have nothing to do with the location of a subterminal elevator. Nevertheless, they are important. Changes in production or transportation conditions tend to compound any traffic impacts due to subterminal development. For example, a subterminal may create a new traffic stream of ten CO–5AX trucks a day on a collector highway. If regional production increases at 5 percent a year, this initial stream may grow to twenty truck a day in fifteen years. Consequently, the impacts on the collector highway may be much greater than a simple analysis would project. Variations in production and transportation can also obscure cost responsibilities. For example, the highway analyst may wish to evaluate land-use controls (such as zoning changes or a developer's fee) as policy options. In such cases, the effects of the subterminal must be clearly distinguished from the effects of changes in the broader agricultural economy.

For the reasons cited above, a multiyear analysis of traffic flows is usually necessary. So, typically subterminal output and market area production must be forecast for some horizon year. The *horizon year* is the farthest year into the future for which the highway analyst can reasonably expect to forecast land-use values.

In addition to the horizon year, two other years are of particular importance in the land-use study. The *base year* is the year prior to or during which the subterminal begins operations. The *impact year* is the first year during which the first substantial impacts are generated. If there is a start-up phase in which the subterminal is moving toward long-run output levels, then the impact year may not directly follow the base year. Instead, the impact year may be three to five years in the future. Any traffic changes that occur between the impact year and base year are only partially related to the facility. In fact, any such shifts may be due to production changes or economic shifts.

The Devils Lake subterminal began initial operations in June 1985 (the base year). However, the facility had only a minimal effect on grain flows during the last half of 1985. Little (if any) change was discernible in grain movements during 1986, and only moderate growth was evident in 1987. Because of the gradual pace of change in the region, 1990 was projected as the first year of significant impacts.

The subterminal manager was asked to make some operational projections for the impact year based on his knowledge of the market area, the cost structure of his elevator, and competition from nonmember elevators in the region. Specifically, he was asked to supply a pessimistic, moderate, and optimistic estimate of the anticipated 1990 subterminal volume, as well as subjective probabilities for each projection. The subterminal manager's projections are summarized in Table 6.1. Since he gave equal weights or probabilities to each of the forecasts, the expected value of the subterminal's volume in the impact year is equal to the mid-range estimate.

**Table 6.1**        Impact-Year Subterminal Volume Projections

|                      | Scenario | | |
|                      | Pessimistic | Mid-Range | Optimistic |
|----------------------|-------------|------------|------------|
| Projected<br>Bushels | 8,000,000   | 11,000,000 | 14,000,000 |
| Probability          | 0.33        | 0.33       | 0.33       |

Source: An interview with Mr. Alfred Bareksten, Manager, Lake Region Cooperative, Devils Lake, North Dakota, June 17, 1987.

Figure 6.4 illustrates the gradual pace of growth in subterminal output in the Devils Lake region, starting from a base year volume of 3,614,494 bushels in 1985 and growing to a projected impact year volume of 11 million bushels in 1990. These data underscore the need for differentiating between the impact year and the first year of operations.

Horizon-year forecasts were developed in the Devils Lake study through means of a Delphi survey. A committee of six people was assembled, each familiar with agricultural policy and production expectations in the region. The committee was supplied with historic production statistics and trends, and asked to estimate production levels (by commodity) for the year 2006. Instead of a single estimate, the participants were asked to supply a range of estimates (low, medium, and high) that might occur given different policy, market, and weather assumptions. Each participant was then asked to attach probabilities (or likelihoods) to each of the three scenarios. Using these probabilities, an "expected value" of future production levels was calculated.[6]

The output of the land-use submodel consists of an estimate of the number of bushels of each crop produced in each agricultural zone during the base year and the horizon year. These data constitute one of the major inputs to the shipment generation submodel, the next model in the chain. Before plunging into the mechanics of shipment generation procedure, the overall impact assessment process is highlighted, beginning with the land-use procedure and culminating with the pavement cost module.

**Figure 6.4**     Devils Lake Subterminal Volume:  1985-1990

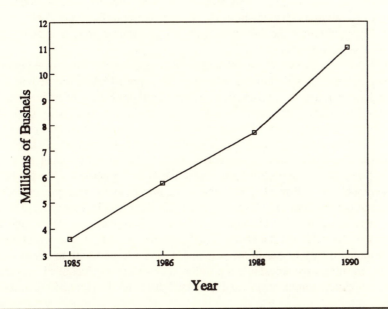

## SUBTERMINAL IMPACT ASSESSMENT PROCESS

As depicted in Table 3.2,  the subterminal impact assessment process entails a battery of submodels or procedures, such that the output of one model essentially becomes the input to the next.  The purpose of this section is to enumerate the steps in the impact assessment process, and to  highlight the major assumptions underlying the models.

**Overview of the Impact Assessment and Computational Process**

The end objective of the land-use, traffic generation, shipment distribution, truck distribution and network assignment procedures is to isolate and model grain truck flows in the impact region. When these procedures are properly applied, the highway analyst will have information regarding the number of grain truck trips of each type on each highway section in the impact zone. Again, these data are not isolated in automatic vehicle classification or weigh-in-motion studies. Furthermore, since the grain truck statistics are generated by a set of models, the analyst can simulate changes in truck traffic patterns at the individual highway level. Thus, although the subterminal impact assessment process is complex, it can be a powerful analytic tool.

As Figure 6.5 shows, the initial step in the impact assessment process consists of the projection of agricultural production and shipment levels for the base year, the impact year, and the horizon year. Agricultural production estimates must be generated for each supply zone in the region. Outbound commodity shipments must be projected for each elevator, using inbound elevator volumes as a proxy (or some other source of data). Once production and shipment levels have been estimated, the analyst is in a position to project the level of annual interzonal traffic flows in the region (for each year in the planning period). The projection of interzonal traffic flows is a key step in the impact assessment process. Once the interzonal volumes have been forecast, grain flows can be converted to annual truck trips and assigned to the highway network. Then (based on the average axle weights of the vehicles) the annual ESALs applied to each highway section can be computed for each year in the planning period. Armed with the incremental ESALs, the highway analyst is in a position to predict any reductions in pavement service life that might occur, and evaluate the need for upgrading impacted highways.

In summary form, the subterminal impact assessment process entails the following steps or computations:

1.  Base year production levels are projected (by commodity) for each agricultural supply zone in the region;
2.  Horizon–year production forecasts are developed (by commodity) for each supply zone;
3.  Annual growth factors are computed for each commodity in the impact region;
4.  Zonal production levels are estimated for each year in the planning period (using the annual growth factors and base–year production projections);
5.  Base–year and impact–year shipments are estimated for each elevator in the impact region;
6.  Farm-to-elevator traffic flows are modeled for both the base year and the impact year;

7.      Outbound (elevator-to-market) flows are simulated for the base year and the impact year;

8.      Annual (unadjusted) interzonal volumes are projected for each flow type for the duration of the planning period;

9.      The projected annual interzonal volumes are adjusted for changes in production levels over time;

10.     The projected (annual) commodity flows are distributed among grain truck types;

11.     The projected annual flows are converted to annual trips (by truck class);

12.     Axle load factors are computed for each annual flow (by truck type);

13.     The projected annual trips are assigned to the highway network;

14.     The annual level of grain truck ESALs is calculated for each year in the planning period (for each highway in the impact study);

15.     The ESAL life of each highway section is projected for the baseline traffic stream and the impact scenario;

16.     Any reductions in pavement life that occur during the current replacement cycle are computed for each highway section.

17.     Any build-sooner costs that might result are estimated in the manner described in chapter 4;

18.     Each section is evaluated with respect to the need for upgrading; and

19.     Upgrading costs (if applicable) are computed using a modification of Purnell's method.

The purpose of this chapter has been to illustrate the analytic techniques employed in a rural land-use study, and to present an overview of the remainder of the highway impact assessment process. The next three chapters focus on the various submodels, starting with the shipment generation procedures.

**Figure 6.5**     Flow of Subterminal Impact Assessment Process

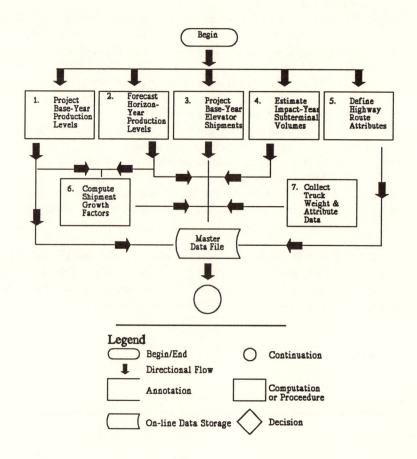

**Figure 6.5**      (continued)

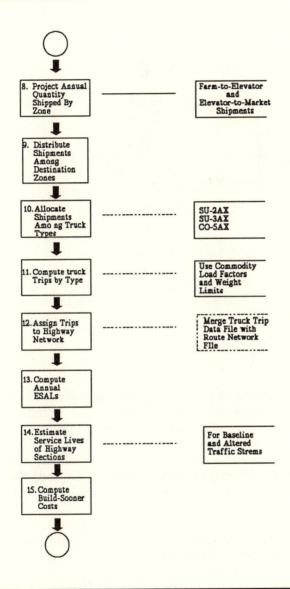

**Figure 6.5**      (continued)

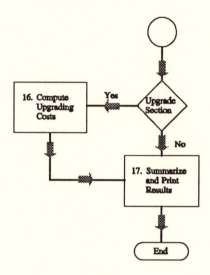

**NOTES**

1. The Devils Lake North Dakota case study was conducted in 1987 and 1988 as part of a North Dakota Highway Department project conducted by the author. For a detailed description of the project see Tolliver (1989).

2. This information was obtained during an interview with Alfred Bareksten, manager of the Lake Region Cooperative, Devils Lake, North Dakota, June 17, 1987, or in subsequent telephone conversations or written correspondence with Bareksten and employees of the organization.

3. Interview with Alfred Bareksten, June 17, 1987, or subsequent telephone conversations and written correspondence.

4. A given subterminal-satellite system is typically subject to two sources of demand-point competition. The first is from noncooperative or nonmember elevators located within the subterminal's trade area. The second is from elevators or competing subterminals that lie outside of the subterminal's market boundary and that apply competitive pressure at the periphery of the trade area.

5. Historic production and crop yield data were obtained from a series of reports titled *North Dakota Agricultural Statistics*, 1984-1987, published by the North Dakota Agricultural Statistics Service, Fargo. The extent of nonagricultural land-uses in the area and the approximate number of acres under cultivation in each zone were developed from land-use maps published by the U.S. Geological Survey, and/or from highway maps published by the NDHWD.

6. The Delphi forecasts were complied on a county basis. The horizon–year production levels for each zone were estimated by assuming that the rate of growth (or decline) in county agricultural production (over the planning horizon) would hold true for each zone in the county.

# 7

# Shipment Generation Procedure

This chapter illustrates the shipment or traffic generation procedure. In the subterminal case study, the traffic generation procedure has a dual purpose. The first objective is to predict the volume generated from each agricultural production zone in the region for each year of the analysis period. The second objective is to project the outbound volume from each elevator during each year of the planning period.

The traffic generation procedure does not assign flows to destinations. It simply projects the volume available for shipment in each zone. The shipment generation model is analogous to (although different from) the trip generation model in urban transportation planning. The essential difference between the two is that the shipment generation model is concerned with predicting the *volume* or quantity shipped from each zone rather than the *trips*. The number of annual trips required to haul a fixed volume of a particular commodity (from a given zone) will depend on the type of truck used. Thus, the number of trips cannot be determined until the annual quantity shipped is projected and allocated among flow-types 1 and 2. Therefore, a logical sequence of events in the modeling of farm-to-elevator shipments is:

1. the volume available for shipment in each supply zone is projected;
2. the potential volume in each supply zone is distributed among flow types and destination zones;
3. the interzonal commodity flows are distributed among truck types; and
4. interzonal truck volumes are converted to truck trips using average commodity payload factors.

In the subterminal example, the initial step consists of projecting the level of shipments generated from each production zone (and each elevator) for two intervals in time: the base year and the horizon year. Once the base year and horizon year shipments are known, the analyst can project the volumes generated during each year of the analysis period.

## COMPUTATION OF BASE-YEAR AND HORIZON-YEAR VOLUMES

Most production estimates are in bushels. However, truck loads and axle weights must be expressed in tons or kilopounds. Thus, the initial step in the estimation of base-year and horizon-year volumes is the conversion of crop production estimates (which are in bushels) to hundreds of pounds (cwts). Algebraically, the computation of the base-year shipment volume for a given agricultural production zone in the impact region is given by:[1]

$$VB_{co} = BB_{co} \times CF_c \qquad (7.1)$$

where:

$VB_{co}$ = Base-year volume of commodity $c$ generated from zone $o$

$BB_{co}$ = Bushels of crop $c$ produced in zone $o$ during the base year

$CF_c$ = Factor for converting bushels of commodity $c$ to hundred-pounds (cwts)

Similarly, the horizon-year volume generated from a given production zone is computed as:

$$VH_{co} = BH_{co} \times CF_c \qquad (7.2)$$

where:

$VH_{co}$ = Horizon-year volume of commodity $c$ generated from zone $o$

$BH_{co}$ = Bushels of crop $c$ produced in zone $o$ during the horizon year

The conversion factor in the formula $(CF_c)$ reflects the density of the commodity being shipped. The conversion factor is computed for a given commodity as follows:[2]

$$CF_c = \frac{LB_c}{100} \qquad (7.3)$$

where:

$LB_c$ = The pounds per bushel of commodity $c$

## COMPUTATION OF SHIPMENT GROWTH FACTOR

The purpose of a shipment growth factor is to calculate the increase (or decrease) in traffic that occurs during each year of the analysis period due to changes in regional production levels. A shipment growth factor may conceivably take many different forms (linear or nonlinear). In the Devils Lake case study, the following functional form was used to represent the annual growth in shipments over time:[3]

$$GF_c = \left(\frac{VH_c}{VB_c}\right)^K \tag{7.4}$$

where:

$$GF_c \quad = \quad \text{Annual volume growth factor, commodity } c$$

$$K = \frac{\ln\left(\frac{VH_c}{VB_c}\right)}{N} \tag{7.5}$$

$$N \quad = \quad \text{Number of years in planning period}$$

## COMPUTATION OF ANNUAL SHIPMENT VOLUMES

Given the base-year volume and a shipment growth factor, it is possible for the analyst to predict the volume generated from each production zone during each year of the analysis period. The volume shipped from a given production zone during any year other than the base year is computed as:

$$V_{coy} = V_{co(y-1)} e^K \tag{7.6}$$

where:

$$V_{coy} \quad = \quad \text{The predicted volume of commodity } c \text{ shipped from production zone } o \text{ during year } y$$

$$V_{co(y-1)} \quad = \quad \text{The predicted volume of commodity } c \text{ shipped from production zone } o \text{ during year } y - 1$$

Equation (7.6) represents the basic formula used to project annual farm-to-elevator commodity flows in the Devils Lake region. However, equation (7.6) represents only one part of the traffic generation procedure. Outbound elevator volumes must also be projected for each year in the analysis period.

In subterminal impact assessment, a given elevator can constitute both an originating and a terminating zone. In order to avoid confusion, some new notation is introduced. In the case of inbound commodity flows (where the elevator functions as a destination zone) a given facility is denoted by the subscript $d$. Thus, the inbound commodity volume for any given year in the analysis period is given by:

$$V_{cdy} = \sum_{O} V_{cody} \qquad\qquad (7.7)$$

where:

$$
\begin{array}{lll}
V_{cdy} & = & \text{Annual inbound volume of commodity} \\
        &   & c \text{ to elevator } d \text{ during year } y \\
V_{cody} & = & \text{Annual volume of commodity } c \text{ shipped} \\
        &   & \text{from origin zone } o \text{ to elevator } d \text{ during} \\
        &   & \text{year } y
\end{array}
$$

As equation (7.7) suggests, the inbound flow to a given elevator is equal to the sum of the flows from each origin zone in the market region. This balance condition will become very important later in the book when the traffic distribution submodels are introduced.

In the case of outbound commodity shipments (where the elevator functions as an originating traffic centroid), a given facility is denoted by the subscript $e$. Outbound elevator volumes are primarily a function of two items: the inbound elevator flows and the amount of grain that is stored or held over during the year. Thus, the outbound flow from a given elevator for a given year in the analysis period may be computed as follows:

$$V_{cey} = V_{cdy} - ST_{cey} + ST_{ce(y-1)} \qquad\qquad (7.8)$$

where:

$$
\begin{array}{lll}
V_{cey} & = & \text{Outbound volume of commodity } c \\
        &   & \text{during year } y \\
V_{cdy} & = & \text{Inbound volume of commodity } c \text{ during} \\
        &   & \text{year } y \\
ST_{cey} & = & \text{Inbound quantity of commodity } c \text{ that is} \\
        &   & \text{not reshipped from elevator } e \text{ during} \\
        &   & \text{year } y
\end{array}
$$

$$ST_{ce(y-1)} \quad = \quad \text{Quantity of commodity } c \text{ held over from previous year at elevator } e \text{ that is reshipped during year } y$$

The primary function of grain elevators is the merchandising of grain (as opposed to storage). So, it is reasonable to assume that most of the volume that flows into an elevator during a particular time period will flow out shortly thereafter (Zink and Casavant, 1984). While there may be a time lag involved, the outbound flows should closely approximate the inbound flows over a multiyear period. Even if there is a sizable lag, so long as the holdover is consistent from year to year the predicted result will be approximately correct. Thus, with little loss of explanatory power, equation (7.8) may be condensed to:

$$V_{cey} = V_{cdy} = \sum_{O} V_{cody} \qquad (7.9)$$

The output of the shipment generation submodel is a year-by-year estimate of the volumes of each commodity shipped from each production zone as well as from each elevator in the region. The next submodel in the chain (the shipment distribution model) allocates these predicted flows among the competing destination zones.

## NOTES

1. This formulation implicitly assumes that all grains and oilseeds produced in a given zone will be shipped out during the same year. This is not completely true, because some on-farm storage will occur, plus there will be a natural time lag involved. But, so long as the hold over and the time lag are consistent from year to year, the computation shown in equation (7.1) will be approximately correct.

2. Volumes for commodities may also be expressed in cubic feet (there are approximately 1.24 cubic feet in a bushel). A 1979 ICC study entitled *A Study to Perform An In-Depth Analysis of Market Dominance and Its Relationship to Other Provisions of the 4-R Act* contains density factors for most commodities.

3. Adapted from FHWA (1986). Equation (7.4) translates the total change in production from the base year to the horizon year into an annual change in quantity shipped.

# 8

# Traffic Models

The purpose of this chapter is to describe and illustrate the shipment distribution, truck distribution, and truck-weight procedures. Specific applications to the subterminal problem are presented throughout.

## SHIPMENT DISTRIBUTION SUBMODEL

The shipment distribution procedure lies at the heart of the impact assessment process. Because of its importance, the mechanics of the process and the choices that are open to the analyst are covered in detail. The intent of the discussion is to: (1) present a synopsis of the potential models evaluated during the study; (2) summarize the chief benefits and drawbacks associated with each technique (so that highway analysts will have a base of information from which to work); and (3) document the basic modeling techniques which were used in the Devils Lake case study.

### Modeling Dimensions

The basic purpose of the shipment distribution procedure is to project *interzonal* traffic volumes for each year in the planning period. The modeling process has four major dimensions:

1. the type of flow;
2. the motivations of the traveler or shipper;
3. the time at which the trip occurs; and
4. the scope of the analysis.

The shipment distribution procedure must allocate both inbound (farm-to-elevator) shipments and outbound (elevator-to-market) flows among competing destinations. In the case of inbound flows, the competing destinations are the elevators, and the transporter is generally the producer. As stated in chapter 4, the primary motivations of the farmer are to maximize the net price received for the commodity (the elevator price minus the farm truck cost), and to minimize the time and inconvenience associated with travel (particularly during periods of peak work demand, such as harvest). In addition, the farmer may patronize certain elevators because he or she is a member of a local cooperative.

In the case of outbound flows, the destination is another elevator, a processing center, or a terminal market, and the shipper is an elevator manager. The primary motivation of an elevator manager is to maximize the net price received for a given commodity (the market price minus the distribution cost). A major concern of elevator managers is with minimizing distribution costs between the elevator and each market where grain is sold. The motivations of a general (subterminal) manager are fundamentally the same as those of the elevator manager except that the general manager is concerned with minimizing distribution costs for the system of elevators as a whole. This objective is consistent with (although not necessarily the same as) minimizing the cost from any given elevator in the system.

The shipment distribution analysis must allocate inbound and outbound elevator volumes in the base year, the impact year, and all other future years. The distinction between time periods is important for several reasons. First, the base year represents a pre-subterminal environment. As such, the traffic patterns are likely to be different than in the impact year (or any other future year), when there may be substantial levels of trans-shipments. Second, more information is typically known in the base year than in the impact year. The actual volume handled at each elevator in the impact region, the amount shipped to each market, and the actual production levels in the region may be known. All of these values must be forecast for future years.

### Base-Year Farm-to-Elevator Shipment Distribution Model

The purpose of the base-year shipment distribution procedure is to simulate interzonal traffic patterns prior to the development of a grain subterminal in the region. The primary purpose is to build a frame of reference for evaluating changes (or potential changes) in traffic patterns caused by the subterminal. However, the base-year analysis meets another important objective: to estimate the grain truck trips at various locations in the impact area.[1] This latter objective cannot be achieved entirely within the bounds of the shipment distribution submodel, for it requires that shipments be allocated among truck types and routed over the highway network. Nevertheless, the estimation process begins with the base-year shipment distribution model.

The isolation of grain truck traffic within the baseline traffic stream is quite important in subterminal impact analysis because the formation of a subterminal-satellite system will change the *existing* pattern of flows (as well as create new ones). As a result, the analyst may have to reallocate some of the baseline grain truck traffic to other highways and routes during the impact year. This can only be accomplished if the approximate number of average annual daily trips (AADT) accumulated by grain trucks is known for each monitoring site in the region during the base year.

The base-year shipment distribution procedure in the Devils Lake study employs a modified version of the spatial interaction model introduced in chapter 4. The model was modified for three basic reasons:

1.      to formulate the allocation process as a nonlinear problem;
2.      to account for detailed information concerning elevator shipments that were available in the base year; and
3.      to apply regional supply and demand constraints to the model.

### Farm-to-Elevator Impedance Function

The impedance function in equation (4.11) of chapter 4 was represented by farm truck cost ($FT_{od}$). In this theoretical model, the transport impedance was implicitly assumed to be a linear function of distance (with an origin intercept). Thus, the farm truck cost between a given supply zone and elevator was given by:

$$FT_{od} = FM \times D_{od} \qquad (8.1)$$

where:

$$FM = \text{the unit cost per mile (\$1.038)}$$
$$D_{od} = \text{distance between zones } o \text{ and } d$$

However, the assumption of linearity may not be appropriate within the context of farm-to-elevator shipments. Farm truck costs *per se* may be a linear function of distance.[2] However, the impedance function must also reflect the value of the farmer's time, the inconvenience, boredom, and fatigue associated with long-distance travel, and the effects of patronage on delivery decisions. Because of these effects, the farm-to-elevator impedance function is likely to be nonlinear in nature. Thus, equation (8.1) may be more appropriately stated as:

$$FT_{od} = FM \times D_{od}^{x} \qquad (8.2)$$

Farm-to-elevator traffic flows have not been subjected to the same detailed empirical analysis or scrutiny as urban flows. Consequently, there is no empirical basis for the selection of one form of the impedance function over another.

However, there is an intuitive rational that tends to support the use of a power function with an exponent of 1.5.

The calibration of urban transportation models has been a common practice in the past, wherein the exponent of the power function has been empirically derived. The work or business trip in urban transportation is perhaps the closest corollary to the farm-to-elevator trip in rural transportation. In both instances, the traveler wishes to minimize the distance, travel time, and cost of the journey. Blunden and Black (1984, page 60) note that the exponent for the work-related urban trip is usually found in the 0.5 to 2.5 range. Thus, 1.5 would represent a mid-range estimate.[3]

Graphic inspection of the impedance curves formed by exponents in this range tends to support this analogy. Figure 8.1 presents a plot of three impedance functions at various distances, using Griffin's industry unit cost of $1.04 (Griffin, Wilson and Casavant, 1984). As Figure 8.1 portrays, the transport impedance (which is perceived by producers when delivering their crops to elevators) varies considerably with the value of the exponent over a range of distances. An exponent of 2.0 places a relatively high impedance on any movement over thirty miles. This probably reflects the situation that exists at harvest time, where the opportunity cost of a farmer's time is quite high. However, at other times during the year, when the demands on a producer's time are much less, an exponent of 2.0 might overstate the trip impedance. A modest price differential in off-peak periods might induce the producer to travel much farther than during harvest (perhaps up to 50 miles). Thus, an exponent of 1.5 appears be a reasonable compromise, reflecting the average tendency during the year. This function was used to represent the transport impedance in the Devils Lake study.

### Revised Spatial Interaction Model

The following information was known (or estimated) for the base year (1985) in the Devils Lake region:

1. the amount of each commodity available for shipment in each production zone ($S_{coy}$);
2. the amount of each commodity shipped from each elevator in the region ($V_{cey} \approx V_{cdy}$);
3. the total amount shipped from all production zones in the region, by commodity ($S_{cy}$); and
4. the total amount shipped from all elevators in the region ($V_{cy}$).

**Figure 8.1**          Plot of Farm-to-Elevator Impedance Functions

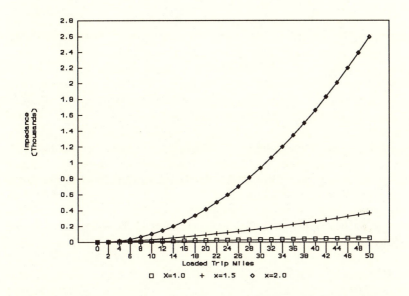

Given this information, it was possible to revise the basic interaction model presented in equation (4.11) so that a more precise estimate of flows could be developed.

The function in equation (4.11) represents a supply-constrained spatial interaction model. The formulation of the model ensures that the total quantity demanded at all elevators in the region will equal the total amount shipped from all origin zones. However, there is no destination or demand-constraint in the equation. Since the actual volume handled by each elevator in the base year is known, it makes sense to further constrain the interaction model so that the amount demanded at each elevator equals the sum of the inbound flows, as stated in equation (7.9). In other words, the spatial interaction model in equation (4.11) should be reformulated so that:

$$\sum_{d} V_{cody} = S_{coy} \qquad\qquad (8.3)$$

$$\sum_{o} V_{cody} = V_{cdy} \qquad\qquad (8.4)$$

where:

$V_{cody} =$       Volume of commodity $c$ shipped from zone $o$ to elevator $d$ in year $y$

$S_{coy} =$       Supply of commodity $c$ in zone $o$ during year $y$

$V_{cdy} =$       Volume of commodity $c$ shipped out of elevator $d$ in year $y$

Applying both the origin and destination constraints to the model leads to the following formulation:

$$V_{cody} = S_{coy} \, V_{cdy} \, RA_{od} \qquad\qquad (8.5)$$

where:

$RA_{od} =$       Relative attractiveness of elevator $d$ for supply zone $o$, which is given by:

$$\frac{A_{od}}{\sum_{d} A_{od}} \qquad\qquad (8.6)$$

$$A_{od} = \frac{P_{cd}}{\sqrt{FT_{od}^3}} \qquad\qquad (8.7)$$

$FT_{od} =$       Farm truck cost between zones $o$ and $d$

Although correct, equation (8.5) contains a redundant term. The attractive force at zone $d$ is represented by the bid price for the commodity (which is part of term $A_{od}$). However, the attractive force is also reflected in the actual quantity demanded (which is in turn a function of price). So, the level of attraction at elevator $d$ may be stated as $V_{cdy}$, which reflects the bid price for the commodity, the size of the firm, and other measures of economic attraction exerted by the elevator. Consequently, equation (8.5) may be reformulated as follows:

$$V_{cody} = A_o B_d S_{coy} V_{cdy} F_{od} \qquad (8.8)$$

where:

$$F_{od} = \frac{1}{\sqrt{FT_{od}^3}} \qquad (8.9)$$

$A_o =$ \qquad a constant representing the supply constraint

$B_d =$ \qquad a constant representing the demand constraint

The term $F_{od}$ in equation (8.8) is generally referred to as a "friction factor." In this form, the spatial interaction model assumes the form of a doubly-constrained gravity model, which is common in urban transportation analysis. $A_o$ and $B_d$ represent balancing factors that are computed so as to satisfy the origin and destination constraints. The supply constraint $A_o$ is arrived by substituting equation (8.8) into equation (8.3), which yields:

$$\sum_d A_o B_d S_{coy} V_{cdy} F_{od} = S_{coy} \qquad (8.10)$$

Solving for $A_o$, the result is equation (8.11).

$$A_o = \frac{1}{\sum_d B_d V_{cdy} F_{od}} \qquad (8.11)$$

Substituting equation (8.8) into equation (8.4) and performing a similar computation yields the balancing equation for $B_d$ (the destination constraint):

$$B_d = \frac{1}{\sum_o A_o S_{coy} F_{od}} \qquad (8.12)$$

The solution to equation (8.8) is derived through an iterative process. The process is initiated by assuming that the value of $B_d$ equals 1.0 for all zones, and by solving for $A_o$. The values of $V_{cody}$ are then computed, representing the output of the first iteration. In the second iteration, the values of $B_d$ are computed using the calculated values of $A_o$ from the first iteration. New values are then computed for $A_o$, and the estimates of $V_{cody}$ are recomputed, concluding the second iteration. This process continues until the value of $V_{cody}$ from the previous iteration is approximately equal to the value of $V_{cody}$ for the current iteration.

## Impact-Year Farm-to-Elevator Model

The purpose of the impact-year shipment distribution analysis is to provide a "snapshot" of grain traffic patterns in the impact region under the "altered" traffic stream (the traffic stream that exists after the subterminal has reached its long-run operating volume). As in the case of the base-year analysis, the analyst is concerned with forecasting grain truck AADT at various highway locations throughout the region. If the subterminal has a significant effect on traffic in the area, then several of the sites can be expected to show either an increase or decrease in grain truck AADT.

In the impact year (and other future years) the volume of each elevator is unknown. It cannot be assumed that the elevator volumes will remain the same as in the base year. In fact, they will almost surely change because of the formation of the subterminal. So, the model presented in equation (8.8) cannot be used. Instead, the (original) supply constrained version of the model presented in equation (4.11) must be applied.

## Elevator-to-Market Model

In the Devils Lake study, the base–year shipments from each elevator to each market were compiled from UGPTI grain and oilseed movement statistics (or were collected in a survey administered to the subterminal manager). This approach is feasible for the base year (where outbound volumes can typically be obtained through survey or from historic shipment records). However, shipments in future years are unknown and must be projected using some modeling technique or forecast. In the Devils Lake study, impact-year (and other future-year) shipments were estimated using the trans-shipment model.

The trans-shipment model is a mathematical programming technique that minimizes the distribution cost between a set of origins and destinations. In this study, the objective of the trans-shipment model is to minimize the distribution cost for the system of elevators as a whole. In doing so, the procedure determines when it is cheaper to trans-ship the grain through the subterminal (as opposed to shipping it directly from the satellite elevators to terminal market). Thus it identifies the optimal allocation of grain between flow-types 3 and 4.

One of the key inputs to the trans-shipment model is the distribution cost. The distribution costs in the model ($TC_{od}$) include not only the transportation rate but the cost of double-handling grain at the subterminal (in cases where the commodities are trans-shipped). The transportation rates may be obtained from rail tariffs (or through interviews with elevator managers). However, double-handling costs usually require a special study.

Zink and Casavant (1982) compiled cost data for various sizes of elevators operating at various levels of output. These data were used to compute unit costs for double-handling grain at elevators in the Devils Lake region. These costs (shown in Table 8.1) may provide reasonable approximations of elevation costs for other areas in the Upper Great Plains in instances where more specific estimates are not available.

**Table 8.1**    Cost of Double-Handling Grain and Oilseeds at North Dakota Elevators

| Storage Capacity (Bushels) | Volume Handled (Bushels) | Average Variable Cost per Bushel ($) |
|---|---|---|
| 300,000 | 5,000,000 | 0.0500 |
| | 8,000,000 | 0.0451 |
| | 11,000,000 | 0.0430 |
| 500,000 | 5,000,000 | 0.0548 |
| | 8,000,000 | 0.0477 |
| | 11,000,000 | 0.0445 |
| | 16,000,000 | 0.0418 |
| 850,000 | 5,000,000 | 0.0585 |
| | 8,000,000 | 0.0493 |
| | 11,000,000 | 0.0451 |
| | 16,000,000 | 0.0416 |
| 1,110,000 | 5,000,000 | 0.0653 |
| | 8,000,000 | 0.0533 |
| | 11,000,000 | 0.0477 |
| | 16,000,000 | 0.0432 |

The mechanics of the trans-shipment model were overviewed in chapter 4 (and are detailed in Lee, Moore, and Taylor, 1985). The model is simply a special case of the transportation problem that utilizes an expanded tableau to derive an optimal solution. The problem is typically solved by a heuristic process. An initial basic feasible solution is obtained using the Northwest Corner Rule, Vogel's Approximation Method (VAM), or the Minimum Cell Cost Method. The initial solution is improved upon through an iterative technique such as the stepping stone or modified distribution method.[4]

The final outputs of the flow distribution submodel are:

1.      the allocation of inbound elevator shipments between farm-
        to-satellite elevator and farm-to-subterminal flows;
2.      the distribution of farm-to-elevator shipments among competing
        elevators;
3.      the allocation of outbound elevator flows between trans-
        shipments and satellite elevator-to-market shipments; and
4.      the distribution of elevator-to-market shipments among potential markets
        and processing centers.

While inbound elevator shipments occur exclusively by truck, outbound elevator shipments may originate by rail or by truck. The next step in the process consists of allocating outbound elevator shipments among alternative modes.

## MODAL SPLIT

The distribution of traffic among modes typically depends on a range of variables. The primary factors are the service attributes of each mode, the cost of service to the carrier, and the relative rates charged. The cross-price elasticity of demand for truck transport and the own-price elasticity of demand for truck transport can be estimated from shippers' demand schedules. The same is true for rail transport demand. A demand schedule would show the volumes that a shipper consigned to each mode at different rate levels. A hypothetical demand schedule for railroad and truck transportation is shown in Table 8.2. From these data, functions for the price elasticity of transport demand could be computed as:

$$\eta_{TR} = \frac{\partial TV}{\partial RR} \tag{8.13}$$

$$\eta_{TT} = \frac{\partial TV}{\partial TR} \tag{8.14}$$

where:

$$\eta_{RR} = \frac{\partial RV}{\partial RR} \qquad\qquad (8.15)$$

$$\eta_{RT} = \frac{\partial RV}{\partial TR} \qquad\qquad (8.16)$$

$TR$ = Truck Rate
$RV$ = Rail Volume
$\eta_{TR}$ = Cross-price elasticity of demand for truck transport
$\eta_{TT}$ = Own-price elasticity of demand for truck transport
$\eta_{RT}$ = Cross-price elasticity of demand for rail transport
$\eta_{RR}$ = Own-price elasticity of demand for rail transport
$TV$ = Truck Volume
$RR$ = Railroad Rate

**Table 8.2**    Hypothetical Shipper Demand Schedule for Railroad and Truck
Transport

| Rate Per CWT | | CWTs Shipped Per Week | |
|---|---|---|---|
| Railroad | Truck | Railroad | Truck |
| $1.00 | $1.10 | 50,000 | 12,000 |
| $1.00 | $1.20 | 52,000 | 10,000 |
| $0.95 | $1.20 | 54,000 | 8,000 |
| $1.05 | $1.10 | 45,000 | 17,000 |
| $1.05 | $1.07 | 42,000 | 20,000 |
| $1.05 | $1.05 | 40,000 | 22,000 |
| $1.05 | $1.00 | 38,000 | 24,000 |

Although important, cross-price elasticity is only a component of a shipper's demand equation. The service attributes of each mode are also important. In fact, in the hypothetical case shown above, it is apparent that the service levels of the two modes vary. Even though the rail rate exceeds the truck rate by five cents in the final row, railroads are still the dominant mode. In short, railroads have a distinct service advantage for this shipper. A detailed review of the literature and available models on this subject is beyond the scope of this book. For a more detailed development of the theory and a more extensive set of references, see Kananafi (1983), Dickey (1984), Mannhiem (1980), or Wilson (1981).

Since actual elevator shipments (by mode) were known for the Devils Lake region, a predictive model was not developed. Instead, the distribution of base-year shipments between modes was calculated directly from grain and oilseed movement statistics. The modal split in future years was approximated from historical data and market trends. The results of this process (as well as some of the issues involved in modal split analysis) are outlined in the following paragraphs.

In subterminal traffic analysis, the analyst must be concerned with the modal allocation of three types of flows:

1.  satellite elevator-to-market shipments (#3);
2.  trans-shipments (#4); and
3.  subterminal-to-market shipments (#5).

Trans-shipments (flow-type 4) have traditionally occurred by truck. However, short–line railroads, with their low labor and train-mile operating costs, may be able to compete with trucks for satellite elevator-to-subterminal traffic in certain markets. At the time of the case study, no short-line carriers were operating in the Devils Lake region. So, flow-type 4 was allocated exclusively to truck.

Flow-type 5 occurs almost exclusively by rail. Because of lower trainload or contract rates, trucks typically cannot compete with railroads in long-haul markets. For example, less than 1 percent of the outbound shipments from the Devils Lake subterminal occurred by truck during crop-year 1986–1987.[5] This type of dominance by railroads is typical of the shipping patterns of large subterminals where the rail share is 90 percent or higher.[6]

While flow-type 3 occurs primarily by rail (in North Dakota), there are still some truck movements. As Figure 8.2 depicts, railroads have steadily increased their market share in North Dakota, from 73% in crop year 1983-1984 to 79 percent in crop year 1986–1987.[7] However, there is a practical maximum (in terms of market share) that railroads can hope to achieve. Trucks will always be competitive in short-distance markets (such as movements to domestic processing plants).

Once the highway portion of the outbound elevator traffic has been determined, the forecasted commodity flows can be translated into truck trips. However, a prerequisite to the calculation of truck trips is the distribution of inbound and outbound elevator shipments among truck types.

## TRUCK DISTRIBUTION SUBMODEL

Recall from chapter 3 that the frequency of SU–3AX and CO–5AX trucks in the impact area will increase with distance and with the relative proportion of grain moving directly from farms to the subterminal elevator (flow-type 2).[8] One way for the analyst to estimate the volume of grain shipped in each type of truck is to project the frequency of use in each subterminal market zone.

Table 8.3 shows the estimated distribution of farm-to-subterminal shipments (by truck type) in the Devils Lake region.[9] As the data depict, farm-to-subterminal shipments in the area are dominated by SU–3AX trucks. However, there are two other trends that deserve mention. First, as the distance from the subterminal elevator increases, the share of grain shipments in SU–2AX trucks declines. Second, as the distance from the subterminal increases (to around forty miles) there is an increased tendency towards the use of CO–5AX trucks in the region.

The subterminal manager expects to see in future years greater use of CO-5AX trucks to transport grain from farms to the subterminal elevator. One possible scenario is that the cooperative will lease or operate a fleet of CO-5AX trucks that will provide pickup service at farms in the area.

**Table 8.3**   Distribution of Farm-to-Subterminal Shipments Among Truck Types in the Devils Lake Region by Market Zone

| Zone | Distance Interval | Truck Type | | |
|------|-------------------|--------|--------|--------|
|      |                   | SU-3AX | SU-2AX | CO-5AX |
| 1    | 25 miles          | 75%    | 25%    | 0%     |
| 2    | 26 to 38 miles    | 82%    | 13%    | 5%     |
| 3    | over 38 miles     | 85%    | 5%     | 10%    |

**Figure 8.2**     Historic Modal Distribution of Grain and Oilseed Shipments in
                   North Dakota

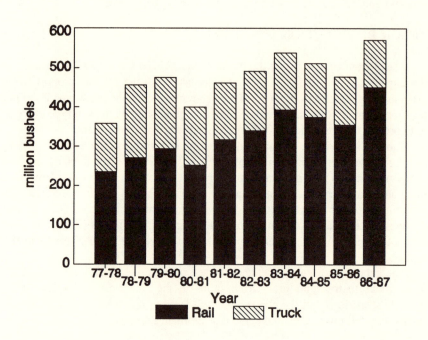

The information presented in Table 8.4 (and graphically in Figure 8.3) helps to explain why these trends are evident in the data. As Table 8.4 depicts, the transportation cost incurred by the farmer in a SU–3AX truck is less than the for-hire rate (for a CO–5AX truck) at trip-distances of less than twenty-one miles. However, at thirty-five miles the reverse is true, and this trend continues over distance.

The subterminal manager estimated that roughly 60 percent of the grains and oilseeds moving to the satellite elevators in the system were being transported in SU–2AX trucks, with the remainder moving in SU-3AX trucks.

While this is a subjective estimate, it tends to fit the results of previous studies and paints a realistic picture of the composition of the farm truck fleet and historic patterns of use.[10] At relatively short distances (such as from farms to satellite elevators) there is a higher probability that farmers will use SU-2AX trucks because there are simply more of them, and because the cost discrepancy between SU-2AX and SU-3AX trucks is less at shorter distances. For example,

**Table 8.4** Grain Trucking Costs per Bushel by Truck Type at Various Distance Intervals (in cents)

| | | Truck Type | | |
|---|---|---|---|---|
| Zone | Distance | SU-2AX* | SU-3AX* | CO-5AX* |
| 1 | 10 miles | 3.64 | 2.33 | 3.51 |
| 2 | 20 miles | 7.28 | 4.66 | 5.13 |
| 3 | 35 miles | 12.74 | 8.16 | 7.56 |
| 4 | 50 miles | 18.20 | 11.65 | 9.99 |

* Source: Griffin, Wilson, and Casavant (1984)

the transportation cost differential between two-axle and three-axle farm trucks is only a penny per bushel at eight miles, but increases to seven cents at fifty miles. In spite of these cost differentials, the majority of farm trucks in North Dakota are of the SU-2AX variety.[11] Thus, as farm-to-subterminal volumes increase, the number of SU-2AX trips may also increase.

Outbound grain shipments from North Dakota elevators occur almost exclusively in CO-5AX trucks, so truck distribution is of little or no concern for flow-types 4 and 5. In the Devils Lake study, all outbound elevator shipments were assumed to occur in CO-5AX trucks.

Once the interzonal trips have been allocated among vehicle types, it is possible to calculate the annual trips required. The annual trips between a given origin zone and elevator are a function of two items: (1) the volume of each commodity shipped, and (2) the distribution of the volume among truck types. If the type of grain truck used is denoted by the subscript $g$, then the annual trips (AT) for a given year can be projected as:

$$AT_{coydg} = V_{coyd} \times \frac{TS_g}{PL_{cg}} \qquad (8.17)$$

where:

$TS_g$ = Truck share or percent of type "$g$"

$PL_{cg}$ = Average payload for commodity "$c$" in truck-type "$g$"

**Figure 8.3**        Transport Cost by Truck-Type and Distance

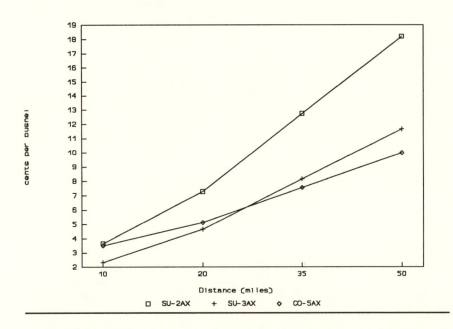

The average payload by truck type was determined from a survey of North Dakota subterminal managers in the spring of 1988. The information presented in Table 8.5 illustrates the differences that can occur for different combinations of commodities and truck types.

The average payload for a CO–5AX truck typically will not vary substantially across commodities. Due to vertical extensions and hopper bottoms on trailers, most truckers are able to reach the legal load limit of 80,000 pounds on even light-loading commodities before the capacity of the payload area is reached. Thus, the average payload for grains and oilseeds can be obtained by subtracting the tare or empty weight of the vehicle from the gross weight. As noted in Table 3.2, the average tare weight for a CO–5AX truck in North Dakota is roughly 26,650 pounds, leaving an average net weight of 53,350 pounds (or 534 cwt). Using this value, the annual outbound trips from a given elevator during a particular year ($AT_{ey}$) can be computed by:

$$AT_{ey} = \frac{V_{ey}}{534} \cdot TS \qquad (8.18)$$

The output of the truck distribution submodel consists of the projected interzonal trips by type of grain truck. The projected annual trips, in conjunction

**Table 8.5**     Average Commodity Payload in Pounds, by Truck Type

|           | Truck Type | |
|-----------|--------|--------|
| Commodity | SU-2AX | SU-3AX |
| Wheat     | 18,000 | 31,800 |
| Barley    | 15,380 | 27,800 |
| Sunflower | 10,992 | 20,372 |
| Other     | 15,593 | 28,329 |

with the vehicle axle weights, are used to estimate annual ESALs. But before ESALs can be calculated, the annual trips must be assigned to the highway network, the next step in the process.

**NOTES**

1. Recall from chapter 2 that grain truck traffic is normally not identified during the vehicle classification and weigh-in-motion process. As a result, the analyst will probably need a method of approximating grain truck AADT at monitoring sites throughout the region. This can be achieved through the modeling process described in this chapter, starting with the shipment distribution submodel and culminating with the network assignment procedure.

2. Fuel costs, maintenance, depreciation, and most other elements of farm truck costs can logically be stated on a per-mile basis. An imputed wage per hour (based on comparable trucking wages for local movements) can also be computed and placed on a per-mile basis. However, the imputed wage will not necessarily capture the value of the producer's time or the inconvenience associated with travel.

3. This analogy is not intended to justify the selection of the farm-to-elevator exponent (in absolute terms). It is only meant to show that an exponent of 1.5 falls clearly within the range of what has been found to be reasonable in previous studies.

4. The SAS TRANS procedure (found in the SAS-OR package) was used to derive the optimal solution in the Devils Lake study. For a detailed description of this procedure, see SAS (1985). Other packages are available that the analyst may wish to evaluate.

5. Source: unpublished UGPTI grain and oilseed movement statistics.

6. This information was developed from unpublished UGPTI grain and oilseed movement statistics. The five largest subterminals in the state all shipped 90 percent or more of their grains and oilseeds by rail. The rail share for the largest facility in the state was 98 percent.

7. Source: unpublished UGPTI grain movement data.

8. In general, the economies of larger payloads make the SU-3AX and CO-5AX trucks more attractive to farmers over long distances. In addition, the greater payload capacity of the trucks makes them attractive to the subterminal manager. Larger trucks reduce the number of trips required to accumulate a fixed amount of grain, thus minimizing the queuing and unloading time at the subterminal.

9. Interview with Alfred Bareksten, manager of the Lake Region Cooperative, Devils Lake, North Dakota, June 17, 1987, or subsequent telephone conversations and written correspondence. The estimates were based partly on historic shipment data and partly on the manager's knowledge of the market area.

10. Griffin et al. (1984) found that the majority of the farm truck fleet (over 80 percent) consisted of SU-2AX trucks. Zink (1988) found that the average distance from farms to the nearest satellite elevator ranged from 6.3 to 13.9 miles. Both are important factors in determining the distribution of farm-to-satellite elevator traffic among truck types.

11. In an interview conducted June 17, 1987, Alfred Bareksten estimated that most of the outbound grain shipments from elevators in the system occurred in CO-5AX trucks. This fits the traditional picture of grain transport in North Dakota, where the predominant vehicle has been the combination five-axle semi. In the Devils Lake study, all elevator-to-market shipments were assumed to occur in CO-5AX trucks.

# 9

# Network and Impact Models

The purpose of this chapter is to detail the mechanics of the network assignment, equivalent axle load, and pavement cost procedures. Because the subterminal case study employs weigh-in-motion (WIM) data, the truck weight and equivalent axle load procedures are considered together. In addition, a modified truck weight procedure is introduced in this chapter that utilizes both weigh-in-motion and truck weight (scale) data. A modified truck-weight approach may prove useful to the highway analyst in situations where WIM data have been collected in the impact region prior to the exogenous change. Where WIM data are unavailable, the standard truck weight procedure can be employed.

The chapter begins with an overview of the functional types or classifications of rural highways. The functional classes are important in understanding differences in intended usage and structural design among highways. Furthermore, they provide a convenient means of summarizing highway impacts.

## HIGHWAY FUNCTIONAL CLASSES

Five rural highway functional classifications relate to low-volume roads:

1.  local roads;
2.  major collectors;
3.  minor collectors;
4.  minor arterials; and
5.  principal arterials.

The primary function of local roads is to provide access to land. Beyond that, they support travel over relatively short distances. In the rural highway network, local roads serve individual farms and other rural land uses. Some general characteristics of local rural roads are:

1.  they have very light traffic densities;
2.  they generally have low-type surfaces;
3.  they are discontinuous and limited in distance; and
4.  they are typically designed for low speeds (thirty miles per hour for roads with less that two hundred average daily trips (ADT)).

Collectors (in contrast to local roads) directly serve small towns, connecting rural communities to the arterial network. They are primarily characterized by intra-county travel (as opposed to statewide or interstate travel). Rural major collectors serve traffic generators of relatively major proportions on the intracounty level (such as major shippers, rural mines, other extractive industries, or schools). Minor rural collectors serve smaller communities and connect localized traffic generators with farms and other outlying rural areas.

Rural arterials typically provide direct service between cities and larger rural towns. The trip distance on rural arterials is generally much longer that it is on collectors, some of it being statewide (or even interstate) in nature. Rural arterials are categorized as either principal or minor arterials. Principal arterials are further differentiated between "freeways" and "other principal arterials."[1] Principal arterials are typically (but not always) multilane rural highways connecting major cities. They usually constitute the most heavily traveled routes in the rural network. Rural minor arterials are generally not as heavily traveled as the principal arterials, and provide for a shorter trip length and lower traffic densities. Rural minor arterials essentially allow for intercounty travel and tie the principal arterial network into the collector and local road system.

A typical farm-to-satellite (local) elevator trip will involve the use of the local, minor collector, major collector and/or minor arterials systems. The trip generally begins with a short journey (typically five miles or less) over a local road that leads to a minor or major collector. The length of the journey on the collector network is generally greater than on local roads, sometimes exceeding twenty miles but more likely falling in the neighborhood of five to ten miles. The loaded journey may conclude at this point (as many grain elevators are connected to the rural hinterland by major or minor collectors). Or the trip may proceed on a rural minor arterial (or in some instances a rural principal arterial).

Elevator-to-market shipments generally entail a different combination of road use. Elevators are major rural traffic-generators, which are typically located on major collectors or minor arterials. Some are even situated on principal rural arterials. A truck journey from elevator-to-terminal market (flow-type 3) may begin on a major collector (or a minor arterial). But the traffic is quickly funneled onto a principal rural arterial or interstate highway where the majority of the trip miles occur.

Subterminal elevators are generally located on arterial highways.[2] So the outbound truck traffic usually travels on the principal arterial and interstate system. The satellite elevator-to-subterminal traffic (flow-type 4) may occur largely on the arterial network. Such a truck journey might begin on a major collector or minor arterial and conclude on a principal arterial. However, this is not always so. Sometimes the most direct route between the satellite and subterminal involves a "short-cut" across minor rural collectors (or even portions of local roads).

Each component of the rural highway system is designed to serve a particular function. Each class is designed for a certain level of traffic (ADT) and traffic mix (percent trucks). The perceived traffic mix will determine the design strength (structural number or slab thickness), which in turn determines the ESAL-life. As depicted in Table 5.4 of Chapter 5, the average ESAL life for a typical rural arterial is 1.5 million, while an average ESAL lifetime is roughly 400,000 for rural collectors and 80,000 for local roads respectively.

Although rural functional classes are not completely homogenous in nature, the highways that comprise the classes are generally quite similar in design. Thus, rural functional classes generally reflect (at an aggregate level) the traffic and pavement design characteristics of the individual highways.

## NETWORK ASSIGNMENT SUBMODEL

Truck trips are assigned to the highway network through means of a highway network (link-node) model. In the Devils Lake study, a computer file was created that defined the routes and highway characteristics between each origin-destination combination. The centroids of the supply zones and the elevators in the system were treated as possible origins, with the elevators in the system comprising the destinations. For each feasible origin-destination combination, a data record was created consisting of the highway "links" in the route. The definition of highway links considered the number of highways in the route and any appreciable changes in roadway condition that occurred from section-to-section. Some origin-destination pairs were assigned as many as eight links (for a distance of fifty miles or less). For each link, the beginning and ending mileposts, the distance, and the structural number were derived from the highway department files.

A given highway link may be part of more than one route. In fact, some links turned out to be common to many different origin-destination routes. So, an algorithm was written that accumulated the annual trips (by truck type) for each highway link in the network. Once the trips were accumulated, the grain ESALs on each link were computed. Because the beginning and ending mileposts of each link were known, the annual grain truck ESALs at each traffic monitoring site in the region (which were referenced by milepost number) could be determined.

The highway routes between agricultural production zones and elevators (and between satellite elevators and the subterminal) were estimated from highway maps using two criteria: (1) distance, and (2) the level of transportation services over the route. At first glance, the ideal highway route might appear to be the shortest possible path between origin and destination. A shortest path algorithm exists that could be employed to find the route of minimal distance. However, focusing exclusively on distance could result in a suboptimal routing pattern. Truck operators are sensitive to the average speed of a highway and to the condition or quality of the road. Both factors affect operator costs.

In the Devils Lake study, differences in travel time and highway condition were factored into the equation. The process used to determine the most likely route is as follows. First, the feasible routes between an origin-destination pair were determined. Second, the travel times were estimated for each route in the set. Third, the quality of each route was approximated by calculating a weighted-average structural number. This value represents the average of the SNs of the various links, weighted by mileage. Fourth, the weights given to travel time versus highway quality by drivers were set. In the Devils Lake study, a weight of .75 was attached to travel time and .25 to highway quality. This means that a truck operator (in deciding which route to select) will attach a greater significance to travel time than to highway quality. This procedure is analogous to calculating a generalized cost for each route.

A standardized score was computed for each attribute for each route. The standardized scores for highway quality and travel time were then multiplied by the weights to compute a composite score or rank. The route with the highest composite rank was selected.

## TRUCK WEIGHT AND AXLE LOAD PROCEDURES

The purpose of the truck weight submodel is to compute average truck axle weights. However, in the Devils Lake study, axle weights and ESALs were computed simultaneously from WIM data. Consequently, the two procedures are discussed together in this section.

The fully loaded axle weight of a given truck is a function of:

1.   the number and configuration of axles;
2.   legal gross weights and axle weights;
3.   the average commodity payload; and
4.   the distribution of the gross weight among axle groups.

On SU–2AX and SU–3AX trucks, the density of the commodity will help determine the axle weights. Not all commodities will load to the legal limits, particularly on the SU–2AX truck. Table 9.1 shows the tare and gross axle weights for wheat, the major commodity transported in the Devils Lake region.

The tare weights in Table 9.1 were obtained from a special study of grain trucks conducted at North Dakota weigh stations in the spring of 1988[3]. The loaded axle weights represent the maximum legal axle weights in North Dakota for the type of axle and tire. In the case of SU–2AX and SU–3AX trucks, the sum of the possible payload capacity (shown in Table 8.5) and the tare weight (shown in Table 9.1) exceeds the maximum axle weights. So, a constraint was built into the model to cap the axle weights at the legal limit for each axle group. In the case of lighter–loading commodities, the loaded axle weights for SU–2AX and SU–3AX trucks were less than the maximums.

**Table 9.1** Loaded and Empty Axle Weights for Wheat by Truck Type, in Thousands of Pounds

| Axle Group | Tare Weight | | | Loaded Weight | | |
|---|---|---|---|---|---|---|
| | SU–2AX | SU–3AX | CO–5AX | SU–2AX | SU–3AX | CO–5AX |
| 1 | 5.2 | 7.0 | 8.9 | 9.9 | 11.0 | 12.0 |
| 2 | 7.2 | 9.8 | 11.2 | 20.0 | 34.0 | 34.0 |
| 3 | - | - | 7.6 | - | - | 34.0 |

Estimating truck axle weights is a central part of subterminal impact analysis. There are generally three ways to arrive at usable estimates:

1. through the use of truck weight (scale) data;
2. through the use of weigh-in-motion statistics; and
3. through a hybrid (modified) truck weight approach.

The Devils Lake case study employs a modified truck weight approach in which both weigh–in–motion data and grain truck axle weight factors are utilized.

### The Truck Weight Method

The highway analyst may not always have access to weigh-in-motion data in the impact region. However, annual ESALs can still be computed for a sample of highway sections using static truck weight data. Typically, data that describe the gross and tare weights of trucks (as well as the distribution of the tare and gross weights among the axle groups) are collected at weigh stations in a given state or region. These data can be combined with vehicle classification (non-WIM) data to estimate average daily ESALs (ADE) for each monitoring site in the impact region. The process is essentially as follows.[4]

1. The average empty and loaded weights on each axle group are obtained from state-wide or regional truck weight data;
2. The AASHTO traffic equivalency formulas are used to convert the raw axle loads to ESALs (given the strength and condition rating of the highway section);
3. The empty ESALs for each axle group are summed to obtain ESALs per empty VMT;

4.  The loaded ESALs for each axle group are calculated in a similar manner;
5.  The loaded ESALs for each axle group are summed to obtain ESALs per loaded VMT;
6.  The hypothetical empty ESALs per day (for a given vehicle class) are calculated by multiplying the number of empty truck trips per day by the empty ESALs per VMT;
7.  The hypothetical loaded ESALs per day are calculated by multiplying the number of loaded truck trips per day by the loaded ESALs per VMT; and
8.  The loaded and empty ESALs are summed to obtain an estimate of total daily ESALs for a given vehicle class.

## Weighing-in-Motion

The shortcoming of the truck weight approach is that it uses average axle weight factors obtained from "static" or stationary weighings at a limited number of locations throughout the state or region. If the equipment and resources are available, in-motion weighing can represent an attractive alternative to the truck weight approach. When a vehicle is weighed in motion, the number of axles and the spacing between the axles are determined.[5] From the spacing between the axles, the type or configuration of each axle group is ascertained (e.g., single axle, tandem axle, or tridem). Using this information, the vehicle is placed into a general category or class (for example, one of the thirteen classes shown in Table 9.2). At the same time that the number of axles is being recorded, the dynamic weight of each axle group is being determined.

Once the weight and configuration of each axle group is known, the AASHTO traffic equivalency formulas described in Appendix C are used to convert the raw axle weights into 18–kip ESALs. The ESALs for each axle group are then summed to obtain the total for each vehicle. This is all done automatically through electronic data transmission from the WIM scale pads to a computer. The computer software executes predetermined data calculations and classification procedures. The advantages of weighing-in-motion are:

1.  dynamic rather than static weights are calculated;
2.  actual weights and axle loads are obtained (as opposed to average factors); and
3.  local traffic conditions and factors are accounted for.

The shortcoming of weighing-in-motion is that the process cannot determine the commodity being transported in the vehicle. Thus, grain truck traffic is typically not identified at the time the data are collected.

**Table 9.2**     Vehicle Classification Records

1. *Motorcycles (Optional)*—All two– or three–wheeled motorized vehicles. Typical vehicles in this category have saddle–type seats and are steered by handle bars rather than a wheel. This category includes motorcycles, motor scooters, mopeds, motor–powered bicycles, and three–wheel motorcycles. This vehicle type may be reported at the option of the state.

2. *Passenger Cars*—All sedans, coupes, and station wagons manufactured primarily for the purpose of carrying passengers and including those passenger cars pulling recreational or other light trailers.

3. *Other Two–Axle, Four–Tire Single–Unit Vehicles*—All two–axle, four–tire vehicles, other than passenger cars. Included in this classification are pickups, panels, vans and other vehicles such as campers, motor homes, ambulances, hearses, and carryalls. Other two–axle, four–tire single–unit vehicles pulling recreational or other light trailers are included in this classification.

4. *Buses*—All vehicles manufactured as traditional passenger-carrying buses with two axles and six tires or three or more axles. This category includes only traditional buses (including school buses) functioning as passenger-carrying vehicles. All two–axle, four–tire minibuses should be classified as other two–axle, four–tire single–unit vehicles. Modified buses should be considered to be a truck and be appropriately classified.

5. *Two-Axle, Six-Tire, Single–Unit Trucks*—All vehicles on a single frame, including trucks, camping and recreational vehicles, and motor homes, having two axles and dual rear wheels.

6. *Three–Axle Single–Unit Trucks*—All vehicles on a single frame including trucks, camping and recreational vehicles, and motor homes, having three axles.

7. *Four or More Axle Single–Unit Trucks*—All trucks on a single frame with four or more axles.

**Table 9.2**      (continued)

8. *Four–or–Less–Axle Single–Trailer Trucks*—All vehicles with four or less axles consisting of two units, one of which is a tractor or straight truck power unit.

9. *Five–Axle Single–Trailer Trucks*—All five–axle vehicles consisting of two units, one of which is a tractor or straight truck power unit.

10. *Six–or–More–Axle Single–Trailer Trucks*—All vehicles with six or more axles consisting of two units, one of which is a tractor or straight truck power unit.

11. *Five–or–Less–Axle Multi–Trailer Trucks*—All Vehicles with six or more axles consisting of two units, one of which is a tractor or straight truck power unit.

12. *Six–Axle Multi–Trailor Trucks*—All six–axle vehicles consisting of three or more units, one of which is a tractor or straight truck power unit.

13. *Seven–or–More–Axle Multi–Trailer Trucks*—All vehicles with seven or more axles consisting of three or more units, one of which is a tractor or straight truck power unit.

## Modified Truck Weight Approach

The application of class averages derived from truck weight data or WIM sessions to grain traffic will not yield specific estimates of grain truck ESALs per VMT in the impact region. There are general differences between grain trucks and other vehicle types within the same broad class. Furthermore, there may be regional variations in farm truck ESALs due to differences in the pattern of commodity shipments within a given area.

The modified truck weight approach uses a combination of WIM or truck weight data (by vehicle class) and specific grain truck factors developed from special studies. For non-grain traffic, vehicle class averages are used to estimate the ADE on impact highways. However, for grain traffic, the specific tare weights, load factors, and axle weights shown in Table 8.4 and Table 8.5 are used.

Nongrain ESALs and AADT in the Devils Lake region were computed from WIM and vehicle classification data collected by the North Dakota Highway Department (NDHWD). The following section of the chapter discusses the data collection practices employed in the Devils Lake study and the adjustments necessary to derive usable data. Some common types of classifiers are discussed and the concept of seasonal variation in grain traffic is introduced.

## COLLECTION OF VEHICLE CLASSIFICATION AND AXLE WEIGHT DATA

In the Devils Lake study, vehicle classification data were compiled at thirty monitoring sites by the North Dakota Highway Department (NDHWD) using two types of portable equipment: (1) Streeter–Richardson weigh-in-motion (WIM) equipment, and (2) Streeter-Richardson tube-style (NonWIM) classifiers.[6] WIM data were collected for the majority of the thirty sites at various intervals during 1985 and 1986. Thus, the actual ESALs per VMT (by vehicle class) were known for most impacted highway sections on the arterial network. However, "tube-style" classifiers were deployed in lieu of WIM classifiers at several monitoring sites. Tube-style classifiers determine the classification of a vehicle but do not weigh it in motion. So, at sites where WIM equipment was never deployed, an alternative method of estimating ESALs had to be devised. In these instances, the ESAL factor at the closest WIM site on the same highway was used to approximate the ADE.

The vehicle classification process in the Devils Lake case study utilized the thirteen primary FHWA categories shown in Table 9.2 (with one minor modification). A separate (fourteenth) category was introduced to account for vehicles that did not fall into one of the thirteen FHWA classifications.[7]

The NDHWD data collection effort covered the arterial highway network in the impact region. However, it did not address minor collectors and local roads. In order to assess the impacts on collectors and local roads, a data collection program was launched to obtain analogous information for these types of highways. The data collection effort is described later in this chapter. But first, the next section describes the process by which raw traffic counts were adjusted.

### Adjustment of Raw Traffic Data

In order to provide usable information, the raw traffic counts must be turned into estimates of average annual daily trips (AADT). This adjustment process is essentially as follows:

1.   multiple traffic counts within a given month are averaged to arrive at monthly average daily trips (ADT);
2.   the monthly ADT are adjusted for seasonal variance; and
3.   where multiple months of observations existed, the adjusted monthly ADTs are averaged to produce an estimate of AADT.

The adjustment of raw traffic counts to reflect seasonal variations in shipments is particularly important in subterminal traffic analysis. As Figure 9.1 depicts, monthly variations in grain shipments can be substantial. Consequently, the ADT (and ADE) derived from vehicle classification activities during any given month may bear little relationship to the annual mean. Therefore, the raw ADT must be factored by a seasonal adjustment index.

**Figure 9.1**       North Dakota Monthly Grain and Shipment:  1986–87

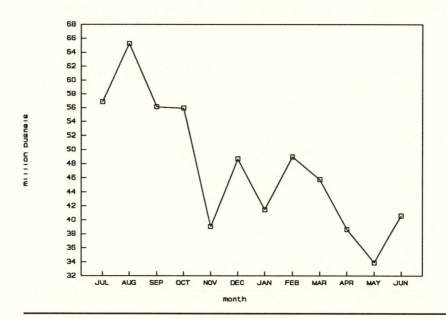

The data for the adjustments came from Minnesota DOT and UGPTI data. The Minnesota DOT maintains a continuous weigh-in-motion station near Bemidji, Minnesota.  Information regarding monthly ADT and ADE were obtained from the Minnesota DOT for 1985 and 1986 (by vehicle class). From the raw statistics, a seasonal adjustment factor was calculated for each vehicle class as follows:

$$SAF_{jk} = \frac{ADT_{jk}}{\overline{ADT}_j} \tag{9.1}$$

where:

$SAF_{jk}$ = seasonal adjustment factor for vehicle class $j$, month $k$

$ADT_{jk}$ = ADT for vehicle class $j$, month $k$

$\overline{ADT}_j$ = Mean monthly ADT for vehicle class $j$

Such WIM data can yield good baseline estimates of ADT and ESALs by vehicle class. However, the application of class averages to grain flows is inappropriate. In the Devils Lake study, specific indexes were computed from grain shipment data in the region. Once the grain truck ADT was approximated at each site, a weighted-average set of monthly indexes was computed for vehicle classes 5, 6, and 9 (which include SU–2AX, SU–3AX, and CO–5AX trucks, respectively). The indexes were weighted by the estimated percentage of grain traffic (as opposed to non–grain traffic) in the Devils Lake region. The CO–5AX grain truck seasonal index was computed from the values shown in Figure 9.1. In addition, monthly indexes for farm–to–elevator shipments were developed from information concerning the average percentage of various crops sold on the open market in each month.[8] These indexes were used in conjunction with Minnesota DOT seasonal control data to compute weighted–average seasonal adjustment factors for vehicle classes five and six (Table 9.3).

Expanding upon the notation introduced earlier, equation (9.2) depicts the computation of adjusted ADTs for each monitoring session.

$$ADTJ_{ijkl} = \frac{ADT_{ijkl}}{SAF_{ijk}} \tag{9.2}$$

where:

$ADTJ_{ijkl}$ = Adjusted at monitoring site $i$ for vehicle class $j$ during month $k$, session (day) $l$

$ADT_{ijkl}$ = Raw (unadjusted) ADT

**Table 9.3**    Seasonal Adjustment Factors for CO-5AX, SU-2AX and SU-3AX
Grain Trucks

| Month | CO-5AX Index | SU-2AX and SU-3AX Index |
|-------|--------------|-------------------------|
| January | 1.12763 | 0.82558 |
| February | 0.7388357 | 1.24348 |
| March | 0.8222269 | 0.67125 |
| April | 0.8486768 | 1.03600 |
| May | 0.7198375 | 0.91921 |
| June | 1.04513 | 1.27225 |
| July | 0.6685787 | 0.92259 |
| August | 2.194321 | 1.21461 |
| September | 1.362976 | 0.83123 |
| October | 1.248131 | 1.16563 |
| November | 1.02862 | 0.78574 |
| December | 0.7916829 | 0.61038 |

In many instances, multiple observations of ADT existed for a particular monitoring site during a given month. So in order to obtain the average adjusted ADT for a given month, vehicle class, and site, the arithmetic mean was computed as shown in equation (9.3).

$$ADTJ_{ijk} = \frac{\sum_l ADTJ_{ijkl}}{n} \qquad (9.3)$$

where:

$n$    =    number of measurements within a given month

Data in the Devils Lake region were typically collected for more than one month at a given monitoring site. Thus, in computing the average annual daily trips, the arithmetic mean of the adjusted monthly ADT was calculated (as follows).

$$AADT_{ij} = \frac{\sum_{k} ADTJ_{ijk}}{n} \tag{9.4}$$

where:

$AADT_{ij}$   =   Average annual daily trips at monitoring site $i$ for vehicle class $j$

Equation (9.4) represents the culmination of an adjustment process turning the number of average daily trips generated from a given traffic monitoring session into a usable estimate of AADT. An analogous process was followed with respect to the adjustment of ESALs. But because the seasonal variation in ESALs was unknown, an indirect (rather than a direct) approach was taken. First, the ESAL factor (ESALs per VMT) was computed for each vehicle class at each monitoring site, as shown in equation (9.5).

$$EAL_{ijk} = \frac{\left(\dfrac{\sum_{l} ADE_{ijkl}}{\sum_{l} ADT_{ijkl}}\right)}{n} \tag{9.5}$$

where:

$EAL_{ijk}$   =   ESAL factor for site $i$, vehicle class $j$, and month $k$

$ADE_{ijkl}$   =   Average daily ESALs at monitoring site $i$, for vehicle class $j$, month $k$, and session $l$

Once the average ESALs per VMT was calculated for a given month, this factor was applied to the adjusted monthly ADT to produce an estimate of monthly ADE adjusted for seasonal variance. This computation is depicted in equation (9.6).

$$EALJ_{ijk} = ADTJ_{ijk} \times EAL_{ijk} \qquad (9.6)$$

where:

$EALJ_{ijk}$ =    Adjusted monthly ADE for monitoring
site $i$, vehicle class $j$, and month $k$

In the final step, the average annual daily ESALs (AADE) were calculated as the arithmetic mean of the adjusted monthly values.

The principal assumption underlying this adjustment is that the primary source of variance in ADEs is the variance in ADT. That is to say, the average ESALs per VMT for a given type of truck type hauling a given commodity will not vary significantly throughout the year. Rather, it is the number of average daily trips (by truck type and commodity) that vary. With the possible exception of spring load restrictions on some highways, there is no reason to believe that the average payload of a CO-5AX truck transporting wheat will be substantially different in July than it is in September.

## Extension of the Analysis to Collector Roads

In the Devils Lake study, the data base initially consisted of information collected by the NDHWD. This information provided a sound basis for analyzing the impacts of subterminal development on principal arterials and minor rural arterials in the area. However, it provided little (if any) insight into the impacts on collectors and local roads. Yet, rural collectors may be the most heavily impacted highways because they are typically low-design roads not built for heavy traffic. Part of the problem is that they are frequently part of the most direct route to an elevator, or constitute a "short-cut" to the subterminal.

In order to account for minor collector and local road impacts, additional data were collected (beyond that supplied by the NDHWD). Information was developed for twenty–three collectors (which comprise some of the most essential links in the farm-to-elevator flow chain in the region). The condition and attributes of the highways were determined from interviews with district engineers at the Devils Lake regional office (of the NDHWD), as well as through interviews with county engineers. For each highway section, the type of surface, the thickness of surface layers, the thickness of the aggregate base, and the general age and condition of the pavement were determined. From this information, the SN and PSR were approximated.

Baseline traffic characteristics were approximated for minor collectors in the region by using statewide averages (where available) and mean functional class values (where statewide averages were not available).[9] The average AADT on collectors and local roads was calculated from statewide statistics as depicted in Table 9.4.

**Table 9.4**     Computation of AADT for North Dakota Minor Collectors and
Minor Roads

| Item | Source | Minor Collectors | Local Roads |
|------|--------|------------------|-------------|
| 1. Miles of Highway | Table HM-220* | 7,504 | 59,838 |
| 2. Annual VMT | Table VM-202* | 185,000,000 | 720,000,000 |
| 3. Average Annual VMT | Line 2 ÷ 365 | 506,849 | 1,972,603 |
| 4. AADT | Line 3 ÷ Line 2 | 68 | 33 |

While it cannot be contended that the use of statewide averages for rural minor collectors and local roads provides for an exact representation of thetrue baseline traffic characteristics on each highway section, these values should provide highway analysts with reasonable approximations. Using information contained in Table 9.5 VM-201A of (FHWA, 1985), the proportion of truck traffic on rural collectors and local roads has been computed at 3.6 percent for single-unit trucks and 3.0 percent for combination trucks. Given these proportions, the average baseline truck AADT and AADE can be computed for single-unit (SU) and combination (CO) trucks, as shown in Table 9.5. Given the relative homogeneity of rural minor collectors and local roads, these values should constitute usable approximations.

**Table 9.5**     Computation of AADE for Rural Minor Collectors and Local Roads

| Item | Source | Minor Collector | Local Roads |
|------|--------|-----------------|-------------|
| 1. AADT | Table 15, Line 4 | 68.000 | 33.00 |
| 2. Proportion: SU Trucks | FHWA (1985) | 0.036 | 0.036 |
| 3. SU-AADT | Line 1 x Line 2 | 2.500 | 1.200 |
| 4. Proportion: CO Trucks | FHWA (1985) | 0.030 | 0.030 |
| 5. CO-AADT | Line 1 x Line 4 | 2.000 | 1.000 |
| 6. ESALs/VMT: SU Trucks | Calculated | 0.818 | 0.818 |
| 7. ESALs/VMT: CO Trucks | Calculated | 1.275 | 1.275 |
| 8. AADE: SU Trucks | Line 3 x Line 6 | 2.045 | 0.982 |
| 9. AADE: CO Trucks | Line 5 x Line 7 | 2.550 | 1.275 |
| 10. Estimated AADE | Line 8 x Line 9 | 4.595 | 2.256 |

## FINANCIAL IMPACT ANALYSIS

The previous discussion has outlined all of the submodels in the chain (up to the final procedure) and has documented the data collection and adjustment process that took place in the Devils Lake study. The chapter concludes with a synopsis of the financial impact procedure.

As noted in chapter 5, pavement impact costs include two components: (1) build-sooner costs, and (2) potential upgrading costs. Both concepts are employed in subterminal case study. The flow of computations within the submodel is as follows:

1.   The ESAL life of each sample section is computed;
2.   The (baseline) ESALs are computed in the base year;
3.   The incremental ESALs are computed for the impact year;

4.  ESALs under the altered traffic stream are computed for each year of the analysis period;

5.  The years of remaining service life are computed under the base case;

6.  The years of remaining service life are computed under the altered traffic case;

7.  The replacement cost is computed under each scenario and discounted to present value, with the difference comprising the build–sooner cost;

8.  The incremental pavement thickness required (if any) is computed; and

9.  Upgrading costs are computed for any incremental thickness of half an inch or more.

The process must be repeated for any new or different scenario analyzed.


**NOTES**

1.  The primary difference is that freeways provide full control of access while other principle arterials do not.

2.  This is not always the case, as subterminals are sited according to rail rather than highway access.

3.  The weights and tare axle loads in Table 11 were obtained from a survey conducted at Grand Forks and Fargo weigh stations by the Truck Regulatory Division.  The reasonableness of the survey estimates were verified by the professional judgment of Dennis Erickson, director of the division.

4.  Typically, vehicle classification data do not tell the number of empty versus loaded trips.  Consequently, an average ratio of empty-to-loaded truck trips must be used to factor the ADT at a given monitoring site into loaded and empty trips. If the ratio of empty-to-loaded truck trips at each site is assumed to be 1.0, then the above computations may be simplified by first averaging the empty and loaded ESALs per VMT and applying this average to the ADT derived through vehicle classification.

5.  The spacing between the axles determines the axle type (single axle, tandem axle, or tridem).

6.  In the Devils Lake case study, WIM data were collected for the majority of the thirty monitoring sites at some time during 1985 or 1986, thus providing the actual ESALs per VMT at most sites.  However, for the non–WIM sites, the ESALs per VMT were not available.  In order to attribute an approximate ESAL value per VMT to the non–WIM sites, they were generally correlated with the

closest WIM site (that had WIM data). Directions and years were matched up as closely as possible during the process. For a detailed description of the data collection sites and methods see *The Impacts of Grain Subterminals on Rural Highways, Volume II*; Denver Tolliver, 1989.

7. The vehicle classes which are of primary importance to this study are: 5, 6, and 9. SU-2AX farm trucks fall into category 5. SU-3AX farm trucks belong to vehicle class 6. And CO-5AX trucks are included in vehicle class 9.

8. The underlying source of the information is: *North Dakota Agricultural Statistics*, 1987, page 69.

9. All values or averages that were attributed to local roads and minor collectors were calculated from *Highway Statistics*, FHWA, 1985. Data for three major collectors were available from the NDHWD's collection efforts. When other major collectors were added to the data file, their attributes were obtained by survey if possible. If not, the average of the attributes for the three major collectors in the data base were used.

# 10

# Subterminal Case Study & Conclusions

Chapters 6–9 focused on the analytic techniques employed in highway impact assessment. Each technique was illustrated in depth using the subterminal problem. This chapter continues the theme of those chapters. Its purpose is to describe the findings of the subterminal case study. In doing so, it draws upon some of the data and formulas presented in the four previous chapters.

The chapter is organized as follows. First, a set of impact scenarios utilized in the Devils Lake study are introduced. Second, the dimensions of the analysis are highlighted, including a description of major effects and cross-effects. Third, an assessment of the subterminal's effects on the problem dimensions is presented. Fourth, the projected short-run and long-run incremental costs under the primary impact scenario are summarized. Fifth, the results of the alternative scenarios and the sensitivity of the findings are evaluated. Sixth, the conclusions of the case study are summarized, and other applications of the procedures are discussed.

## IMPACT SCENARIOS

The subterminal case study utilizes the technique of scenario analysis introduced in chapter 2. Altogether, four major scenarios are analyzed. The scenarios are designed to account for the uncertainty created by several major forces in the agricultural, transportation, and marketing environment.

### Major Variables or Forces of Uncertainty

The environment of grain transportation is subject to considerable uncertainty. In addition to subterminal development, several major forces could affect flows in the impact region. Three of the most important are:

1.    rationalization of the grain elevator industry;
2.    changes in truck utilization patterns; and
3.    railroad restructuring and abandonment.

An implicit assumption in the subterminal impact study is that the system of elevators will remain intact throughout the analysis period. This assumption actually involves two suppositions: (1) the price relationships between the subterminal and the satellite elevators will remain the same, and (2) all satellites (substations) will remain operative. Although valid, there is some uncertainty surrounding these assumptions. Cobia et al. (1985, page 86) feels that many substations will be shut down in the future: "Satellite stations will, with few exceptions, decline in use and will in many cases be eliminated as receiving stations." If this occurs, two events will materialize that have implications for grain flows. First, more direct farm-to-subterminal shipments will occur because the substations will no longer be available as receiving points. Second, with the closing of substations, fewer trans-shipments and satellite elevator-to-market shipments will be made.

In addition to affecting the allocation of traffic among flow types, elevator rationalization can impact the distribution of traffic among truck types. Under a rationalization scenario, the subterminal manager may engage in differential pricing, providing producers with incentives to deliver grain to the subterminal. Thus, the price at the substations may no longer be the price at the subterminal minus the grain trucking rate from the satellite elevator to the subterminal. Instead, the subterminal price may be higher, designed to attract grain from producers located at greater distances from the main facility. As the relative price at the subterminal increases and substations begin to close, producers will truck from even greater distances to the main facility. As the trip distance increases, the cost per bushel-mile in CO-5AX trucks becomes substantially lower than in SU-2AX or SU-3AX trucks. Consequently, elevator rationalization is likely to go hand-in-hand with increased CO-5AX farm-to-elevator shipments. Since the receivers (elevator managers) prefer larger payloads, there may be a dual incentive for a shift to CO-5AX truck utilization in the impact region. However, the majority of farm trucks are of the older SU-2AX variety. Instead of contracting with commercial carriers or investing in newer equipment, some producers may continue to utilize their existing truck fleet for longer trips to subterminals. SU-2AX trucks generate the most ESALs per loaded ton-mile. Thus, if this shipment pattern evolves, farm-to-subterminal impacts could be greater than if CO-5AX trucks are used.

Most satellite elevators are located on branch lines. These rail lines could conceivably be abandoned during the analysis period. If this occurs, projected grain flows and highway impacts may change considerably.

Altogether, four major impact scenarios were analyzed in the Devils Lake case study:

1.  the primary impact scenario (based on a cooperative elevator model and
    static truck utilization patterns);
2.  a modified farm-to-elevator scenario (where increased utilization of CO-
    5AX trucks is simulated);
3.  an elevator rationalization scenario, in which four of the seven satellite
    elevators are assumed to be closed in the future; and
4.  an abandonment scenario.

These scenarios are all contrasted to a base case, referred to as "Scenario Zero."

### Base-Case Scenario

Scenario Zero reflects the baseline grain flow pattern in the Devils Lake
region.    Base-year farm-to-elevator flows are projected using the doubly
constrained spatial interaction model described in chapter 4.  Outbound elevator
flows are modeled using actual elevator-to-market shipment data.

### Scenario 1:  Primary Impact Scenario

Under scenario 1, farm-to-elevator shipments are projected using the spatial
interaction model defined in chapter 9.  The model (as detailed previously) is
based on the "law of relative attraction" and utilizes elevator bid prices, satellite-
subterminal price relationships, and farm truck costs.  Outbound elevator flows
are projected using the trans-shipment procedure.

The major assumptions underlying the inbound allocation of flows are:  (1)
the distribution of grain among truck types will remain relatively static over time,
and (2) the cooperative system of elevators will remain intact (having basically
the same relationships throughout the impact period).  These assumptions are
allowed to vary in scenarios 2 and 3 which address the implications of changes
in future farm-to-elevator truck use patterns and possible elevator rationalization.

### Scenario 2:  Increased CO-5AX Farm Truck Usage

The exact allocation of future traffic among truck types is unknown.  The
elevators could acquire their own fleet of CO-5AX trucks and begin to operate
them between the subterminal and area farms.  The objective of scenario 2 is to
isolate the effects of increased combination five-axle shipments (within the farm-
to-elevator traffic stream) on annual ESALs and highway costs.

Table 10.1 shows a likely allocation of traffic among truck types if this
scenario comes to pass.  These allocation factors are based on the relative

**Table 10.1**    CO-5AX Truck Use as a Percentage of Total Shipments Under the
                  Base Case and Scenario 2

| | Flow Type 2 | | | |
| | <25 miles | 25-38 miles | >38 miles | Flow Type 1 |
|---|---|---|---|---|
| Scenario 1 | 0 % | 5 % | 10 % | 0 % |
| Scenario 2 | 50 % | 75 % | 90 % | 15 % |

Source:  Interview with Subterminal Manager

economies of truck classes as well as the distances from the subterminal. It is unlikely that CO-5AX trucks will become prevalent in the farm-to-satellite elevator traffic stream. As discussed in chapter 3, the cost per bushel-mile in single-unit farm trucks is typically lower than the for-hire CO-5AX truck rate at short distances. Thus, flow-type 1 will probably continue to be dominated by SU-2AX and SU-3AX trucks. However, the economies of combination trucks increase with distance. Consequently, for long-distance shipments to the subterminal (flow-type 2), the CO-5AX's share of grain may increase dramatically.

In summary, scenario 2 entails the following assumptions:

1.    farm-to-elevator shipments reflect the CO-5AX percentages shown
      in Table 10.1; and
2.    outbound elevator shipments are modeled in the same manner as in
      scenario 1.

**Scenario 3:  Elevator Rationalization**

Scenarios 2 and 3 are closely related. Scenario 3 entails all of the assumptions of scenario 2, plus the additional assumption that some substations will be closed during the impact period.

In the Devils Lake study, four satellite elevators were identified that might be eliminated if the system is rationalized. These four "non-essential" satellites have historically shipped small volumes of grain, are relatively close to the subterminal, and do not perform any specialized functions. The remaining three satellites either perform specialized functions or provide cost-effective farm-to-elevator transfer points for grain in competitive parts of the region. So, it is unlikely that any of the three would be eliminated as receiving points under a rationalization strategy.

### Scenario 4: Rail-Line Abandonment

The first three scenarios assume that the branch-line network will remain in place for the duration of the analysis period. Thus, satellite elevators will have the option of shipping directly to market by rail. However, the future of the light-density branch-line system in rural areas is uncertain. As the process of railroad rationalization continues, many light-density lines in rural areas may be dropped. The purpose of scenario 4 is to assess the change in flow patterns and highway costs that would result from abandonment. In doing so, the trans-shipment rule introduced in chapter 5 is used to allocate grain flows from the satellite elevators. Since rail transport is not an option, the long-haul truck rate is substituted for the rail rate in the equation.

In summary, scenario 4 entails the following assumptions:

1. the branch lines on which the satellite elevators are located are abandoned in the impact-year;
2. the distribution of farm-to-elevator shipments is the same as in scenario 2; and
3. outbound elevator shipments from *satellite* elevators are allocated between flow types 3 and 4 using a variant of the decision rule in equation 4.19.

### DIMENSIONS OF SUBTERMINAL IMPACTS

As described in chapter 3, grain subterminals generate a fairly intricate set of impacts and cross impacts. Subterminals can affect market share, grain flows, truck utilization/distribution, and highway utilization. There are some important cross-effects as well. For example, the allocation of grain among flow types will impact the distribution of shipments among truck types, as well as the types of highways utilized.

In this section, grain flow effects are evaluated by contrasting the allocation of grain among the five types of flows between the base case and the impact scenarios. Truck-type effects are modeled in a similar fashion using the three truck classes introduced in chapter 3. Highway class effects are simulated by compiling data at the functional class level.

**Major Cross-Effects**

The interaction between functional class and flow type is only one possible cross-effect in subterminal impact analysis. Two others which determine (in large part) the extent of highway impacts:

1.    flow types and truck types; and
2.    truck types and functional classes.

Each of the these effects and cross-effects were analyzed in the Devils Lake case study. The results of this dimensional analysis are presented next.


## DIMENSIONAL ANALYSIS

Table 10.2 depicts mean annual shipments for the analysis period. These data illustrate the potential effects of the subterminal on grain flows in the region. As Table 10.2 shows, the eight elevators that comprise the cooperative system


**Table 10.2**    Projected Distribution of Grain Between Co-op and Non-Co-op Elevators

|                        | Scenario | |
|------------------------|----------------------------|--------------------------------------|
| Elevator Status        | Base Case CWT (000)        | Primary Impact Case CWT (000)        |
| Non-Co-op Elevators    | 15,280                     | 13,484                               |
| Co-op Elevators        | 6,070                      | 9,184                                |
| Total                  | 21,350                     | 22,668                               |

collectively drew 6 million hundred-pounds (cwts) during 1985 (when the subterminal was operational for only five months of the year).[1] This volume comprised only 28 percent of total production in the market region. In contrast, the subterminal-satellite system is projected to draw over 9 million cwts from the surrounding area under the impact scenario.[2] This amounts to over 40 percent of the grain produced annually during the impact period. The reason for this market shift lies with the transportation rate advantage and the size economies of the subterminal. Since the price at the satellite elevator is assumed to be the price at the subterminal minus the grain trucking cost, a great deal of the subterminal's economies will be passed on to the satellites. Thus, all of the elevators in the cooperative will enjoy some price advantage over noncooperative elevators.

Impacts on market share are important. However, it is the aggregate change in grain flows brought about by the subterminal-satellite system that constitute the first major link in the chain of cause-and-effect. Table 10.3 and Table 10.4 show the before and after patterns of flow in the impact area.[3] The tables graphically illustrate the projected change in flow patterns predicted by the traffic models. As the subterminal moves toward its long-run market and operating position, trans-shipments are projected to reach 34 percent of total shipments within the impact region. Farm-to-subterminal and satellite elevator-to-market shipments, meanwhile, are projected to decline. These trends underscore the fallacy of focusing solely on early volume and shipment patterns.

**Table 10.3**    Distribution of Shipments Among Flow Types

| Flow Type | Scenario | |
| --- | --- | --- |
| | Base Case CWT (000) | Primary Impact Case CWT (000) |
| Farm-to-Satellite | 14,550 | 18,052 |
| Farm-to-Subterminal | 4,823 | 2,385 |
| Satellite-to-Market | 1,977 | 1,397 |
| Trans-shipment | . | 11,913 |
| Subterminal-to-Market | . | 834 |
| Total | 21,350 | 34,581 |

**Table 10.4**    Percentage Distribution of Shipments Among Flow Types

|  | Scenario | |
| --- | --- | --- |
| Flow Type | Base Case CWT (000) | Impact Case CWT (000) |
| Farm-to-Satellite | 68% | 52% |
| Farm-to-Subterminal | 23% | 7% |
| Satellite-to-Market | 9% | 4% |
| Trans-shipment | . | 34% |
| Subterminal-to-Market | . | 2% |
| Total | 100% | 100% |

Changes in flow types are the catalyst of the impact process. However, the highway impacts themselves are actually generated by changes in truck traffic within the impact region. Table 10.5 and Table 10.6 depict the distribution of traffic among truck types during the base case and the impact scenario. As Table 10.6 shows, CO-5AX truck trips are projected to increase from 4 percent of annual truck trips in the base case to 21 percent under the impact scenario. Meanwhile, SU-2AX and SU-3AX truck trips are expected to decline by seven and ten percentage points, respectively. Much of this reallocation of shipments among truck types is due directly to changes in flow types (particularly flow-type 4). Most trans-shipments represent traffic that previously moved by rail from satellite elevators to markets.

**Table 10.5**    Annual Trips by Truck Class

| Truck Type | Scenario Annual Trips | |
| | Base Case | Primary Impact Case |
|---|---|---|
| CO-5AX | 7,774 | 53,174 |
| SU-2AX | 115,590 | 135,252 |
| SU-3AX | 67,792 | 64,256 |
| Total | 191,156 | 252,682 |

**Table 10.6**    Percent of Annual Trips by Truck Class

| Truck Type | Percent of Annual Trips | |
| | Base Case | Primary Impact Case |
|---|---|---|
| CO-5AX | 4% | 21% |
| SU-2AX | 61% | 54% |
| SU-3AX | 35% | 25% |
| Total | 100% | 100% |

Table 10.7 and Table 10.8 present an analogous display of highway usage patterns. Annual trips are projected to increase within all functional classes during the impact scenario (see Table 10.7). The largest increases occur on principal and minor arterial highways. This is primarily the result of trans-shipments between the satellite elevators (situated mostly on minor rural arterials) and the subterminal (located on a principal arterial).

**Table 10.7**     Truck Trips by Functional Class

|                     | Annual Trips | |
|---------------------|--------------|-------------------------|
| Functional Class    | Base Case    | Primary Impact Scenario |
| Major Arterial      | 120,262      | 184,030                 |
| Minor Arterial      | 186,690      | 235,508                 |
| Major Collector     | 59,422       | 79,064                  |
| Minor Collector     | 24,764       | 34,274                  |
| Total               | 291,138      | 532,876                 |

**Table 10.8**     Percent of Truck Trips by Functional Class

|                     | Percent of Annual Trips | |
|---------------------|-------------------------|-------------------------|
| Functional Class    | Base Case               | Primary Impact Scenario |
| Major Arterial      | 30%                     | 35%                     |
| Minor Arterial      | 48%                     | 44%                     |
| Major Collector     | 15%                     | 15%                     |
| Minor Collector     | 6%                      | 6%                      |

Table 10.8 indicates that the distribution of truck trips among functional classes is projected to remain relatively unchanged throughout the impact period. However, this finding can be somewhat misleading, because the table does not show the change in CO-5AX truck traffic on various functional classes of highways.  So, perhaps a better indicator of changes in highway utilization patterns is the increased annual vehicle miles of travel (VMT) attributable to each truck class on each functional system.  Table 10.9 and Table 10.10 present a

breakdown of annual VMT by truck-type and functional class for the base case and the impact scenario. As the tables depict, annual CO-5AX VMT are projected to increase substantially on minor and principal arterials. At the same time, SU-2AX and SU-3AX VMT are projected to decline on both classes of highways. Collector highways are also likely to experience increases in CO-5AX VMT.

**Table 10.9**    Grain Truck VMT by Truck Type and Functional Class

| Scenario | Functional Class | Truck Type | | | Total |
| | | Co-5AX | SU-2AX | SU-3AX | |
| | | Annual VMT (000) | | | |
|---|---|---|---|---|---|
| Base Case | Major Arterial | 162 | 208 | 233 | 604 |
| | Minor Arterial | 74 | 756 | 556 | 1386 |
| | Major Collector | 37 | 239 | 136 | 412 |
| | Minor Collector | 2 | 98 | 47 | 147 |
| | Total | 277 | 1,302 | 971 | 2,549 |
| Primary Impact Case | Major Arterial | 598 | 184 | 149 | 931 |
| | Minor Arterial | 663 | 704 | 385 | 1,752 |
| | Major Collector | 86 | 267 | 125 | 477 |
| | Minor Collector | 13 | 93 | 41 | 148 |
| | Total | 1,359 | 1,249 | 701 | 3,308 |

**Table 10.10**     Percent of Annual Truck VMT by Truck Type and Functional
                    Class

| Scenario | Functional Class | Truck Type | | | All |
|---|---|---|---|---|---|
| | | CO-5AX | SU-2AX | SU-3AX | |
| | | Annual VMT (000) | | | |
| Base Case | Major Arterial | 6% | 8% | 9% | 24% |
| | Minor Arterial | 3% | 30% | 22% | 84% |
| | Major Collector | 1% | 9% | 5% | 16% |
| | Minor Collector | 6% | 4% | 2% | 6% |
| Primary Impact Case | Major Arterial | 18% | 6% | 5% | 28% |
| | Minor Arterial | 20% | 21% | 12% | 53% |
| | Major Collector | 3% | 8% | 4% | 14% |
| | Minor Collector | 0% | 3% | 1% | 4% |

It is interesting to note that the distribution of annual VMT is somewhat
different than that of annual truck trips.  A larger percentage of VMT are logged
on rural minor arterials (as opposed to truck trips).  Relatively lengthy trips from
the satellite elevators located on State Highway 20 to the subterminal are the
primary reason for the difference.

Changes in truck distribution and highway usage are translated into incremental highway costs through changes in ESALs. Table 10.11 shows the incremental average annual daily ESALs (AADE) by road and functional class for the impact scenario. The principal arterial in the impact region (Highway 2) shows substantial projected increases in AADE. So does Highway 20 north and south of Devils Lake. Three major collectors (3618, 3627, and 3630) will also be impacted, as well as three minor collectors.

Several items in Table 10.11 are particularly noteworthy. First, the highway on which the subterminal is located (2W) is projected to experience a substantial increase in grain AADE. This is to be expected, since both direct farm-to-subterminal shipments and trans-shipments will traverse parts of the highway. Second, Highway 20 (on which three of the satellite elevators are located) will also be heavily impacted. Again, this is primarily due to trans-shipments under the impact case. Third, Highway 3627 (a major collector) is likely to incur substantial incremental cost. This is because one of the major satellite elevators in the system is located on a section of the highway. As a result, the road is likely to experience both heavy inbound and outbound truck shipments.

Negative or decremental values are possible in Table 10.11. This is because as the subterminal exerts its influence over the market region, traffic will be diverted from some highways, actually reducing impacts. However, in the final analysis Table 10.11 shows a net gain of 204 incremental grain truck AADE in the area.

The purpose of the previous discussion was to formulate an analytic chain of cause-and-effect in subterminal impact analysis. Table 10.12 brings the financial impacts into sharper focus by displaying the projected replacement costs for the analysis period, by functional class and road. These replacement costs are employed in the build-sooner analysis, discussed next.

**Table 10.11**    Incremental Grain AADE

| Road | Major Arterial | Minor Arterial | Major Collector | Minor Collector | Total |
|------|------|------|------|------|------|
| | | | **Functional Class** | | |
| | | | **Grain AADE** | | |
| 1 | . | -4 | . | . | -4 |
| 15 | . | -10 | . | . | -10 |
| 19 | . | 0 | . | . | 0 |
| 2e | 9 | . | . | . | 9 |
| 2w | 135 | . | . | . | 135 |
| 66 | . | -16 | . | . | -16 |
| 17e | . | 0 | . | . | 0 |
| 17w | . | -4 | . | . | -4 |
| 20n | . | 47 | . | . | 47 |
| 20s | . | 17 | . | . | 17 |
| 3604 | . | . | . | 8 | 8 |
| 3607 | . | . | . | 2 | 2 |
| 3614 | . | . | 0 | . | 0 |
| 3617 | . | . | . | 5 | 5 |
| 3618 | . | . | 4 | . | 4 |
| 3627 | . | . | 16 | . | 16 |
| 3630 | . | . | 6 | . | 6 |
| 3633 | . | . | 1 | . | 1 |
| 4819 | . | . | . | -12 | -12 |
| Total | 144 | 30 | 27 | 3 | 204 |

**Table 10.12**     Base-Case Replacement Cost by Functional Class

| Road | Major Arterial | Minor Arterial | Major Collector | Minor Collector | Total |
|---|---|---|---|---|---|
| | | **Functional Class** | | | |
| | | Replacement Cost (000) $ | | | |
| 1 | . | 5,712 | . | . | 5,712 |
| 15 | . | 3,927 | . | . | 3,927 |
| 19 | . | 834 | . | . | 834 |
| 2e | 5,054 | . | . | . | 5,054 |
| 2w | 4,118 | . | . | . | 4,118 |
| 66 | . | 3,927 | . | . | 3,927 |
| 17e | . | 595 | . | . | 595 |
| 17w | . | 476 | . | . | 476 |
| 20n | . | 3,453 | . | . | 3,453 |
| 20s | . | 2,536 | . | . | 2,536 |
| 3604 | . | . | . | 4,998 | 4,988 |
| 3607 | . | . | . | 3,248 | 3,248 |
| 3614 | . | . | 580 | . | 580 |
| 3617 | . | . | . | 3,248 | 3,248 |
| 3618 | . | . | 580 | . | 580 |
| 3627 | . | . | 4,408 | . | 4,408 |
| 3630 | . | . | 1,044 | . | 1,044 |
| 3633 | . | . | 4,408 | . | 4,408 |
| 4819 | . | . | . | 4,988 | 4,988 |
| Total | 9,172 | 21,460 | 11,020 | 16,472 | 58,124 |

## INCREMENTAL COST ANALYSIS

Eighty-two of the 126 highway sections in the Devils Lake study had some grain truck traffic routed over them during either the base case or the impact scenario. As Table 10.12 depicts, over $58 million in replacement costs were forecast for the 82 sections between 1990 and 2006. These sections collectively comprise 452 miles of highway. The forecasted replacement cost increased to over $59 million under the impact scenario. The accelerated replacement cost (or build-sooner cost) totals $1.14 million. Much of it is concentrated on the major collector system and two minor rural arterials subject to the heaviest trans-shipments.

The projected short-run incremental costs for the analysis period are displayed in Table 10.13. As Table 10.13 shows, the collector and minor arterial system is likely to be most heavily impacted by future subterminal operations. This finding is born-out by an analysis of heavily-impacted highways such as 3627 and 20S.[4]

**Table 10.13**     Short–Run Incremental Cost

| Road | Functional Class | | | | Total |
|------|------------------|--|--|--|-------|
|      | Major Arterial | Minor Arterial | Major Collector | Minor Collector | |
|      | SRIC (000) $ | | | | |
| 1    | .  | 0   | .   | .   | 0   |
| 15   | .  | 0   | .   | .   | 0   |
| 19   | 11 | 0   | .   | .   | 0   |
| 2e   | 75 | .   | .   | .   | 11  |
| 2w   | .  | .   | .   | .   | 75  |
| 66   | .  | 0   | .   | .   | 0   |
| 17e  | .  | 0   | .   | .   | 0   |
| 17w  | .  | 0   | .   | .   | 0   |
| 20n  | .  | 124 | .   | .   | 124 |
| 20s  | .  | 286 | .   | .   | 286 |
| 3604 | .  | .   | .   | 82  | 82  |
| 3607 | .  | .   | .   | 22  | 22  |
| 3614 | .  | .   | 0   | .   | 0   |
| 3617 | .  | .   | .   | 49  | 49  |
| 3618 | .  | .   | 51  | .   | 51  |
| 3627 | .  | .   | 345 | .   | 345 |
| 3630 | .  | .   | 64  | .   | 64  |
| 3633 | .  | .   | 29  | .   | 29  |
| 4819 | .  | .   | .   | 0   | 0   |
| Total | 86 | 410 | 489 | 153 | 1,138 |

The build-sooner costs represent only the short-run impacts of subterminal traffic incurred during the current replacement cycle. In addition to the SRIC, upgrading or LRIC were computed in the Devils Lake region. The projected LRIC for the impact area are displayed in Table 10.14. Not all highways in the impact region will have to be strengthened. With the exception of Highway 20 (and 2W in the vicinity of the subterminal), the arterial network in the region appears to be sufficient to support future changes in truck traffic generated by the subterminal. However, the collector system is under-designed in terms of the level and mix of future traffic it will be required to bear. Certain major impact highways (such as 3627) are likely to incur significant long-run costs because of low structural numbers and old pavements. Altogether, $8.3 million in upgrading costs are projected.

**Table 10.14**     Long–Run Incremental Cost

| Road | Functional Class | | | | |
|------|------------------|--|--|--|--|
|      | Major Arterial | Minor Arterial | Major Collector | Minor Collector | Total |
|      | LRIC (000) $ | | | | |
| 1    | .   | 0   | .   | .   | 0   |
| 15   | .   | 0   | .   | .   | 0   |
| 19   | .   | 0   | .   | .   | 0   |
| 2e   | 63  | .   | .   | .   | 63  |
| 2w   | 111 | .   | .   | .   | 111 |
| 66   | .   | 0   | .   | .   | 0   |
| 17e  | .   | 0   | .   | .   | 0   |
| 17w  | .   | 0   | .   | .   | 0   |
| 20n  | .   | 249 | .   | .   | 249 |
| 20s  | .   | 800 | .   | .   | 800 |
| 3604 | .   | .   | .   | 1,213 | 1,213 |
| 3607 | .   | .   | .   | 2,104 | 2,104 |
| 3614 | .   | .   | 0   | .   | 0   |
| 3617 | .   | .   | .   | 1,133 | 1,133 |
| 3618 | .   | .   | 283 | .   | 283 |
| 3627 | .   | .   | 1,416 | .   | 1,416 |
| 3630 | .   | .   | 218 | .   | 218 |
| 3633 | .   | .   | 729 | .   | 729 |
| 4819 | .   | .   | .   | 0   | 0   |
| Total | 174 | 1,049 | 2,646 | 4,450 | 8,319 |

## DISTRIBUTION OF IMPACTS

The results of the case study were somewhat mixed. Collector highways (as a class) incurred the greatest build-sooner costs. Although the overall impacts were relatively modest, individual highways within the class were heavily impacted. The results were also mixed for arterials. Only one minor arterial (Highway 20) incurred any SRIC at all under the impact scenario. Similarly, only Highway 2W in the vicinity of the subterminal incurred any significant short-run costs within the principal arterial grouping. Perhaps the best generalization that can be drawn from these results is that some SRIC are likely to occur from subterminal development. The impacts will be significant on a localized scale, particularly on collector highways and on arterials in the vicinity of the subterminal or on major trans-shipment routes.

As Table 10.14 shows, the majority of the LRIC will fall to the collector network. These highways were designed for low traffic levels. Thus, they have correspondingly low structural numbers. Collectors will require more resources in the future and more attention from state and local highway planners. These are the highways that need to be closely monitored in a subterminal impact region.

As Table 10.14 shows 85 percent of the long-run incremental costs are projected to occur on the collector network. Perhaps more significant, 53 percent are projected to occur on the minor collector system alone. Meanwhile, only 2 percent of the projected long-run costs will fall to the principal arterial network. In essence, rural collector and minor arterial highways can be expected to incur significant LRIC as a result of subterminal development (perhaps even catastrophic on a localized scale). However, principal arterials may not be impacted at all. This distribution of impacts is logical, since principal arterials are designed to higher standards.

## SENSITIVITY ANALYSIS

Table 10.15 and Table 10.16 summarize the SRIC and LRIC under each of the four alternative scenarios. As the tables indicate, the greatest LRIC would occur under scenarios 2 and 4. The SRIC costs show little fluctuation from the values forecast under the primary impact scenario. Scenario 3 (the elevator rationalization scenario) actually has the lowest projected cost. As substations are eliminated, fewer trans-shipments occur. Concurrently, more direct farm-to-subterminal shipments will be made, particularly from the areas closest to the subterminal. Since the subterminal elevator is located on a principal arterial, a different mix of highway utilization will materialize under scenario 3 than under scenario 1.

**Table 10.15**     Short–Run Incremental Cost

| | SRIC (000) $ | | | | |
| | Functional Class | | | | |
| Scenario | Major Arterial | Minor Arterial | Major Collector | Minor Collector | Total |
|---|---|---|---|---|---|
| Scenario 2 | 85 | 383 | 391 | 141 | 1,000 |
| Scenario 3 | 64 | 410 | 420 | 0 | 894 |
| Scenario 4 | 7 | 410 | 489 | 153 | 1,125 |

**Table 10.16**     Long–Run Incremental Cost

| | LRIC (000) $ | | | | |
| | Functional Class | | | | |
| Scenario | Major Arterial | Minor Arterial | Major Collector | Minor Collector | Total |
|---|---|---|---|---|---|
| Scenario 2 | 185 | 913 | 2,700 | 6,473 | 10,271 |
| Scenario 3 | 102 | 1,071 | 2,846 | 0 | 4,019 |
| Scenario 4 | 193 | 1,049 | 2,646 | 4,450 | 8,338 |

Several additional insights may be gleaned from the sensitivity analysis. First, increased CO-5AX truck use between farms and the subterminal as envisioned in scenario 2 would not significantly affect SRIC. In many instances, CO-5AX trips would be substituted for SU-2AX trips. As illustrated in Table 3.1 (of chapter 3), an SU-2AX generates more ESALs per ton-mile than a CO-5AX truck. Second, the difference between scenario 1 and 2 primarily results from changes in projected costs for collector highways. Some gravel surface collector highways will have to be upgraded to handle CO-5AX trucks. Moreover, thicker pavements will be needed on thin collector highways to maintain the same life cycle as before. Thus, the projected LRIC on collector highways is greater under scenario 2 than in the primary impact scenario. Third, a significant decrease in SU-2AX truck use as envisioned in scenario 3 would reduce highway impacts. Moreover, a significant reduction in trans-shipments (also envisioned in scenario 3) will further reduce highway impacts. One of the satellite elevators in the Devils Lake system is located on collector roads. Thus, the elimination of movements into and out of these substations will reduce overall highway costs. Fourth, since most of the shipments from satellite elevators are trans-shipments under the primary impact scenario, the abaondonment of branch lines as envisioned in scenario 4 will not significantly affect the projected costs. However, this finding should not be interpreted as a general rule of abandonment impacts. In the Devils Lake simulation, most of the satellite elevator shipments already moved by truck to the subterminal under scenario 1.

## CONCLUSIONS

The construction of the grain subterminal elevator at Devils Lake will cause localized short-run impacts, resulting in $1.14 million in build-sooner costs. The LRIC will be more substantial, totaling $10.3 million in the worst-case scenario. Scenario 3 (in which the elevator system is rationalized) shows the lowest projected SRIC and LRIC. This points out the potentially large reductions in highway costs brought about by the elimination of trans-shipments. The greatest SRIC would be generated under scenario 2 and scenario 4.

The conclusions of the study are consistent with engineering and economic logic. Changes in traffic patterns caused by the grain subterminal are likely to generate more local trips and annual miles, much of which will be concentrated on collector highways not designed for heavy truck traffic. This mismatch between traffic and highway classes will result in localized short-run impacts, as well as significant long-run costs on the collector network.

As the case study points out, the construction of a single grain subterminal can result in highway costs of between $9.7 and $11.3 million. However, less than 2 percent of the rural minor arterial and collector highway mileage in the state is represented in the case study. If the Devils Lake region is a microcosm of rural North Dakota, the statewide accelerated replacement and upgrading costs could be in the vicinity of $57 million and $420 million, respectively. Regional variations within the state may result in either higher or lower per-mile costs for a given elevator system than those experienced in the Devils Lake region. Many parts of the state do not have the extensive coverage and quality of service provided by the arterial and collector network in the Devils Lake region. In these areas, the impacts are likely to be much greater.

The analytic procedures utilized in the subterminal study are transferable to many other types of problems. In chapter 11, a railroad abandonment case study is introduced that utilizes this same process. Fortunately, the land-use and traffic distribution procedures are more straightforward than in the subterminal example.

## NOTES

1. This figure is based on actual grain shipment data.

2. Horizon-year estimates take into account: (1) increased production, (2) changes in elevator relationships, and (3) increased market penetration by the subterminal.

3. The 1985 figures reflect farm shipments to the existing Devils Lake elevator in the first half of the year, and farm-to-subterminal shipments during the last half of the year.

4. Highway 3627 provides access to one of the satellites that has trainloading capabilities. As the table depicts it is perhaps the most-heavily impacted of all roads. This is because: (1) the facility both receives and trans-ships grain on the same highway, and (2) the highway is not designed to arterial standards.

# 11

# Branch-Line Abandonment
# Case Study

The basic process illustrated in chapters 4 to 9 is applicable to a wide range of exogenous land–use, transportation, and regional economic changes. One of the most significant transportation examples is railroad branch-line abandonment.

As stated in chapter 1, over 61,000 miles of railroad lines have been abandoned since 1960. The passage of the Staggers Rail Act of 1980 streamlined the abandonment process. In a deregulated environment, carriers are apt to file more applications in future years. Over 60,000 miles of railroad currently operated by Class I carriers in America have traffic densities less than or equal to 5 million gross ton-miles per mile.[1] Class I railroads would like to rid themselves of much or all of this trackage. For example, the strategic plan of one large railroad calls for the possible abandonment of 7,000 miles of track in the near future.[2]

Abandonment was once thought to apply only to branch lines. However, rationalization is also impacting railroad mainlines. In a recent example (1991), the Chicago and Northwestern (CNW) filed for abandonment of a 324–mile secondary mainline across northern Nebraska. The traffic on this line averaged nearly 4,000 carloads a year between 1988 and 1990. If the line is abandoned, this rail volume will translate into approximately 15,000 annual incremental CO-5AX truck trips.[3] The geography of the area, the types of highways involved, and the distances to rail transloading facilities make this line an excellent case study of railroad abandonment.

The purpose of this chapter is to illustrate the highway impact assessment process within the context of abandonment impact studies. In the first section of the chapter, some background concepts in abandonment impact analysis and state rail planning are introduced. Section two describes the case study. This description includes a land-use study and a history of traffic and operations on the line. Section three describes the data sources and surveys utilized in the case study, and highlights the shipment generation, shipment distribution, truck weight, highway network and equivalent axle load procedures. Section five presents the analytic approach and pavement deterioration models.

## BACKGROUND

### Forecasting Abandonments

Railroads are required by law to indicate which lines are being contemplated for abandonment prior to filing with the ICC. Each carrier publishes a Systems Diagram map annually.[4] These maps are filed with state departments of transportation or regulatory commissions.[5] Each state receives maps for all Class I carriers operating within its boundaries.

There are three important categories on a Systems Diagram map. Category 2 contains lines under study for future abandonment. However, no definitive abandonment time-frame has yet been established for these lines. Lines in Category 1 are under analysis for possible abandonment within three years. However, an application can be filed as quickly as four months after a carrier places a line in Category 1. Abandonment applications have already been filed on lines in Category 3. These applications are pending before the ICC, and will usually be resolved within a matter of days.

The Systems Diagram map is a valuable tool for highway analysts. It constitutes a highway impact warning system of sorts. Highway analysts can use these maps to identify potential impact zones. Furthermore, highway planners can conduct preliminary impact analyses of rail lines appearing on the map prior to abandonment. Some states perform such preliminary analyses and publish them in state rail plans.[6] However, there are several problems associated with exclusive reliance the Systems Diagram map as a warning device. First, most highway expenditures are programmed over a multi-year period (e.g. five). On these grounds alone, the four–month warning period guaranteed by the Systems Diagram map can be problematic. Second, most lines are downgraded in terms of service and maintenance frequencies several years prior to being placed on the Systems Diagram map. Consequently, some highway impacts may occur before the line is classified.

A line does not necessarily have to be on the Systems Diagram map to warrant the attention of highway planners. Previous studies have shown that lines with less than thirty-four cars per mile are circumspect.[7] The Federal Railroad Administration currently requires that a line have at least twenty cars a mile before public funds can be used to rehabilitate the track. The Nebraska rail line highlighted in this chapter averaged approximately eleven cars a mile in the last complete year of operations. The Union Pacific recently abandoned a rail line in Washington with a projected traffic density of twelve cars a mile during the forecast year.[8] The traffic mix of these two lines was similar. Agricultural commodities comprised most of the traffic on both lines. But in spite of these commonalities, there is no universal formula for computing the break-even volume of a railroad line. The Burlington Northern operates many miles of track in rural North Dakota with traffic densities less than twenty cars a mile.

The viability of a rail line depends upon a range of revenue, traffic, operational, and maintenance factors. In the absence of a break-even density, some sort of early warning abandonment system could prove helpful for highway planners. One method of constructing such a warning system is to use threshold traffic densities. When the traffic on a rail line drops below thirty-five cars a mile, highway analysts should label the line as a potential future abandonment. In essence, a density of thirty-five cars a mile could comprise the initial threshold of the warning system. When the traffic density drops below twenty cars a mile, the chances of an abandonment increase substantially. Thus, this traffic level could form the inner threshold of the early warning system. Rail-line traffic densities could serve another useful purpose in an early warning highway impact system. Recent railroad traffic levels can quickly be converted to equivalent truckloads, thus providing the highway planner with a sense of the probable scale of impacts.

## State Rail Planning Process

As mentioned previously, the downgrading of railroad lines prior to abandonment can create substantial highway impacts. The Federal Railroad Administration and most state DOTs have railroad planning programs that target deteriorating light-density lines. Most of these programs have been in existence since 1980. Most of the rail programs in western states were started in responses to the Local Rail Services Assistance Act of 1978. In this act, Congress provided funding to the states to deal with railroad restructuring and abandonments. The Local Rail Freight Assistance (LRFA) program of 1990 provided renewed funding to states and focused more attention on the process of rail planning. Most states have developed loan programs that are used to acquire or rehabilitate light-density rail lines.

Under the rail assistance programs, states invest public funds in rail-line rehabilitation, restoration, or upgrading. In some instances, states have purchased light-density rail lines, or facilitated a transfer of ownership. Many former Class I branch lines are now being operated by local or regional railroads.

Before public funds can be invested in rail lines, a comprehensive benefit-cost study must be undertaken. In these studies, the alternative to rehabilitation or acquisition is usually abandonment. Rail-line studies typically simulate the effects of a line being abandoned in some future year. *Avoidable highway impacts* are one class of potential benefits considered in rail planning studies. In some cases, the transportation agency can avoid future highway costs by rehabilitating or acquiring a rail line.[9]

Since rail planning studies simulate abandonment, they are not distinguished from abandonment impact studies in this book. The primary difference between the two types of analyses is the time frame. Rail planning studies are generally conducted much earlier in the history of a line. In general, highway planners can provide valuable input to the state rail planning process using the impact assessment techniques illustrated in this chapter.

## CASE STUDY DESCRIPTION AND LAND-USE ANALYSIS

In 1991, the CNW placed the O'Neill to Chadron line in category 1 on its Systems Diagram map. This move alerted Nebraska transportation planners and shippers to the possible loss of rail service over a large section of the state. The Nebraska Department of Roads (DOR) initiated a set of studies to identify and evaluate alternatives, working closely with shippers located on the line. The DOR and a major shipper association announced their intentions to acquire the rail line from the CNW and rehabilitate portions of it. The shippers felt that some traffic currently moving by truck would be shipped by rail after rehabilitation, thus enhancing the viability of the rail line.

The highway impact assessment process illustrated in this chapter is based on this scenario. The analysis considers rail traffic, plus traffic currently moving by truck in the rail-line market area. The avoidable costs attributable to both classes of traffic are highlighted later in the chapter.

### Land-Use Analysis

There are similarities between a subterminal and a rail-line land-use study. However, there are also differences. The subterminal land-use study in chapter 6 encompassed one group of elevators that belonged to the same firm. The study focused primarily on the markets and production characteristics of the elevators and potential patterns of flow among the facilities. The potential drawing powers of elevators was a major concern of the land-use study. In contrast, rail-line studies focus primarily on traffic currently moving by rail and truck from elevators on the line. The drawing powers of elevators and farm-to-market shipment patterns are of secondary concern. Instead, a major objective is to identify traffic that could be diverted from highways to railroads if a rail investment is made (and the line is not abandoned). Moreover, a major task of rail-line studies is the identification of potential trans-shipment points that impacted shippers might use after abandonment.

Like the subterminal land-use study, a rail-line analysis begins with a description of the market area.

## Market Area

The line in question, the *Northern Line,* extends across the northern part of Nebraska (Figure 10.31). The Northern Line serves Madison, Antelope, Holt, Rock, Brown, Cherry, Sheridan and Dawes Counties in Nebraska. In addition, the line is in proximity to Boyd and Keya Paha Counties in Nebraska, and Gregory, Tripp, Todd, Bennett, and Shannon counties in South Dakota. These counties are all part of the Northern Line market area. The Burlington Northern (BN) provides service to Antelope and Dawes Counties. Madison county is also served by the Union Pacific (UP).

**Figure 11.1    CNW Northern Line**

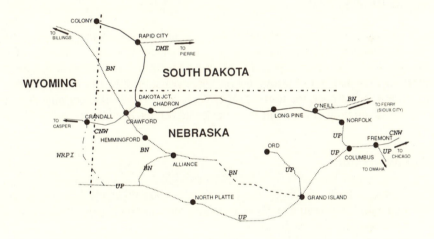

The businesses on the line are nearly all agriculturally-oriented, including grain elevators, feed and fertilizer distributors, and farm implement dealers. The primary commodities handled are grains, beans, fertilizers, propane gas, lumber products, and farm machinery.

If the Northern Line is abandoned, alternative railroad services will be limited. The nearest trans-shipping points on the CNW are the two terminals of the line (Chadron and O'Neill) and Norfolk, a major market to the east. The current level of services at Chadron is low. Therefore, it is uncertain whether Chadron would remain a viable trans-shipping point if the remainder of the line to the east is abandoned. Other possible trans-shipping points are located on the BN at Crawford, Alliance, and Hemmingford. The only feasible trans-shipping point on the Union Pacific (UP) is located at Ord. However, Ord is 72 miles south of the closest on-line shipper at Atkinson. In general, the distances from on-line elevators to these trans-shipping points are considerable, over one hundred miles in many instances.

The primary east–west highway is U.S. 20, that parallels the railroad from Inman to Chadron. U.S. 20 is a low-design asphaltic highway, primarily intended for lighter truck traffic. The weighted average SN of sections within the primary impact zone is less than 3.0.[10] Water transport is not an option. There are no navigable rivers in northern Nebraska. The closest river ports are Sioux City, Iowa, and Omaha, Nebraska, both in excess of two hundred miles.

**Traffic History**

A history of originated and terminated traffic is displayed in Table 11.1. As the data indicate, the line has a history of relatively low traffic density. On average, the CNW originated 2,111 cars and terminated 1,144 carloads each year between 1974 and 1990. During the last three years, the line averaged seventeen cars a mile. However, the traffic density declined to eleven cars per mile during 1990. A description of the grain elevators located on the line is presented in Table 11.2

**Potential Traffic**

Historical traffic levels on the Northern Line are relatively low. However, substantial traffic potential exists in the market area, implying that a large volume of traffic currently moves by truck.[11]

To develop a reasonable assessment of the line's potential, and to identify the current truck market share, agricultural production and consumption statistics were compiled for the region.[12] Data for the major crops produced are presented in Table 11.3 - Table 11.5. In addition, summary statistics for all crops are shown in Table 11.6. Each table has three numeric columns. The first numeric column contains the estimated bushels harvested in each county in the market area in 1989. The second numeric column contains the equivalent carloads that the production totals would yield if the total volume moved by rail. The third numeric column shows the estimated truck loads that would be generated if all of the production moved by truck.

**Table 11.1**   Traffic Originating and Terminating on CNW Line Between but Excluding Norfolk and Chadron

| Year | Cars Originated | Cars Terminated | Total Cars |
|------|------|------|------|
| 1974 | 2,388 | 2,032 | 4,420 |
| 1975 | 1,178 | 1,644 | 2,822 |
| 1976 | 1,043 | 2,232 | 3,275 |
| 1977 | 650 | 1,715 | 2,365 |
| 1978 | 1,266 | 1,547 | 2,813 |
| 1979 | 2,513 | 1,492 | 4,005 |
| 1980 | 3,844 | 986 | 4,830 |
| 1981 | 2,516 | 807 | 3,323 |
| 1982 | 1,837 | 620 | 2,457 |
| 1983 | 2,773 | 405 | 3,178 |
| 1984 | 3,251 | 399 | 3,650 |
| 1985 | 1,512 | 351 | 1,863 |
| 1986 | 1,261 | 360 | 1,621 |
| 1987 | 1,974 | 781 | 2,755 |
| 1988 | 2,947 | 1,043 | 3,990 |
| 1989 | 2,741 | 1,623 | 4,364 |
| 1990 | 2,187 | 1,420 | 3,607 |
| Average | 2,111 | 1,144 | 3,255 |

Source:  Chicago and North Western Transportation Company

**Table 11.2**    Major Northern Line Elevators

| Location | Elevator | Storage Capacity (Bushels) |
|---|---|---|
| Hay Springs | Lewin Grain | 3,500,000 |
| Hay Springs | Farmers COOP Grn | 856,000 |
| Rushville | Nor'west Grn, Ltd. | 1,221,000 |
| Clinton | Retzlaff Grain Co. | 440,000 |
| Gordon | Magowan Grain | 2,058,520 |
| Gordon | Retzlaff Grain | 440,000 |
| Gordon | Ag. Pro. COOP | 1,600,000 |
| Merriman | Non-Stock Gr | 1,389,000 |
| Crookston | Crookston Grn & F | 1,112,000 |
| Valentine | Valentine Feed Sr | 15,000 |
| Long Pine | Bassett Grain | 2,463,000 |
| Long Pine | Deaver-Stockham | 966,000 |
| Ainsworth | Farmers Ranchers | 990,000 |
| Atkinson | Segran Grain, Inc. | 1,000,000 |
| Atkinson | Grasslands Grain | 2,400,000 |
| Atkinson | Curry Grain Inc. | 1,887,000 |
| Emmet | Emmett Fer & Grn. | 698,000 |
| Clearwater | Clearwater Elev Co | 200,000 |
| Clearwater | Clearwater Feed/Gn | 80,000 |
| Oakdale | White Grain Co. | 1,294,000 |
| Tilden | Tilden Feed & Grn | 914,000 |
| Meadow Grove | Meadow Grove Grn | 354,000 |
| Meadow Grove | Warrick & Sons | 275,000 |
| Battle Creek | Battle Ck F.COOP | 3,311,000 |
| TOTAL | | 29,463,520 |

Equivalent carloads and truck loads are a function of the density of the commodity and the type of equipment used. The equivalent carloads shown in Table 11.3 - Table 11.6 assume the use of large covered hopper cars (e.g. C113). Covered hopper car capacities were estimated from the internal dimensions of the car and the density of the commodity. For example, corn has a density of 60 pounds per bushel, resulting in an average load of 99 tons per rail car. The equivalent truck loads reflect the use of CO-5AX trucks. Average CO-5AX loads for grain usually range from 25 to 28 tons. The values shown in Tables 11.3 to 11.6 reflect the midpoint of this range (26.5 tons). As these data show, the transport capacity of a grain covered hopper car is approximately 3.7 times that of a CO-5AX truck.

A portion of the crops produced in the market area are typically consumed on farm or stored for later shipment. In addition, some crops stored from previous years on farms or in grain elevators were probably shipped out during 1989. So, there is not a perfect correlation between 1989 production and 1989 shipments. However, there is an approximate relationship. The best way to interpret these production totals is as the maximum volume that could have been shipped from the market region in 1989.

As Table 11.6 shows, the equivalent of 33,193 railroad covered hopper cars were produced in the market region in 1989. In contrast, only 4,364 carloads were handled on the CNW line (not all of which were grain shipments). This large disparity between production and shipments underscores some important points. First, there is undoubtedly much greater traffic potential on the line than historical shipment data would imply. Second, a substantial amount of grain traffic is already moving in the impact region by truck. Third, some of the traffic currently handled by trucks is probably moving considerable distances to terminal markets or to trans-shipment points on the BN, UP, or the CNW. Therefore, if the line is retained and upgraded instead of being abandoned, some of this traffic may be recaptured by the CNW or a new local rail operator.

In addition to grain, fertilizer products have traditionally moved into the area by rail. However, much of the CNW's traffic base has eroded in recent years. Barges now move large amounts of phosphates from the Gulf of Mexico to river ports at Sioux City or Omaha. From there, the fertilizers are trans-shipped by truck to their final destinations. Table 11.7 provides a summary of fertilizer sales in the impact region during 1989, by county. Equivalent carload and truckload figures are also shown.

The purpose of Tables 11.3 to 11.7 is to identify the potential traffic in the market area in terms of equivalent rail cars and truckloads, and to estimate the amount currently handled by truck. The data and techniques used to construct the tables can be replicated in most rail-line studies. Similar agricultural production statistics are compiled for each state. When combined with a shipper survey and historical rail traffic volumes, these statistics can be useful tools in abandonment impact studies.

**Table 11.3**     Summary of Harvest—Nebraska/South Dakota Counties Along
                   CNW Northern Line, 1989:  Soybeans

| State County | Bushels Harvested | Equivalent Carloads | Equivalent Trucks |
|---|---|---|---|
| NEBRASKA | | | |
| Madison | 2,178,280 | 681 | 2,519 |
| Antelope | 1,480,390 | 463 | 1,712 |
| Knox | 843,360 | 264 | 975 |
| Holt | 709,650 | 222 | 821 |
| Boyd | 164,450 | 51 | 190 |
| Rock | 49,400 | 15 | 57 |
| Keya Paha | 15,200 | 5 | 18 |
| Brown | 72,000 | 23 | 83 |
| Cherry | 46,020 | 14 | 53 |
| Sheridan | 0 | 0 | 0 |
| Dawes | 0 | 0 | 0 |
| SOUTH DAKOTA | | | |
| Gregory | 182,400 | 57 | 211 |
| Tripp | 35,200 | 11 | 41 |
| Todd | 17,500 | 5 | 20 |
| Bennett | 0 | 0 | 0 |
| Shannon | 0 | 0 | 0 |
| Total | 5,793,850 | 1,811 | 6,700 |

**Table 11.4**     Summary of Harvest—Nebraska/South Dakota Counties Along
CNW Northern Line, 1989:  Corn

| State<br>County | Bushels<br>Harvested | Equivalent<br>Carloads | Equivalent<br>Trucks |
|---|---|---|---|
| NEBRASKA | | | |
| Madison | 4,748,750 | 4,338 | 16,050 |
| Antelope | 23,064,750 | 6,784 | 25,100 |
| Knox | 8,821,890 | 2,595 | 9,600 |
| Holt | 25,449,600 | 7,485 | 27,695 |
| Boyd | 1,694,700 | 498 | 1,844 |
| Rock | 4,191,240 | 1,233 | 4,561 |
| Keya Paha | 589,780 | 173 | 642 |
| Brown | 5,487,440 | 1,614 | 5,972 |
| Cherry | 1,777,570 | 523 | 1,934 |
| Sheridan | 2,848,320 | 838 | 3,100 |
| Dawes | 248,530 | 73 | 270 |
| SOUTH DAKOTA | | | |
| Gregory | 2,111,200 | 621 | 2,297 |
| Tripp | 1,231,400 | 362 | 1,340 |
| Todd | 410,400 | 121 | 447 |
| Bennett | 340,800 | 100 | 371 |
| Shannon | 16,200 | 5 | 18 |
| Total | 93,032,570 | 27,363 | 101,241 |

**Table 11.5**    Summary of Harvest—Nebraska/South Dakota Counties Along
CNW Northern Line, 1989:  Wheat

| State<br>County | Bushels<br>Harvested | Equivalent<br>Carloads | Equivalent<br>Trucks |
|---|---|---|---|
| NEBRASKA | | | |
| Madison | 14,820 | 5 | 17 |
| Antelope | 8,010 | 3 | 9 |
| Knox | 41,650 | 13 | 48 |
| Holt | 83,640 | 26 | 97 |
| Boyd | 44,030 | 14 | 51 |
| Rock | 9,900 | 3 | 11 |
| Keya Paha | 35,140 | 11 | 41 |
| Brown | 0 | 0 | 0 |
| Cherry | 17,600 | 6 | 20 |
| Sheridan | 1,719,900 | 537 | 1,989 |
| Dawes | 1,199,900 | 375 | 1,387 |
| SOUTH DAKOTA | | | |
| Gregory | 514,800 | 161 | 595 |
| Tripp | 2,057,850 | 643 | 2,379 |
| Todd | 193,200 | 60 | 223 |
| Bennett | 1,566,060 | 489 | 1,811 |
| Shannon | 682,500 | 213 | 789 |
| Total | 8,189,000 | 2,559 | 9,469 |

**Table 11.6**   Summary of Harvest—Nebraska/South Dakota Counties Along CNW Northern Line, 1989:  Total Crops

| State County | Bushels Harvested | Equivalent Carloads | Equivalent Trucks |
|---|---|---|---|
| NEBRASKA | | | |
| Madison | 17,104,850 | 5,071 | 18,763 |
| Antelope | 24,728,950 | 7,300 | 27,012 |
| Knox | 10,597,900 | 3,131 | 11,583 |
| Holt | 26,505,690 | 7,810 | 28,898 |
| Boyd | 2,242,180 | 662 | 2,451 |
| Rock | 4,250,540 | 1,251 | 4,630 |
| Keya Paha | 658,420 | 195 | 720 |
| Brown | 5,569,640 | 1,639 | 6,066 |
| Cherry | 1,857,190 | 547 | 2,025 |
| Sheridan | 5,065,920 | 1,524 | 5,640 |
| Dawes | 1,570,063 | 484 | 1,791 |
| SOUTH DAKOTA | | | |
| Gregory | 4,271,821 | 1,263 | 4,675 |
| Tripp | 4,302,600 | 1,289 | 4,770 |
| Todd | 639,500 | 192 | 709 |
| Bennett | 1,980,960 | 609 | 2,254 |
| Shannon | 729,300 | 226 | 837 |
| Total | 112,075,524 | 33,193 | 122,824 |

**Table 11.7**    Fertilizer Sold in the Impact Area During 1989

| State County | Estimated Total Tons Sold | Equivalent Carloads | Equivalent Trucks |
|---|---|---|---|
| NEBRASKA | | | |
| Madison | 34,043 | 358 | 1,362 |
| Antelope | 46,595 | 717 | 1,864 |
| Knox | 10,452 | 161 | 418 |
| Holt | 51,483 | 792 | 2,059 |
| Boyd | 2,501 | 38 | 100 |
| Rock | 0 | 0 | 0 |
| Keya Paha | 0 | 0 | 0 |
| Brown | 0 | 0 | 0 |
| Cherry | 0 | 0 | 0 |
| Sheridan | 0 | 0 | 0 |
| Dawes | 0 | 0 | 0 |
| SOUTH DAKOTA | | | |
| Gregory | N/A | N/A | N/A |
| Tripp | N/A | N/A | N/A |
| Todd | N/A | N/A | N/A |
| Bennett | N/A | N/A | N/A |
| Shannon | N/A | N/A | N/A |
| Total | 145,074 | 2,066 | 5,803 |

## TRAFFIC AND NETWORK ASSIGNMENT PROCEDURES

In the subterminal case study, farm-to-elevator flows were simulated with a spatial interaction model, while outbound elevator flows were distributed among markets using the trans-shipment algorithm. Only outbound elevator shipments are analyzed in the abandonment case study. Some abandonments may cause farmers to change elevators, bypassing elevators on the abandoned line in favor of more distant facilities with rail access. However, in most cases impacted elevators will market their grains through the closest large elevator with rail access. Thus, farm-to-elevator shipping patterns frequently remain the same after an abandonment. Typically, the major highway impacts of an abandonment result from the trans-shipment of grains from elevators located on the abandoned line to other railheads.

Because abandonment impact studies focus on outbound elevator shipments, the traffic and network assignment procedures are somewhat different than those used in the subterminal case study. This section of the chapter highlights the traffic and network assignment procedures. In addition, it documents the primary data sources utilized in the case study. Most of the data were derived from eight sources:

1.  Shipper surveys,
2.  Nebraska Department of Roads (DOR) Pavement Management System (PMS) file,
3.  Nebraska Highway Performance Monitoring System (HPMS) file,
4.  Nebraska highway and railroad maps,
5.  CNW company traffic data,
6.  CNW and BN tariffs,
7.  Nebraska railroad waybill sample, and the
8.  Nebraska DOR staff.

### Traffic Volumes

Railroads compile detailed traffic data for lines placed in category 1. These data are typically accessible by state transportation planners several months prior to the actual filing of an abandonment application. In the Nebraska case study, the CNW provided current and historical traffic data (by station) for the 1974–1990 period. The total carloads for each year were summarized in Table 11.1.

Railroad traffic data are important inputs to an abandonment impact study. However, they are usually insufficient to perform detailed highway impact assessments. Therefore, railroad company data must usually be supplemented by a shipper survey or secondary data sources.

A detailed set of shipper surveys was developed for the Nebraska study. The shipper surveys were primarily designed to obtain information regarding present and historical volumes, modal split, truck types, operating characteristics, commodities handled, terminal markets and trans-shipment points. A separate survey was designed for elevators (as opposed to other types of businesses).[13]

Both shipper survey and railroad company data were used to derive estimates of originated traffic volumes. Most of the large-volume shippers responded to the survey. Approximately two-thirds of the grain volume on the line was accounted for in the surveys. Since all traffic originated on the line during 1990 consisted of grains and oilseeds, it was relatively easy to compare shipper survey and railroad company data. Moreover, since the elevator surveys provided data on truck shipments, several key relationships could be established. These relationships were used to forecast truck and rail market shares and estimate the potential traffic that could be diverted from highways to railroads after rehabilitation.

The 1990 outbound rail volume reported in the survey (1,379 carloads) comprised 63 percent of the originated carloads reported by CNW (2,187) for the same year. The survey respondents also originated 4,900 truck loads in 1990. In tonnage, this is roughly the equivalent of 1,325 rail cars. Thus, the modal split in 1990 was approximately 49 percent. When the survey results were expanded to the population of elevators, it appeared that roughly 2,100 additional equivalent rail cars were originated along the line during 1990 (1,325/0.63). However, these shipments moved by truck instead of by rail. Much of the current truck traffic previously moved railroad, but was diverted as a result of declining service levels and poor car supply. Thus, much of it could probably be diverted back to the rail line after rehabilitation.

Because service was downgraded on the line in 1990, a three-year average (1988–1990) was used to project rail traffic volumes. The use of a multi-year average also tends to smooth out year-to-year fluctuations in grain productions and sales due to droughts and market conditions. From 1988 to 1990, an average of 2,808 carloads of traffic was originated on the line. A comparable three year average for terminated traffic is 1,366 cars.

## Traffic Distribution

In the subterminal case study, the farm-to-market grain flows were distributed among destinations using a spatial interaction model. A similar process was followed in the abandonment case study. Although the CNW provided originated traffic data, by station, the railroad did not identify the destination or market. The shippers were asked to provide detailed market and trans-shipping data in their surveys. In some cases, the data were specific and completely usable. In other cases, the answers were sketchy or incomplete. Thus, a third data source (the

Nebraska railroad waybill sample) was used to analyze markets for grains and oilseeds.

All major railroads must submit an annual waybill data file to the Interstate Commerce Commission. State transportation or public utility agencies may obtain state waybill files from the ICC. The state files contain traffic that originates in, terminates in, or passes through the state. The Nebraska DOR authorized the use of its 1987 and 1988 state waybill samples in the study. All of the traffic that originated or terminated on the Northern Line was identified from the state file, and the origin and destination Standard Point Location Codes were decoded so that the actual stations could be determined. Almost all of the shipping points on the line were reflected in the waybill sample. From these data, a history of recent rail markets and the distribution of traffic among markets was developed. Many of the markets listed by shippers appeared in the waybill file.[14]

Once the originated volumes were allocated among markets, the traffic was distributed between trans-shipping points and the terminal market. After abandonment, shippers will have two options: (1) truck their grain directly to terminal market, or (2) truck the grain to a nearby rail transhipping point. Many abandonment studies assume that the diverted traffic will be shipped to the closest railhead. However, some of the markets for northern Nebraska shippers (such as Omaha and Freemont) are located within the state. Consequently, some of the diverted traffic may be trucked directly to a terminal market. In addition, there are multiple railroads in the region, each having different markets and different degrees of market access. So, a given shipper may truck to more than one railhead or market.

In the survey, each shipper on the line was asked to identify the two most desirable railheads in the event of abandonment. Each shipper was also asked to identify each major market, and for each market, to project the distribution of diverted rail traffic among the two railheads and the terminal markets. Many of the surveys contained usable data. However, others were incomplete. Therefore, a alternative method of traffic distribution was devised.

The reader will recall that a general trans-shipping rule was introduced in equation (4.19). The rule states *if the sum of the cost of trucking the commodity to the railhead, the cost of double-handling and/or transloading the grain, and the rail rate to terminal market is less than the trucking rate, then the commodity will be trans-shipped.* Otherwise, it will be trucked directly to a market. The trans-shipping rule was used to augment shipper data and to complete the traffic distribution analysis.[15]

**Network Assignment**

Overall, the network assignment process used in the Nebraska study is analogous to the procedure employed in the grain subterminal study. In many cases, routes between origins and railheads and between origins and terminal markets were readily apparent. However, in some cases, several potential highway routes existed. In these instances, the shortest route that did not encompass minor collectors or local roads (except at the origin or destination) was selected. Again, it is reasonable to assume that truckers will take the shortest route except where highway service levels and conditions are relatively poor. In essence, truckers will minimize some generalized cost function, which includes both time and vehicle operating costs.

Several different methods of traffic distribution and network assignment have been described in this chapter. These techniques can be used individually or collectively to distribute rail traffic diverted by an abandonment. Transportation analysts typically have several options for a traffic distribution study. First, they can administer a shipper survey (as was done in the Nebraska case study), asking affected shippers to distribute the traffic among railheads and markets. Since shippers have detailed knowledge of markets and transportation conditions, this may be the preferred approach in abandonment impact studies. However, shipper estimates may be subjective. Furthermore, all shippers may not respond to the survey in a timely manner. Therefore, analysts may need alternative methods and data. One alternative is to use an operations research (OR) software package. Some OR packages will distribute traffic over a network in accordance with user-specified criteria (such as the shortest path or minimal cost path). Alternatively, a computer program could be written that utilizes the trans-shipping rule. Both options require substantial time and resources. Detailed data inputs must typically be developed for the OR software. Alternatively, building and testing a computer-based distribution model could take months. Typically, abandonment studies have to be performed under severe time constraints. For example, the Nebraska study had to be completed in 60 days to avoid a possible filing by the CNW. Thus, analysts must evaluate time and resource constraints when deciding whether to use a survey or develop a computer-based network model.

**Highway and Truck Weight Data**

The attributes of the impacted highway sections were derived from the Nebraska Pavement Management System (PMS) file. The PMS file contained two critical pavement variables: the depths of the pavement layers and the base. The strength rating of each highway section in the post-abandonment routed was computed with these variables.

Table 11.8 shows typical truck and axle weights for combination trucks. Both grain and dry fertilizers are transported almost exclusively in dry van 3S2 trucks. Farm machinery and lumber primarily utilize flat-bed trucks. Liquid fertilizer, sand, or gravel require specialized types of equipment that vary in weights.

**Table 11.8**     Gross Weights and Axle Loads for Major Commodities

| Commodity | Gross Weight | Net Weight | Gross Axle Weights | | |
|---|---|---|---|---|---|
| | | | Axle 1 | Axle 2 | Axle 3 |
| Grain | 80,000 | 26.7 | 12,000 | 34,000 | 34,000 |
| Liquid Fertilizers | 76,000 | 26 | 11,800 | 32,600 | 32,600 |
| Dry Fertilizers | 80,000 | 26 | 12,000 | 34,000 | 34,000 |
| Farm Machinery | 653,00 | 13.5 | 9,900 | 27,700 | 27,700 |
| Lumber | 46,700 | 24 | 7,100 | 19,800 | 19,800 |
| Sand & Gravel | 77,000 | 2,637 | 11,600 | 32,200 | 32,200 |

Source: North Dakota and Washington Truck Survey Data.

## HIGHWAY IMPACTS

This section highlights the analytic techniques used in the abandonment impact analysis.   First, it highlights the general costing approach and the categories of highway costs analyzed.   Second, it presents an overview of pavement analysis techniques. Third, it describes a methodology for estimating highway user costs. Fourth, it outlines the overall highway impact assessment.

**Background**

A substantial amount of traffic is currently moving by truck in the rail-line market area. Therefore, some existing highway costs could be avoided by shifting truck traffic back to the railroad. As mentioned in chapter 5, an incremental (or decremental) method may not accurately predict reductions in current pavement costs. Moreover, an incremental method may assign different costs to grain trucks diverted *from* highways (as a result of rail-line rehabilitation) than to the same class of trucks diverted *to* highways (as a result of abandonment). For these (and other reasons), an alternative approach was used.

Readers will recall that the incremental method computes both the build-sooner costs in the first replacement cycle as well as the long-run incremental cost of increasing the pavement thickness. The approach introduced in this chapter does not compute upgrading costs. Instead, an average pavement cost per ESAL is computed.

The two approaches are similar in some respects. Both methods relate increased pavement costs to increased ESALs. The upgrading method directly computes the change in pavement thickness required for the entire incremental traffic volume. In contrast, the first step in the average cost method is to calculate a pavement unit cost per ESAL. This unit cost is then multiplied by the current rail traffic (or the potential traffic diverted from highways) to estimate changes in pavement costs. Under the average cost approach, each class of traffic can be analyzed separately and the results added together. The same unit cost per ESAL is used for each class. For modest changes in traffic, the incremental and the average cost approaches should produce similar estimates of impacts.

Since build-sooner costs are SRIC, they not part of the average cost method. If the pavement thickness is allowed to vary, build-sooner costs will not exist in the long-run. However, if pavement thickness is not varied in response to increases in ESALs, then build-sooner costs will occur. In fact, build-sooner costs will accrue *until* the pavement is strengthened. A transportation agency's budget may be fixed in the short-run (due to lack of funds and multiyear capital improvement programs). Thus, the agency may not increase the pavement thickness when the first (or even the second) improvement is made. This situation poses a conceptual issue for abandonment impact analysis. The analyst must assume that the pavement will be varied in response to changes in ESALs. Otherwise, only build-sooner costs can be computed. One way of handling this apparent inconsistency is to compute build-sooner costs, but not allocate them to traffic. This is the approach taken in the Nebraska study. Build-sooner costs are computed for illustrative purposes (i.e. to alert the transportation agency to the costs they could face if they do not take action) However, they are not used to assess highway user fees or impact charges. Furthermore, they are not allocated to truck traffic in computing annual unit costs.

Another potential cost of abandonment is an increase in highway user costs. Highway user costs were not analyzed in the subterminal case study, since most of the truck hauls were less than 30 miles, many of them over lightly-trafficked roads. However, U.S. 20 (across northern Nebraska) is a major automobile route through the state. With truck hauls in excess of 100 miles (after abandonment), significant highway user impacts may result. Consequently, user cost were included in the abandonment study.

The three classes of highway costs were computed for two traffic levels. The first level (4,174 carloads) represents the average traffic handled on the rail line during the last three years of operation. The second level (6,274 carloads) includes the 2,100 carloads of grain that moved by truck in 1990 but that shippers would commit to shipping by rail under good service conditions. All highway impacts were calculated for a twenty-five year period. At the time of the analysis, the state of Nebraska was negotiating with the CNW for purchase of the line. The proposed acquisition and rehabilitation costs were to be amortized over twenty-five years. Thus, twenty–five years was selected as the time frame for the benefit–cost study. This period typically encompasses one or two replacement cycles.

## Net Pavement Costs

Truck traffic diverted from rail lines to highways usually generates additional user fees. Similarly, the diversion of traffic from highways to railroads typically reduces highway user fees.

Much of the subterminal impact analysis focused on farm-to-elevator flows. Farmers typically avoid some motor fuel taxes through exemptions for on-farm fuel use. Furthermore, due to the age and assessed value of farm trucks, farmers typically pay only minimal registration fees. Thus, highway user fees were not a significant factor in the subterminal case study. However, commercial truck hauls of over 100 miles (such as in the Nebraska case study) can generate significant fuel tax revenues. Therefore, in abandonment studies, it is usually necessary for the analyst to compute the change in truck user fees. If several classes of vehicles or commodities are involved, highway revenues and costs should be computed for each group.[16] Then, the net cost should be computed by crediting the vehicle registration and motor fuel tax revenues against the pavement impacts. If the incremental revenues are equal to the incremental highway costs, then other highway users and taxpayers are no worse off than before (from a highway infrastructure perspective). Furthermore, if the incremental revenues exceed the highway costs, then there has been a net gain to society. However, if the incremental revenues do not cover the additional costs, then other highway users (and society in general) will have been made worse-off by the abandonment.

The additional resource costs, as noted above, are the variable cost of the overlay or reconstruction. These pavement costs are allocated to all classes of traffic on an ESAL-mile basis. Every ESAL is treated the same in this approach, regardless of whether it is old or new traffic. Thus, a grain truck currently on the highway that would move by rail after the line is upgraded is treated the same as a potential grain truck that would be added to the traffic stream if the line is abandoned. However, not all pavement deterioration costs are allocated to traffic under an average cost approach. To some extent, pavements will deteriorate as a function of time. A natural decay process (not used in the subterminal study) is used to model time-related pavement deterioration. The decline of highway serviceability resulting from time (in the absence of traffic) is isolated and removed from the cost base. Such a model was unnecessary in the subterminal impact analysis because time and environmental costs were already recovered by the baseline traffic.

**Analytic Procedures**

A highway will deteriorate over time in the absence of traffic (as a result of natural decay). The shape of the decay curve is unknown, but Figure 11.2 depicts a likely form for the function (negative exponential). The negative exponential function suggests that pavement condition declines rapidly when initially exposed to the elements, but then deteriorates at a decreasing rate over time. This type of decay process seems to characterize many natural and man-made phenomena, not just highways.

**Figure 11.2**    (Hypothetical) Natural Pavement Decay Process

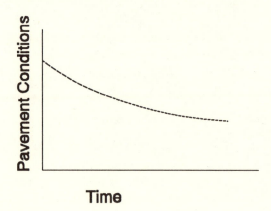

The purpose of a decay model is to simulate the decline in pavement serviceability resulting from climatic and natural forces in the absence of significant traffic levels. In contrast, the purpose of a damage model is to predict the decline in serviceability resulting from axle passes. In the Nebraska study, both models were applied simultaneously to each highway section. When the present serviceability rating (PSR) of a section reached a threshold level, either a resurfacing or reconstruction activity was simulated. Sometimes the activity was triggered by natural decay processes rather than by traffic. This happened on lightly trafficked sections. However, in many instances, the replacement activity was triggered by traffic (e.g., the damage model).

Which model triggers the simulated activity is of no concern to the calculation of build–sooner costs. Build-sooner costs are computed by comparing a base case (reflecting existing traffic levels) to an impact scenario (reflecting the incremental traffic). If the decay model triggers the activity, then the time of the simulated replacement activity under the base case and the impact scenario will be identical. Thus, build-sooner costs will be zero. On the other hand, if the damage model triggers a resurfacing or reconstruction act, then the time at which the activity occurs will be shifted forward. In this case, the build-sooner costs will be positive.

Net resource costs must be handled differently than build-sooner costs. Not all of the responsibility for a resurfacing or reconstruction event can be attributed to traffic. Only the variable component or resource costs can be allocated to trucks. As an example, suppose that the damage model predicts a resurfacing event in 2011. Further suppose that the decay model predicts a decline in PSR from 4.5 to 3.5 over this period, while the damage model predicts a decline from 4.5 to 3.0 (the optimal resurfacing PSR). In essence, the stand-alone decay model has predicted that the serviceability of the highway section will decline by one third regardless of the traffic level. This portion of the consumption of pavement life cannot be attributed to traffic. So, it must be removed from the replacement cost base allocated to highway users.

Two variables must be estimated before the decay model can be operationalized. The first is the annual rate of decay. As equation (11.1) illustrates, the annual rate of natural decay is affected by two factors: the maximum feasible life of a pavement and the remaining pavement life. The annual decay rate ($DR$) is inversely related to maximum feasible life ($MaxLife$), and directly related to the proportion of pavement life previously consumed ($P_t/P_o$). Table 11.9 illustrates maximum feasible pavement lives for types of highways.

$$DR = -(LOG\ (P_t\ /\ P_o\ )\ /\ MaxLife) \qquad (11.1)$$

**Table 11.9**     Maximum Feasible Pavement Lives

| Type of Pavement | Pavement Section | | |
|---|---|---|---|
| | Heavy | Medium | Light |
| Flexible | 35 | 30 | 25 |
| Rigid | 40 | 35 | 30 |

Source: FHWA, 1986

Once computed, the annual rate function is used to forecast the PSR at the end of a typical design life (n). The calculation of this value (referred to as $PSR_e$) is illustrated in equation (11.2).

$$PSR_e = P_o\, e^{\,(-DR \cdot 20)} \qquad\qquad (11.2)$$

Next, the total decline in PSR is estimated based on the original design PSR and the terminal PSR. Then, the time-related decline in PSR is computed. Using these two values, the proportion of PSR loss attributable to traffic is computed as follows:

$$TPSR = 1.0 - \frac{\Delta ESPR}{\Delta PSR} \qquad\qquad (11.3)$$

where:

$TPSR$ = Proportion of PSR loss due to traffic
$EPSR$ = Loss in PSR due to natural decay
$PSR$ = Total loss in PSR

The following example will illustrate the process. Suppose that the cost per mile to resurface the highway section in question is $250,000, and the computed values of TPSR and EPSR are 1.5 and 1.0, respectively. Then, 33 percent of the highway resurfacing costs (or $75,000) is allocated to traffic. In an actual analysis, this value would be divided by the ESAL life of the highway to compute a unit cost per ESAL. The remainder is not allocated to any group, but is assumed to constitute the baseline cost of providing the highway capacity.

As illustrated in chapter 5, the HPMS function yields results consistent with the revised FHWA formula. Since the HPMS is function is based on the AASHTO equations, its form and function are familiar to many highway engineers. The reader will recall that the primary difference between the two models relates to truck tire pressures. However, the results of the HPMS function can be empirically adjusted to account for truck tire factors. Recall from chapter 5 that moving from 75 to 100 psi on a typical low-volume asphaltic highway reduces pavement life by 7 percent. This prediction is consistent with other empirical evaluations (See TRB, 1990). Nebraska highway engineers typically employ a 10 percent adjustment factor. The lower of the two values (the 7 percent factor) was used in the case study.

## Incremental Revenues

Motor fuel tax revenues are a function of the incremental VMT, the fuel efficiency of the vehicle, and the motor fuel tax. At the time of the analysis, the motor fuel tax in Nebraska was 26.67 cents a gallon. At an average consumption rate of five miles a gallon, each incremental truck VMT would generate approximately 10.7 cents in new revenue. The average motor vehicle registration fee in Nebraska at the time of the study was $816. Thus, for every additional truck needed to handle the diverted traffic (in terms of annual capacity), $816 in incremental revenues would be generated.

Before incremental truck revenues can be estimated, the number of (equivalent) trucks (or truck capacity) must be computed. The truck capacity required to transport the diverted traffic depends primarily on two factors: (1) the diverted volume (in terms of equivalent truck loads), and (2) the average time required per round trip. The round trip time, in turn, depends on the mileage, the average operating speed, layovers, and loading and unloading times. Round trip time was computed as follows. The round-trip distance on non-interstate rural highways was divided by the average operating speed. This yields the theoretical running time for a team–driver operation. However, most grain truckers are owner-operators or small firms. A single driver typically accomplishes the over-the-road service for a given movement. To account for mandatory layovers, the theoretical running time is divided by ten (the maximum allowable hours of continuous operation). After ten hours of operation, each driver must (presumably) rest a minimum of eight hours before commencing further operations. Thus, to simulate layovers, eight hours have been added to each ten-hour interval. The sum of the estimated road time plus layovers constitutes the running portion of the estimated round-trip time. The average time at origin and destination is more difficult to model. In the Nebraska study, the time required to load a 3S2 truck at origin was obtained from the grain elevator survey. Elevator managers are usually observant of the loading times at origin, since excessive loading times may generate queues.

Three additional steps were required to calculate incremental registration fees. First, the number of active truck days a year (280) was divided by the average trip time to determine the average number of trips a year that each truck serving the elevators could make. Second, the incremental truck capacity (the number of equivalent trucks required) was computed by dividing the diverted truck loads by the average trips a year. Third, the number of equivalent trucks was multiplied by the average vehicle registration fee to estimate the additional revenues generated (from registration fees).

## Highway User Costs

User costs are heavily influenced by the service levels of highways. The major elements of highway service levels impacted by abandonments are: (1) pavement performance, and (2) capacity. Pavement performance refers to the capability of a highway section to provide a safe, comfortable, and economical ride at or close to the design speed. As pavement performance declines, highway user costs increase. Surface irregularities and roughness (such as rutting and cracking) typically grow in frequency and magnitude as maintenance and resurfacing activities diminish. As a result, the vibrations and oscillations of a vehicle's frame and parts increase. These forces tend to increase normal maintenance costs for the life of the vehicle. In addition, poor pavement performance reduces the life expectancy of vehicles and hastens their replacement. Pavement roughness and irregularities can also increase the vertical and lateral motion of a vehicle along its path of movement. Vertical and lateral motions tend to increase both wind and rolling resistance, requiring more fuel to traverse a given distance at a particular speed.

Highway users may react to poor pavement performance in several ways. As the discomfort associated with rougher rides mounts, travelers may reduce their operating speeds. To the extent that speeds are significantly reduced below the legal level, highway users will face higher opportunity costs.[17]

User costs may also rise due to capacity constraints. Each highway section has a throughput capacity (in terms of vehicles per lane per hour), which is a function of the design speed. As the ratio of existing to maximum utilization increases, vehicle speeds decline. When speeds decline, fuel costs and air pollution tend to increase. Furthermore, travelers incur the costs associated with lost time (as in the case of poor pavement performance).

Changes in highway user costs in the Nebraska study were estimated from equations given by Balta and Markow (1985).[18] The functions were derived through simulations of the computer model EAROMAR.[19] EAROMAR simulates a roadway system in considerable detail (including its structured design, capacity, and traffic characteristics). The model generates estimates of user costs at different levels of capacity traffic mix. The user costs generated by EAROMAR include travel time and vehicle operating costs. The vehicle operating costs include fuel, oil, and tire consumption. However, the model does not simulate accelerated repairs and vehicle replacement. So, the user costs presented in the case study are conservative in nature. The function for estimating annual user costs is:

$$UC = 3.03^6 - 0.212 \; PSR + 1.139 \times 10^{-36} \times ESAL^6 \qquad\qquad (11.4)$$

where:

$$
\begin{array}{lll}
UC & = & \text{Annual user costs} \\
PSR & = & \text{Present serviceability rating} \\
ESAL & = & \text{Annual ESALs}
\end{array}
$$

Changes in user costs were estimated in the following manner. The costs were computed for each year of the twenty–five–year analysis period for the base case and the impact scenario. Since the PSR will probably change during each year of the analysis period, the term $UC$ could assume a unique value for each year. So, in order to compute the change in user costs, each cost stream was translated into present value. The difference between the present value of user costs under the base-case and the impact scenario measures the change in user costs during the analysis period.

In summary, the major concepts presented in this section are:

- The incremental revenues generated by heavy truck traffic on low-volume roads may not cover the incremental pavement costs.

- If a shortfall occurs, funds may have to be diverted from an alternative use, or new user fees and taxes will have to be implemented.

- The ability of the transportation agency to adjust user fees or develop new sources of highway funds is constrained by broader sociopolitical trends and values.

- If funds are constrained and the diversion of monies (or new user fees) is not practical, then the level of highway services may decline.

- A decline in highway serviceability may lead to increased user costs for repairs, replacement, fuel, and lost time.

## Overview of the Highway Impact Assessment Procedures

In the preceding discussion, a set of pavement deterioration, revenue, and user cost procedures was introduced. This section of the chapter presents an integrated overview of the highway impact assessment process employed in the abandonment case study. The reader will notice many similarities between this overview and the subterminal highway impact assessment process described in chapter 6. However, there are some important differences.

The key steps in the abandonment impact assessment process are summarized in the following list.

1. The number of potentially-diverted rail cars of each type of commodity are estimated;
2. The most frequently-used truck types are determined for each major commodity;
3. The number of equivalent trucks required to handle one diverted rail car is estimated for each major commodity and truck type;
4. The gross and tare weights of each truck type, and the tare and gross axle weights for each axle group are determined;
5. Truck routes and mileages to each major market are compiled;
6. The primary routes to each potential alternate rail transloading facility (*railhead*) are identified;
7. The diverted traffic is routed over the highways;
8. The attributes of each highway section in each route are compiled (e.g. structural design rating, present condition, current traffic, etc.);
9. The existing truck traffic base is identified from transportation agency's files;
10. The base-case ESALs are computed for each highway section;
11. The incremental ESALs resulting from the diverted traffic stream are computed for each highway section;
12. Future resurfacing and/or reconstruction events are predicted for each section under the status quo and impact scenarios;
13. The cost of each resurfacing or reconstruction event is estimated for each section under both scenarios based on transportation agency's unit costs and the thickness of the overlay (optional);

14. The future highway costs incurred under both scenarios are expressed in present dollars;
15. Build-sooner costs are computed (optional);
16. The life of each highway section is estimated in ESALs;
17. The proportion of highway deterioration attributable to time and natural decay rather than to traffic is determined and deducted;
18. The proportion of remaining highway deterioration attributable to truck traffic (ESALs) is multiplied by the resurfacing or reconstruction cost for each section to estimate the costs of the resources consumed by this traffic;
19. The number of vehicle miles of travel (VMT) and truck capacity required to transport the diverted commodities are estimated;
20. The additional motor fuel taxes and vehicle registration fees generated by the diverted traffic are computed;
21. The difference between these revenues and the additional highway costs generated by the diverted traffic are calculated;
22. The difference is treated as either a credit against accelerated replacement costs if the additional revenues exceed the additional costs or a cost to other highway users and society if they do not;
23. The present value of highway user costs are computed for the status quo and the impact scenarios;
24. The difference between the two scenarios becomes a change in user costs.

Steps 12, 13 and 15 relate only to build-sooner costs. Thus, they are optional in abandonment impact studies. As noted previously, build-sooner costs should be excluded from truck impact costs or user fee calculations.

## QUANTIFICATION OF HIGHWAY COSTS

The preceding part of the chapter highlighted the specific analytic techniques utilized in the abandonment case study. This section illustrates the computations involved and highlights the findings. The section begins with a discussion of three major budgetary scenarios analyzed in the case study.

### Scenarios

Build-sooner, pavement, and highway user costs are computed under three different budgetary scenarios. The first scenario reflects an unconstrained highway budget. Under this scenario, the DOR will resurface a highway section when the Pavement Serviceability Rating (PSR) drops to 3.0.[20] The second budgetary scenario assumes that all highway sections will be resurfaced at or prior to a PSR of 2.0 (or 2.5 for interstates and freeways). This threshold is known as the *critical* PSR. Beyond this level, pavements will have to be reconstructed at a higher cost per mile. Although the life of a highway section has not completely expired at a PSR of 2.0, this level is usually interpreted as the practical lifetime of a section. Below 2.0, the quality of the ride declines rapidly and routine maintenance and user costs accelerate. Consequently, the period of decline in PSR from 4.5 to 2.0 is interpreted as the maximum economic life of a section by highway analysts. The third scenario (reconstruction) typically reflects a severe budgetary constraint and resulting failure to catch the pavement when resurfacing was still possible. Instead, the PSR is allowed to decline from 4.5 to 1.8 (or 2.0 for interstate highways).

## Build–Sooner Costs

Under the first budgetary scenario (optimal resurfacing) the Nebraska DOR could face $13 million in build-sooner costs during the impact period if the agency is unable to strengthen impacted pavements during the first or second improvement cycle (Table 11.10). These costs only reflect the current rail traffic level. If the rail line is retained and rehabilitated, shippers are likely to consign another 2,100 equivalent rail carloads currently moving by truck. If this occurs, the build-sooner costs could increase to $16 million (Table 11.11).

**Table 11.10**    Build-Sooner Costs for Twenty-Five Years (4,174 Carloads)

(Millions of Dollars)

| Budgetary Scenario | Present Value of Status Quo Needs | Present Value of Impact Case Needs | Build–Sooner Costs |
|:---:|:---:|:---:|:---:|
| 1 | $274.084 | $287.093 | $13.009 |
| 2 | $379.653 | $425.261 | $35.608 |
| 3 | $410.826 | $463.984 | $52.435 |

If the Nebraska DOR allows highways to deteriorate to the critical PSR before rehabilitating them, build-sooner costs could increase substantially. If the PSR declines below 2.0, then pavements will have to be fully reconstructed.

**Table 11.11**   Build–Sooner Costs for Twenty-Five Years (6,274 Carloads)

| | (Millions of Dollars) | | |
|---|---|---|---|
| Budgetary Scenario | Present Value of Status Quo Needs | Present Value of Impact Case Needs | Build–Sooner Costs |
| 1 | $274.084 | $290.036 | $15.952 |
| 2 | $379.653 | $417.649 | $37.996 |
| 3 | $410.826 | $470.227 | $59.401 |

Reconstruction costs are nearly double that of an overlay. Thus, under budgetary scenario 3, build-sooner costs could increase even more.

## Net Pavement Costs

If the CNW rail line is abandoned, 15,444 new CO-5AX trucks will be added to the traffic stream. This new stream will result in a nominal pavement resource cost of $95 million over twenty–five years. This is a net figure. The additional revenues generated from truck fuel taxes and registration fees have already been deducted from this total. This figure translates into an annual equivalent cost of nearly $3.5 million as shown in Table 11.12. Alternatively, if the rail line is rehabilitated, an additional 7,700 CO-5AX trucks may be removed from the existing traffic base. If this occurs, the total avoided pavement costs will exceed $5 million a year (Table 11.13).

**Table 11.12**   Annual Net Pavement Costs for 4,174 Carloads

| Annual Fuel Revenues | Annual Registration Fees | Annual Pavement Cost | Annual Net Resource Cost |
|---|---|---|---|
| $184,723 | $141,984 | $3,812,248 | $3,485,541 |

**Table 11.13**    Annual Net Pavement Costs for 6,274 Carloads

| Annual Fuel Revenues | Annual Registration Fees | Annual Pavement Cost | Annual Net Resource Cost |
|---|---|---|---|
| $275,597 | $212,976 | $5,733,345 | $5,244,722 |

## Highway User Costs

Highway user costs are projected to increase by approximately $3.5 million over twenty–five years. An additional $.382 million in highway user costs will be avoided if the line is rehabilitated and draws additional truck traffic from highways in the area. These avoidable highway costs are shown in Table 11.14 and Table 11.15.

**Table 11.14**    Highway User Costs for 4,174 Carloads

(Millions of Dollars)

| Budgetary Scenario | Status Quo User Costs | Impact Case User Costs | Change In User Costs | Annual Increase In User Costs |
|---|---|---|---|---|
| 1 | $58.431 | $61.944 | $3.513 | $ 0.14052 |
| 2 | $62.020 | $64.814 | $2.794 | $ 0.11176 |
| 3 | $62.595 | $65.219 | $2.624 | $ 0.10496 |

**Table 11.15**     Highway User Costs for 6,274 Carloads

| Budgetary Scenario | Base Case User Costs | Impact Case User Costs | Change In User Costs | Annual Equivalent Net User Costs |
|:---:|:---:|:---:|:---:|:---:|
| 1 | $58.431 | $62.326 | $ 3.895 | $ 0.15580 |
| 2 | $62.020 | $65.226 | $ 3.206 | $ 0.12824 |
| 3 | $62.595 | $65.817 | $ 3.222 | $ 0.12888 |

## Comparison of Results with Other Studies

This section of the chapter compares the results of the Nebraska analysis to recent heavy truck studies in other states.    The intent is to assess the reasonableness of the results and define a range of likely highway impacts. The California Department of Transportation (1990) recently found that the incremental maintenance cost per *heavy* truck mile was $3.73, or approximately 11.3 cents per ton-mile. In a Washington Department of Transportation study, Casavant and Lenzi (1989) quantified the incremental pavement costs of four abandonment case studies. In these studies, the incremental costs ranged from 2 cents per ton-mile to 9 cents per ton-mile, with a mean value of 7.5 cents per ton-mile. In the Nebraska study, the projected incremental pavement (net resource cost) that would result from abandonment was approximately 2.5 cents per ton-mile.[21] This value falls into the range of impacts identified by Casavant and Lenzi, towards the lower end of the range.

This chapter has illustrated the use of highway impact assessment procedures in railroad abandonment cases.   Analysts can replicate many of the analytic techniques and data sources used in the Nebraska analysis. In the concluding chapter, some typical ranges of impacts and analytical issues are discussed.

**NOTES**

1. This statistic was computed from Schedule 720 of the railroads' R-1 reports to the Interstate Commerce Commission.

2. Journal of Commerce, November 20, 1991.

3. An approximate ratio for converting rail covered hopper cars to grain semi trucks is 3.7.

4. See 49 CFR Part 1151.10 and Part 1152.11.

5. See 49 CFR Part 1152.10(b)(1).

6. See Washington State Rail Plan, 1991.

7. See FRA (1977)

8. See AB-33 Sub No. 42.

9. For recent examples of rail planning studies see *Washington State Rail Plan* (1991) and *Preliminary Analysis of CNW's Nebraska Rail Line, (1991)*.

10. Computed from Nebraska pavement management system file.

11. See *Preliminary Analysis of CNW's Nebraska Rail Line,* Tolliver, Denver and Transportation Operations Inc., UGPTI Publication 85, February, 1991.

12. The sources of these data are *Nebraska Agricultural Statistics* and *South Dakota Agricultural Statistics*, 1989.

13. Where the shipper surveys provided usable data that could be verified as reasonable, this information became the primary inputs to the traffic and highway routing procedures. All elevator survey data and much of the general business survey data were reviewed and cross-checked against the storage and throughput capacities shown in Table 11.2 to determine if the values appeared reasonable. All traffic forecasts for future years were compared to historical data in an effort to identify unusual relationships. Other cross-checks and evaluations were also employed.

14. The process of allocating the originated grain volumes among markets is as follows. Default distribution percentages were computed for each station from waybill data. If the shipper surveys contained usable market data, this information

was used to override the default distribution percentages computed from the waybill file. Thus, the distribution of outbound volumes among markets reflected survey data from many of the large shippers. In all cases, the distribution was based on actual data and percentages.

15. The average cost of double handling grain and grain trucking costs per mile were derived from previous studies by Taylor and Casavant (1988) and Tolliver (1989). The railroad rates used in the equation were derived from CNW, BN, and UP tariffs.

16. Vehicle registration fees may vary with the type and age of truck, operating weight, and sometimes distance. Moreover, fuel efficiency may vary among truck types. Therefore, it is advisable to compute separate user fee unit costs for each vehicle class.

17. Each highway user has alternative uses for the time spent in a vehicle (whether it be leisure or income-generating uses). Thus, each highway user has an opportunity cost associated with his or her travel time. Consequently, as trip times increase, so do user opportunity costs.

18. Balta, W.S. and M.J. Markow. *Demand Responsive Approach to Highway Maintenance and Rehabilitation, Vol. 2*, U.S. Department of Transportation Report #DOT/OST/P-34/871054, Washington, D.C. June 1985.

19. For a description of EAROMAR, see M.J. Markow and B. Brademeyer, *Modification of the System EAROMAR*, FHWA Report DOT-FH-11-9350, Washington, D.C. 1981.

20. The PSR is a pavement serviceability rating that theoretically ranges from zero to five. A PSR of 5.0 denotes a newly-built or reconstructed highway. A PSR from 4.0 to 4.9 denotes a highway section in very good condition. A PSR in the 3.0 to 3.9 range is considered good. A PSR from 2.0 to 2.9 is considered fair, while a PSR from 1.0 to 1.9 is considered poor. A PSR below 1.0 denotes a poor highway section. Historically, state DOT's have resurfaced or rebuilt major highways when the PSR reaches a level of 2.5. The trigger PSR has historically been 2.0 for other classes of highways.

21. This figure reflects the net pavement costs divided by the total ton-miles accumulated during the twenty–five year period. If build-sooner costs are added to the net resource costs, the total becomes approximately 3 cents per ton-mile. Although build-sooner costs cannot be allocated to traffic using an average cost method, they are still relevant to the DOR's decision to acquire and rehabilitate the line.

# 12

# Conclusions and Sensitivity Analysis

An average cost procedure was introduced in chapter 11 that can be used to project the impacts of various transportation or land-use changes. In this chapter, some general impacts and sensitivity analysis are presented. In conclusion, some major concepts and issues are reviewed.

## GENERAL IMPACT AND SENSITIVITY ANALYSIS

In both the abandonment and subterminal case studies, detailed network models of highway routes were developed. In addition, the specific attributes of each highway section (e.g. SN and PSR) were developed from PMS data. In both cases, the process required a substantial amount of time and resources. Time and costs are luxuries that analysts may not be able to afford. In some instances, "ballpark" estimates of impacts may be sufficient for preliminary discussion and decision-making. Thus, a general scale of impacts may prove useful to transportation analysts.

The models described in chapter 11 were used to simulate average costs for three classes of rural highways. Table 12.1 lists some typical highway attributes for rural principal arterials (other than interstate), minor arterials, and major collector highways. These attributes were used to estimate unit costs per ton-mile for three different structural designs: high, medium, and low. A typical design period (n) of twenty years was used to simulate the annual rate of time-related pavement decay.

The results of the simulation are shown in Table 12.2. The resurfacing costs per mile used in the calculations are shown in Column (b) while the average costs per ton-mile are shown in columns (c), (d), and (e) for a high, medium, and low structural design, respectively. As the table shows, the cost per ton-mile increases within a given functional class as the structural design moves from high to low. The costs per ton-mile are highest for collector highways because of lower design standards and maximum pavement lives.

Table 12.3 better illustrates the sensitivity of pavement impacts to changes in structural design. This simulation focuses on a rural minor arterial with an assumed maximum feasible life of 30 years. The effects are graphically illustrated in Figure 12.1. As Figure 12.1 shows, the cost per ton-mile declines sharply over the range of SN values.

**Table 12.1**    Typical Highway Attributes for Rural Functional Classes

| Functional Class | $PSR_t$ | $P_o$ | Maximum Pavement Life |
|---|---|---|---|
| Principal Arterials | 2.5 | 4.2 | 3.0 |
| Minor Arterials | 2.0 | 4.2 | 3.0 |
| Major Collector | 2.0 | 4.2 | 2.5 |

**Table 12.2**    Cost Per Ton-Mile (cents) for Rural Functional Class by Design Level

| | Replacement Cost/Mile per $000 | Cost per Ton-Mile (cents) Structural Design | | |
|---|---|---|---|---|
| | | High | Medium | Low |
| Principle Arterials | 150 | 2.1 | 5.4 | 12.7 |
| Minor Arterials | 125 | 2.8 | 7.2 | 14.0 |
| Major Collector | 100 | 5.1 | 9.8 | 16.7 |

**Table 12.3**    Sensitivity of Impacts to Changes in Structural Design

| Strength Rating | Cost per ESAL ($) | Cost per Ton-Mile ($) |
|---|---|---|
| 3.2 | 0.314 | 0.028 |
| 2.5 | 0.817 | 0.072 |
| 2.0 | 1.582 | 0.14 |
| 1.5 | 2.698 | 9.238 |

**Figure 12.1**    Cost per Ton-Mile for a Range of Structural Numbers

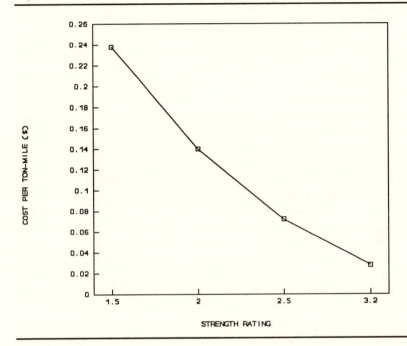

## CONCLUSION

In the preceding eleven chapters, the highway impact assessment process was described and illustrated. Two different case studies were used to illustrate the techniques. The grain subterminal example introduced in chapter 3 represents a major rural land-use change. Many western and midwestern states have experienced elevator restructuring and the location of grain subterminals during the last two decades. Further restructuring of the elevator industry is likely. As illustrated in chapter 10, the construction of a single facility can result in over $10 million of incremental highway costs. In the Devils Lake case study, only one satellite elevator was located on a collector highway. In cases where several substations are located on collector highways, the results could be much worse. The railroad abandonment example introduced in chapter 11 represents a major change in the freight transportation network. Over 30,000 miles of rail line were abandoned between 1980 and 1988.[1] Furthermore, as pointed-out in chapter 11, over 60,000 miles of light-density track remain. Thus, many more abandonments can be anticipated in rural and agricultural areas. As the Nebraska case study illustrated, the highway costs of a major line abandonment can be substantial. Instead of one grain elevator, many facilities can be affected. Furthermore, the trans-shipment distances can be substantially greater than in the subterminal example.

Although different, there are many similarities between the two case studies. The same highway impact assessment process was utilized in both instances. The grain subterminal example was ideal for fully illustrating the land-use and traffic distribution techniques. The subterminal example is complex, generating five types of grain flows and many effects and cross–effects. Fortunately, the land-use and traffic distribution studies are typically more straightforward in abandonment cases. The major traffic allocation question is where on-line businesses will trans-ship to a nearby railhead or to a terminal market. The trans-shipping decision rule presented in equation (4.19) can be used to make this allocation.

The major analytic differences between the two case studies relate to the pavement deterioration model and the highway costing techniques used. The revised FHWA pavement damage model was used in the subterminal case study. This is a promising but largely untested damage function. The major advantages of this model over the HPMS function are the truck tire pressure and subgrade support variables it includes. However, as illustrated in chapter 5, the TTI model is relatively insensitive to moderate changes in the subgrade modulus. This finding is consistent with the results of a recent TRB study (1989). The TRB concluded that except for extreme cases, changes in environmental factors will have little effect on pavement rehabilitation costs.[2] Although the HPMS damage function does not include a tire pressure parameter, the output of the model can be empirically adjusted to reflect 100 psi radial tires. The TRB (1989) estimates that higher truck tire pressures will reduce pavement life by 10 percent.

In the Nebraska study, a natural pavement decay function was introduced. The purpose of the function is to account for time–related or natural decay of highways. In the Nebraska study, the effects of traffic and time on pavement deterioration were projected independently. The proportion of pavement deterioration attributable to time (as opposed to traffic) was removed from the highway cost base. The simultaneous modeling of natural decay and pavement damage represents an improvement over the methods described in chapter 5. However, even this technique treats the effects of time and traffic independently. In reality, there is an interactive effect that compounds pavement deterioration. Further advances in pavement deterioration analysis will undoubtedly address this concern. As noted previously, any pavement deterioration model can be substituted for the HPMS or FHWA functions. The overall process of highway impact assessment will remain the same. The other major difference between the two case studies relates to the costing approach.

An average cost approach was used in the abandonment case study, whereas an incremental cost approach was employed in the subterminal analysis. There is no right or wrong approach per se. However, the method chosen should reflect the objectives of the analysis. In some cases, the relevant impacts will be purely incremental in nature. In other instances, cost responsibilities and user fees will be important issues.

## NOTES

1. Klindworth and Batson, 1991.

2. See *Access for Large Trucks*, Appendix F, 1989.

# Appendix

## TRAFFIC EQUIVALENCY FACTORS

This appendix presents the AASHO axle equivalency formulas for single and tandem axles, and the axle equivalency formula that was used in the updated FHWA model. The AASHO formula (for flexible pavements) for single axles is given by:

$$LOG_{10}\left(\frac{N_r}{N_x}\right) = 4.79\ LOG_{10}(L_x + 1) - 4.79 \times LOG_{10}(L_r + 1) + \frac{G}{\beta_r} - \frac{G}{\beta_x}$$

$$(A.1)$$

where:

$$LOG_{10}(N_r/N_x) = \text{log of the traffic equivalency factor}$$

$$G = LOG_{10}[(P_i - P)/(P_i - P_t)]$$

$$L_r = \text{reference axle weight (kips)}$$

$$L_x = \text{axle weight (kips)}$$

$\beta_r$ and $\beta_x$ are computed in accordance with equation (5.19) in chapter 3.

The AASHO formula for tandem axle (on flexible pavements) is given by:

$$LOG_{10}\left(\frac{N_r}{N_x}\right) = 4.79\,LOG_{10}(L_x + 2) - 4.79\,LOG_{10}(L_r + 1)$$
$$- 4.33 \times LOG_{10}(2) + \frac{G}{\beta_r} - \frac{G}{\beta_x} \tag{A.2}$$

The AASHO formulas for rigid pavements are given in Langsner, Huff, and Liddle (1962).

The load equivalence formula used in the updated FHWA model is given by:

$$LE_x = \left(\frac{\tau_{18}}{\tau_x}\right)\left(-\ln\frac{g}{c}\right)^{EXP} \tag{A.3}$$

where:

$$\tau_x = \text{computed value of } \tau \text{ for axle of interest}$$

$$c = \frac{(P_i - P_f)}{(P_i - P_t)} \tag{A.4}$$

$$g = \frac{(P_i - P)}{(P_i - P_t)} \tag{A.5}$$

$$EXP = \frac{1}{\beta_x} - \frac{1}{\beta_r} \tag{A.6}$$

# Bibliography

Afiesimama, B.T., and A. Garcia-Diaz. "A Model for Evaluating Rehabilitation Costs of Flexible Pavement Under Different Climatic Conditions." Paper presented at the 67th Annual Meeting of the Transportation Research Board, Washington D.C., January 1988.

American Association of State Highway Officials. *AASHO Interim Guide for Design of Pavement Structures*. Washington, D.C., 1986.

American Association of State Highway Officials. *A Policy on Geometric Design of Highways and Streets*. Washington, D.C., 1984.

American Association of State Highway Officials. "The AASHO Road Test." *HRB Special Report 73*. Washington, D.C.: National Academy of Sciences, 1962.

Balta, W. S., and M. J. Markow. *Demand Responsive Approach to Highway Maintenance and Rehabilitation*. USDOT Report No. DOT/OST/P–34/87/054. June 1985.

Bartelsmeyer, R. R., and E. A. Finney. "Use of AASHO Road Test Findings by the AASHO Committee on Highway Transport." *The AASHO Road Test*, Highway Research Board Special Report 73, Washington, D.C., 1962.

Baumal, C. P., J. J. Miller and T. P. Drinka. *An Economic Analysis of Upgrading Rail Branchlines*. USDOT Report FRA–OOPD–76–3, Washington, D.C., 1976.

Benkelman, A. C., R. I. Kingham and H. Y. Fang. "Special Deflection Studies on Flexible Pavement." *The AASHO Road Test*, Highway Research Board Special Report 73, Washington, D.C., 1962.

Bennett, C. J. Load Limitations for Primary and Secondary Roads. *Public Roads* 3, no. 34., 1921.

Bisson, B. G., J. R. Brander and J. D. Innes. "Highway Cost Allocation Methodology For Pavement Rehabilitation and Capacity-Related Costs Occasioned by an Increment in Heavy Truck Traffic." *Freight Papers–1985*, Transportation Research Record 1038: 10–16, 1985.

Black, W. R. "Interregional Commodity Flows: Some Experiments with the Gravity Model." *Journal of Regional Science* 12, no. 2, (1972): 107–118.

Blunden, W. R., and J. A. Black. *The Land-Use and Transport System*, 2 ed. Pergamon Press, 1984.

Casavant, K. L., and G. C. Griffin. *Characteristics and Cost of Operation of North Dakota's Farm Trucks*. UGPTI Staff Paper No. 37. Upper Great Plains Transportation Institute, North Dakota State University, Fargo, 1982.

Casavant, K. L., and G.C. Griffin. *Structure and Operating Characteristics of the North Dakota Grain Elevator Industry*. UGPTI Publication No. 47. Upper Great Plains Transportation Institute, North Dakota State University, Fargo, 1983.

Chase, C. S., and D. H. Helgeson. *Cost Analysis of Potential North Dakota Subterminal Systems*. UGPTI Publication No. 44. Upper Great Plains Transportation Institute, North Dakota State University, Fargo, 1983.

Chase, C. S., D. H. Helgeson and T. L. Schaffer. *Statistical Cost Analysis of the Existing North Dakota Country Elevator Industry*. UGPTI Publication No. 43. Upper Great Plains Transportation Institute, North Dakota State University, Fargo, 1983.

Cobia, D. W., W. W. Wilson, S. P. Gunn and R. C. Coon. *Pricing Systems of Trainloading Cooperative Elevators*. Department of Agricultural Economics Report No. 214. Department of Agricultural Economics, North Dakota State University, Fargo, December, 1985.

Dickey, J. W. *Metropolitan Transportation Planning*. New York: McGraw-Hill, 1983.

Dickey, J. W. *Road Project Appraisal*. New York: John Wiley & Sons, 1984.

Dooley, F. J. "The Theory of Multiplant Firms Applied to Washington Grain Elevators." Ph.D. dissertation, Department of Agricultural Economics, Washington State University, Pullman, 1986.

Elliot, R. P. and M. R. Thompson. "Illi-Pave Mechanistic Analysis of AASHO Road Test Flexible Pavements." *Pavement System Analysis*, Transportation Research Record 1043: 39–49, 1985.

Fernando, E. G., D. R. Lurh and H. N. Sazena. "Analysis of Axle Loads and Axle Types for the Evaluation of Load Limits on Flexible Pavements." Paper prepared for presentation at the 66th Annual Meeting of the Transportation Research Board, Washington, D.C., January 1987.

Greenstein, J. "Pavement Evaluation and Upgrading of Low-Cost Roads." *Design and Upgrading of Surfacing and Other Aspects of Low-Volume Roads*, Transportation Research Record 875: 26–32, 1982.

Griffin, G. C., W. W. Wilson and K. Casavant. *Characteristics and Costs of Operation of North Dakota's Farm Trucks*. UGPTI Publication No. 51. Upper Great Plains Transportation Institute, North Dakota State University, Fargo, 1984.

Halim, A. O. A. and F. F. Saccomanno. "Axle Load Limits in Ontario: Long-Term Analysis." *Freight Papers–1985*, Transportation Research Record 1038: 26–33, 1985.

Henry, G. T. and J. M. Bennett. "Cost Responsibility for Low–Volume Roads in Virginia." *Design and Upgrading of Surfacing and Other Aspects of Low-Volume Roads*, Transportation Research Record 875: 53–60, 1982.

Hillier, F. S. and G. J. Lieberman. *Introduction to Operations Research.* Holden-Day, 1980.

Highway Research Board. *The Truck Weight Problem in Highway Transportation.* Bulletin No. 26. National Research Council, Washington, D.C., 1950.

Hobeika, A. G. and T. K. Tran. "Maintenance Cost-Allocation Study for Virginia's Interstate Highways." *Cost Responsibility, User Charges, and Finance Issues*, Transportation Research Record 858: 20–24, 1982.

Kanafani, A. *Transportation Demand Analysis.* New York: McGraw-Hill, 1983.

Klindworth, K. A., and J. A. Batson. *Economic Impact of Proposed Kansas Rail Abandonments.* U.S. Department of Agriculture, Domestic Services Branch, Transportation and Marketing Division, July 1991.

Langsner, G., T. S. Huff and W. J. Liddle. "Use of Road Test Findings by AASHO Design Committee." *The AASHO Road Test.* Highway Research Board Special Report 73, Washington, D.C., 1962.

Lee, S. M., L. J. Moore and B. W. Taylor. *Management Science.* William C. Brown, 1985.

Lee, C. E. and B. Izadmehr. "Estimating Lanewide Traffic Loading on Multilane Highways From WIM Data." *Pavement Management, Data Storage, Surface Properties, and Weigh-in-Motion.* Transportation Research Record 1048: 65–73, 1985.

Lee, C. E. and R. B. Machemehl. "Weighing Trucks on Axle-Load and Weigh-in-Motion Scales." *Pavement Management, Data Storage, Surface Properties, and Weigh-in-Motion.* Transportation Research Record 1048: 74–82, 1985.

Linsenmeyer, D. "Effect of Unit-Train Grain Shipments on Rural Nebraska Roads." *Design and Upgrading of Surfacing and Other Aspects of Low-Volume Roads.* Transportation Research Record 875: 60–64, 1982.

Lurh, D. R. and B. F. McCullough. "Structural Analysis of AASHO Road Test Flexible Pavements for Performance Evaluation." Structural Performance of Pavement Systems, Transportation Research Record 888: 63–69, 1982.

Manheim, M. L. *Fundamentals of Transportation System Analysis.* Boston: MIT Press, 1980.

McNeil, S., and C. Hendrickson. *Three Statistical Models of Pavement Management Based on Turnpike Data with an Application to Roadway Cost Allocation.* Department of Civil Engineering, Carnegie-Mellon University, Pittsburgh, Penn., September 1981.

Mittleider, J. F., D. D. Tolliver and H. G. Vreugdenhil. *North Dakota Line Segment Analytical Model (NOLAM)—A Technical Description.* UGPTI Publication No. 50. Upper Great Plains Transportation Institute, North Dakota State University, Fargo, 1983.

North Dakota State Highway Department, Planning Division. *North Dakota Highway Funding Needs Through the Year 2000.* February 1988.

Payne, W. F., C. P. Baumel and D. E. Moser. *Estimating Truck Transport Costs for Grain and Fertilizer.* Res. Bull. 1027, Agricultural Experiment Station, University of Missouri, Columbia, 1978.

Purnell, L. O., E. J. Yoder, and K. C. Sinha. "Effect of Railroad Abandonment on Rural Highway Pavement Maintenance." *Civil Engineering for Practicing and Design Engineers*, Vol. 1. Pergamon Press, 1984.

Rauhut, J. B., L. Lytton and M. I. Darter. "Pavement Damage Functions for Cost Allocation: Vol. 1, Damage Functions and Load Equivalence Factors," 1984.

Rauhut, J. B., L. Lytton and M. I. Darter. "Pavement Damage Functions for Cost Allocation: Executive Summary." FHWA/RD-84/117, January 1983.

Riggins, M., R. L. Lytton and A. Garcia-Diaz. "Developing Stochastic Flexible Pavement Distress and Serviceability Equations." *Pavement Management, Data Storage, Surface Properties, and Weigh-in-Motion.* Transportation Research Record 1048: 1–7, 1985.

Rimmer, P. J. and J. A. Black. "Urban Goods and Commercial Vehicle Movements in Sydney: A Research Framework." *Journal Australian Road Research* 11: 15–29, 1981.

Roberts, F. L. and B. T. Rosson. "Effects of Higher Tire Pressures on Strain in Thin AC Pavements." *Pavement System Analysis.* Transportation Research Record 1043: 68–77, 1985.

Rutherford, G. S. and J. Lattemann. "The Use of Future Scenarios in Long-Range Public Transportation Planning." Prepared for the Annual Meeting of the Transportation Research Board, Washington, D.C., January 1988.

Saha, S. K. and J. D. Fricker. "Traffic Volume Forecasting Methods for Rural State Highways." Paper presented at the 67th Annual Meetings of the Transportation Research Board, Washington, D.C., January 1988.

SAS Institute. *SAS/OR Users Guide*, Version 5. Crary, N.C., 1985.

Saskatchewan Highways and Transportation. "A Methodology for Analyzing the Impact of Branch Line Abandonment on the Provincial Road System." Extracted from *The Saskatchewan Submission to the Branch Line Inquiry of the Canadian Transport Commission*, 1987.

Saskatchewan Highways and Transportation. "Preeceville, Dunelm, and Central Butte Subdivisions: Results of an Analysis of Road Impacts on the Provincial Road System Associated with Alternative Rail Line Abandonment Proposals." Paper prepared for A Study of Rail Line Abandonment in Western Canada by the SGTC, December 1987.

Taylor, Richard and Ken Casavant. *Working Papers: Washington Rail Development Commission Study*, 1988.

Thompson, M. R. and R. P. Elliott. "Illi-Pave-Based Response Algorithms for Design of Conventional Flexible Pavements." Pavement System Analysis, Transportation Research Record 1043: 50–57, 1985.

Tolliver, D. D. and Transportation Operations, Inc. *Preliminary Analysis of CNW's Nebraska Rail Line.* UGPTI Publication No. 85. Upper Great Plains Transportation Institute, North Dakota State University, Fargo, 1991.

Tolliver, D. D. and D. L. Zink. *Service and Funding Alternatives for Subterminal Impacted Roads, the Case of Stark and Hettinger Counties, North Dakota.* UGPTI Staff Paper No. 73. Upper Great Plains Transportation Institute, North Dakota State University, Fargo, 1985.

Transportation Research Board. *Truck Weight Limits* Special Report No. 225. Washington, D.C., 1990.

Transportation Research Board. *Twin Trailer Trucks.* Special Report No. 211. Washington, D.C., 1986.

Transportation Research Board. "Freight Modelling and Forecasting." *Transportation Research Record 889.* National Academy of Sciences, 1982.

Transportation Research Board. "Travel Demand Forecasting Procedures." *Transportation Research Record 895.* National Academy of Sciences, 1982.

U.S. Department of Agriculture. "Five Million Motor Cars on Roads of the United States." *Public Roads*, 1, no. 1, 1918a.

U.S. Department of Agriculture. "The Highways of the Country and Burden They Must Carry." *Public Roads*, 1, no. 2, 1918b.

U.S. Department of Transportation. *Highway Performance Monitoring System, Truck Weight Case Study.* Washington, D.C., June 1982.

U.S. Department of Transportation. *Highway Investment Practices and Trends.* Washington, D.C., November 1981.

U.S. Department of Transportation. Federal Highway Administration. *Highway Statistics.* Washington, D.C., 1982, 1983, 1985, 1988, and 1989.

U.S. Department of Transportation. Federal Highway Administration. *Overweight Vehicles—Penalties and Permits: An Inventory of State Practices for Fiscal Year 1987.* Washington, D.C., January 1989.

U.S. Department of Transportation. Federal Highway Administration. *Highway Statistics: Summary to 1985.* Washington, D.C., 1987.

U.S. Department of Transportation. Federal Highway Administration. *Highway Performance Monitoring System.* Washington, D.C., January 1986.

U.S. Department of Transportation. Federal Highway Administration. *The Feasibility of a Nationwide Network for Longer Combination Vehicles.* Washington, D.C., May 1985a.

U.S. Department of Transportation. Federal Highway Administration. *Longer Combination Vehicle Operations in Western States.* Washington, D.C., 1985b.

U.S. Department of Transportation. Federal Highway Administration. *Traffic Monitoring Guide.* Washington, D.C., June 1985c.

U.S. Department of Transportation. Federal Highway Administration. State Highway Cost–Allocation Guide,—Vol. 1, Main Text, Vol. 2, Technical Appendix. Washington, D.C., October 1984.

U.S. Department of Transportation. Federal Highway Administration. *The Final Report on the Federal Highway Cost Allocation Study.* Washington, D.C., May 1982.

U.S. Department of Transportation. Federal Highway Administration. "Performance–Investment Analysis Process." *Technical Report.* Washington, D.C., September 1978.

Van Til, C. J., B. R. McCullough, B. A. Vallerga, and R. G. Gicks. Evaluation of AASHTO Interim Guide for Design of Pavement Structures. Washington, D.C., 1972.

Villarreal, A., A. Garcia-Diaz and R. L. Lytton. *Pavement Cost Allocation Models Updates.* Federal Highway Administration, Washington, D.C., September 1987.

Walters, A. A. *The Economics of Road User Charges.* World Bank Staff Occasional Papers Number Five. Baltimore: Johns Hopkins Press, 1968.

Wang, M. C. "Performance Analysis for Flexible Pavements with Stabilized Base." *Structural Performance of Pavement Systems.* Transportation Research Record 888: 70–76, 1982.

Werner, A. and S. Khalil. "Athabasca Subdivision Rail Line Abandonment Proposal." Alberta Transportation and Utilities, October 1987.

Wilson, A. G., J. D. Coelko, S. M. Macgill and H. C. Williams. *Optimication in Locational and Transport Analysis.* John Wiley & Sons, 1981.

Wilson, W. W., G. C. Griffin and K. Casavant. *Costs and Characteristics of Operating Interstate Motor Carriers of Grain in North Dakota.* UGPTI Publication No. 46. Upper Great Plains Transportation Institute, North Dakota State University, Fargo, 1982.

Wilson, W. W., S. C. Hvinden and J. G. Cosgriff. *Impacts of Seasonal Rail Rates on Grain Flows and Storage in North Dakota.* UGPTI Publication No. 37. Upper Great Plains Transportation Institute, North Dakota State University, Fargo, 1981.

Wilson, W. W., S. C. Hvinden and J.G.Cosgriff. *Seasonal Behavior of Marketing Patterns for Grain from North Dakota.* UPGTI Publication No. 38. Upper Great Plains Transportation Institute, North Dakota State University, Fargo, 1981.

Yoder, E. J. and M. W. Witczak. *Principles of Pavement Design,* 2  ed. New York: John Wiley, 1975.

Zink, D. L. *The Subterminal/Satellite Elevator Cooperative and the Role of the Local Country Elevator.* UGPTI Publication No. 64. Upper Great Plains Transportation Institute, North Dakota State University, Fargo, 1988.

Zink, D. L. and K. L. Casavant. *Feasibility of the Cooperative Subterminal: A Case Study of Bisbee, North Dakota.* UGPTI Publication No. 55. Upper Great Plains Transportation Institute, North Dakota State University, Fargo, 1984.

Zink, D. L. and D. R. Ming. *Grain Drawing Capabilities and Plant Upgrade Analysis of the Mooreton-Dwight Cooperative.* UGPTI Staff Paper No. 60. Upper Great Plains Transportation Institute, North Dakota State University, Fargo, 1984.

# Index

AADE viii, 134-136, 151,
    152, 151
AADT vii, 104, 105, 110,
    129, 130, 133,
    134-136
AASHO 6, 60, 61, 63, 64,
    65, 66, 68, 73, 74,
    75, 74, 203,
    204-207
AASHO road test 63, 66,
    205, 206, 207
AASHTO 49, 53, 60, 71,
    74, 125, 126, 185,
    210
Abandonment vi, v, xii, 3,
    9, 12, 19, 41, 52,
    54-56, 74, 79, 140,
    141, 143, 158, 159,
    161, 162-164, 169,
    175, 176-181, 188,
    189, 193, 197, 199,
    200, 208, 209, 210
American Association of
    State Highway and
    Transportation
    Officials 4
American Association of
    State Highway
    Officials 5, 60,
    205
Average annual daily
    ESALs 134, 151
Average annual daily trips
    105, 129, 133

Axle
Axle vii, viii, 5-8, 11,
    13, 15, 16, 19,
    21-23, 45-50, 56,
    58, 60, 61-63,
    65-67, 90, 91, 98,
    117, 119, 121, 124,
    125, 124, 125-127,
    126, 128, 129, 141,
    161, 179, 183, 188,
    203, 204, 206, 207
Group 13, 56, 58, 59,
    125, 124, 125, 126,
    164, 181, 185, 188
Load 5, 6, 15, 16, 21,
    22, 23, 46, 53,
    60-63, 66, 91, 118,
    121, 124, 128, 134,
    161, 168, 186, 204,
    205-208
Loading 21, 38, 51, 81,
    85, 86, 118, 124,
    185, 186, 207
Pass 8, 13, 22, 39, 48,
    49, 141
Weight 5, 6, 15, 16,
    21, 22, 23, 56, 58,
    62, 103, 118, 121,
    124, 125, 124, 125,
    126, 128, 129, 161,
    178, 179, 181, 203,
    207, 209

Branch Line 50, 56, 209
Build-sooner cost 51, 52,
    54, 55, 153

Build-sooner costs viii, ix,
    51-53, 91, 136,
    154, 156, 158, 180,
    183, 189, 190, 191,
    193

CO-5AX vii, viii, 5, 7, 12,
    21, 23, 50, 68, 115,
    117, 129, 132, 134,
    140, 141, 142, 146,
    147-150, 157, 158,
    161, 168, 169, 191
Combination five-axle 5,
    117, 141

Devils Lake vii, ix, 40, 71,
    73, 74, 79, 80,
    82-89, 99, 103,
    105, 106, 110, 111,
    112, 114, 115, 117,
    123, 124, 125, 129,
    131, 133, 134, 136,
    139, 140, 141, 142,
    144, 145, 151, 153,
    154, 158, 199

ESAL vii, ix, 22, 48-50,
    53, 56, 63, 64, 68,
    71, 72, 71, 73-75,
    74, 91, 123, 129,
    133, 136, 180, 182,
    185, 187, 198
ESALs vii, 15, 22, 23, 47,
    49, 50, 53, 54, 56,
    62, 64, 71, 86, 90,
    91, 119, 123-126,
    128, 129, 131, 133,
    134, 136, 137, 140,
    141, 151, 157, 180,
    187, 188, 189

FHWA vii, ix, 1, 7, 11, 40,
    58, 60, 65, 67, 68,
    70-72, 71, 73-75,
    74, 99, 129, 134,
    135, 136, 184, 185,
    187, 200, 203, 204,
    208
Flow type 91, 142, 144,
    145, 146
Functional class vii, viii, 2,
    73, 75, 134, 143,
    144, 148, 149,
    150-152, 151, 153,
    154, 155, 157, 197,
    198

Incremental cost viii, ix,
    45, 47, 50, 54, 55,
    57, 151, 153, 154,
    155, 157, 180, 200

Land use ix, xi, 4, 24, 85

NDHWD 64, 68, 71, 86,
    129, 134
Nebraska vii, viii, xi, 161,
    162-167, 166, 170,
    171-178, 180, 181,
    183, 185, 186, 187,
    190, 193, 199, 200,
    207, 209
North Dakota vii, ix, xi,
    xii, 2, 19, 23, 24,
    34, 40, 68, 73, 74,
    79, 82, 86, 88, 111,
    114, 116, 115, 117,
    118, 124, 129, 130,
    131, 135, 158, 162,
    179, 206, 208, 209,
    211

Pavement
  Damage  16, 22-24, 35,
    45, 58, 59-69, 74,
    183, 200, 208
  Decay  ix, 45, 51, 61,
    62, 63, 64, 67, 73,
    74, 182-184, 189,
    197, 200
  Design  ix, xi, 4, 5, 11,
    24, 45, 49, 50,
    53-57, 60, 62, 64,
    65, 74, 79, 121,
    123, 134, 166, 184,
    186, 187, 188, 197,
    198, 205, 206,
    207-211
  Deterioration  vi, ix, 4,
    5, 7, 9, 15, 22,
    45-47, 51, 57-60,
    62, 63, 66, 67,
    72-74, 161, 182,
    188, 189, 200
  Pavement  vi, v, viii, ix,
    3-5, 8, 11, 12, 15,
    16, 21-24, 45,
    46-48, 47-52,
    54-68, 71, 72, 73,
    74, 89, 90, 91, 121,
    123, 134, 136, 137,
    161, 166, 175, 178,
    179-193, 197, 198,
    200, 205, 206,
    207-211
  Rehabilitation  1, 3, 4,
    7, 11, 22, 47, 50,
    54, 56, 163, 164,
    176, 180, 181, 187,
    200, 205
  Replacement  viii, ix,
    48, 47, 48, 50, 51,
    52-55, 58, 63, 91,
    137, 151, 153, 154,
    158, 180, 181,
    183, 186,
    187-189, 198
Pavement Serviceability
  Index  64
Present Serviceability
    Rating  vii, 22, 59,
    60, 183, 187
PSI  58, 61, 63-65, 67, 68,
    71, 73, 74, 185,
    200
PSR  vii, 22, 48, 49, 51, 58,
    59, 63, 64, 71, 73,
    134, 183, 184, 187,
    189, 190, 197

Rail  vi, 20, 35, 38, 52, 54,
    55, 56, 111, 112,
    113, 114, 122, 140,
    143, 146, 161-164,
    166, 168, 169, 175,
    176, 177, 178, 180,
    181, 182, 188, 190,
    191, 199, 205, 207,
    209, 210, 211

Satellite  vii, ix, 19-21,
    23-25, 24, 32, 33,
    38-40, 81, 82, 83,
    104, 110, 112, 114,
    116, 122, 123, 140,
    141-143, 145, 146,
    147, 150, 151, 158,
    199, 211
Seasonal  vii, 13, 129, 130,
    131-133, 211
Shipment distribution  16,
    40, 86, 90, 101,
    103, 104, 105, 110,
    161
Shipment generation  vi, v,
    16, 88, 89, 91, 97,
    101, 161

Spatial Interaction 27, 29,
    30-32, 40, 41, 79,
    105-107, 109, 141,
    175, 176
SU-2AX vii, 21, 23, 68,
    115, 117, 116, 117,
    119, 129, 132, 140,
    142, 146, 147, 149,
    150, 157, 158
SU-3AX vii, 21, 23, 68,
    115, 117, 116, 119,
    124, 129, 132, 140,
    142, 146, 147, 149,
    150
Subterminal vi, v, vii, ix,
    xi, 3, 12, 14, 16,
    19, 20, 21, 23, 24,
    25, 24, 25, 27,
    32-41,54-56, 71,
    72, 79, 80, 79, 81,
    82, 83, 84, 83, 85,
    86-90, 92, 97, 100,
    103, 104, 110, 112,
    114, 115-118, 121,
    122, 123, 125, 130,
    134, 136, 139,
    140-147, 150, 151,
    154-159, 164, 175,
    176, 178, 181, 182,
    188, 197, 199, 200,
    206, 209, 211
Systems Diagram map 162,
    164

Time value of money 52,
    54
Trans-shipment
    Algorithm 34-37, 39,
        41, 123, 175
    Model vii, ix, 15, 19,
        22, 27-29, 32,
        33-41, 45, 55, 58,
        60, 63, 65, 66, 67,

        68, 70, 71, 72,
        71, 72-74, 88,
        89, 90, 97, 101,
        104, 105, 106,
        107, 108, 109,
        110, 112, 114,
        123, 124, 141,
        175, 176, 178,
        182, 183, 186,
        187, 200, 203,
        204, 205, 208
    Trans-shipment 20, 25,
        24, 27, 34, 38, 39,
        41, 110, 112, 141,
        143, 145, 146, 156,
        164, 169, 175, 176,
        200
Transportation algorithm
    34, 36, 37, 39
Truck
    Cost vii, viii, ix, xi, 3,
        11, 12, 15, 28, 30,
        32-41, 45, 47,
        48-57, 56, 58, 65,
        74, 87, 89,
        104-106, 108,
        110-112, 116, 117,
        116, 117, 121, 124,
        137, 140, 142, 145,
        151, 153-157, 163,
        177, 178, 180, 181,
        182, 183, 185, 186,
        187, 188, 189, 190,
        191, 192, 193, 197,
        198, 199, 200, 201,
        205, 206, 207, 208,
        210
    Distribution vii, viii, ix,
        1, 4, 7, 9, 12, 15,
        16, 24, 35, 38,
        39-41, 55, 67, 82,
        83, 86, 90, 100,
        101, 103, 104, 105,

101, 103, 104,
105, 110, 112,
114, 115, 116,
115, 116, 117,
118, 124, 125,
140, 141,
143-146, 148,
150, 151, 156,
159, 161, 176,
177, 178, 200
Truck   vi, vii, viii, ix,
xi, 1, 3-8, 11-13,
15, 16, 19, 20-24,
32-37, 40, 41, 45,
50-54, 67, 68, 72,
71, 81, 82, 83, 87,
90, 91, 97, 98, 103,
104, 105, 108, 110,
112-115, 117, 116,
117, 116, 117, 118,
119, 118, 121, 122,
123, 124, 125, 124,
125, 126, 127, 126,
128, 131, 134, 135,
140, 141, 142, 141,
142, 143, 144, 146,
147, 148, 149, 150,
151, 153, 155, 157,
158, 161, 164, 166,
168, 169, 176, 177,
178, 179, 180, 181,
182, 185, 186, 187,
188, 189, 190, 191,
192, 193, 200, 205,
207, 208, 209
Type   vii, viii, ix, 13,
15, 20-22, 25, 29,
40, 46, 47, 50,
61-63, 67-69, 71,
73, 74, 82, 87, 90,
91, 97, 103, 114,
115, 117-119, 118,
121, 122, 123, 124,

125, 126, 127,
134, 142, 143,
144-147,149,
150, 168, 181,
182, 184, 188
Truck distribution  16, 90,
103, 117, 118, 151
Truck type   vii, viii, 22, 71, 91,
115, 117, 118, 119, 123,
125, 134, 147, 149, 150,
188
Truck weight  5, 15, 16, 23,
121, 124, 125, 126,
128, 161, 178, 207,
209

Upgrading costs  50, 52,
53, 54, 91, 136,
137, 155, 158, 180

Vehicle classification  vii,
90, 104, 125, 127,
129, 130
Vehicle miles of travel  12,
148, 189
VMT  viii, 12, 15, 23, 125,
126, 128, 129,
133-136, 148, 149,
150, 185, 189

Washington  vii, xi, 58,
162, 163, 179, 187,
193, 205, 206,
207-210
Weigh-in-motion  13, 15,
90, 104, 121, 125,
129, 130, 207, 208
WIM  13, 15, 121, 124,
125, 126, 128, 129,
131, 207

**About the Author**

DENVER TOLLIVER is a research scientist at the Upper Great Plains Transportation Institute at North Dakota State University. A former railroad planner for the North Dakota Department of Transportation, he has consulted for transportation agencies in Nebraska, Oregon, and Washington State. He has published articles in such journals as *The Logistics and Transportation Review*, *Journal of the Transportation Research Forum*, and *Transportation Law Journal*.